The Pipe Organ

The Pipe Organ

A COMPOSER'S GUIDE

James Mitchell

OXFORD
UNIVERSITY PRESS

Oxford University Press is a department of the University of Oxford. It furthers
the University's objective of excellence in research, scholarship, and education
by publishing worldwide. Oxford is a registered trade mark of Oxford University
Press in the UK and certain other countries.

Published in the United States of America by Oxford University Press
198 Madison Avenue, New York, NY 10016, United States of America.

© Oxford University Press 2023

All rights reserved. No part of this publication may be reproduced, stored in
a retrieval system, or transmitted, in any form or by any means, without the
prior permission in writing of Oxford University Press, or as expressly permitted
by law, by license, or under terms agreed with the appropriate reproduction
rights organization. Inquiries concerning reproduction outside the scope of the
above should be sent to the Rights Department, Oxford University Press, at the
address above.

You must not circulate this work in any other form
and you must impose this same condition on any acquirer.

Library of Congress Cataloging-in-Publication Data
Names: Mitchell, James (Organist) author.
Title: The pipe organ : a composer's guide / James Mitchell.
Description: [1.] | New York : Oxford University Press, 2023. |
Includes index.
Identifiers: LCCN 2023003788 (print) | LCCN 2023003789 (ebook) |
ISBN 9780197645291 (paperback) | ISBN 9780197645284 (hardback) |
ISBN 9780197645314 (epub) | ISBN 9780197645321
Subjects: LCSH: Organ (Musical instrument)—Instruction and study. |
Composition (Music)—Instruction and study.
Classification: LCC MT180 .B57 2023 (print) | LCC MT180 (ebook) |
DDC 786.5/19—dc23/eng/20230126
LC record available at https://lccn.loc.gov/2023003788
LC ebook record available at https://lccn.loc.gov/2023003789

DOI: 10.1093/oso/9780197645284.001.0001

Contents

Foreword by John Rutter • vii
Acknowledgements • ix
About the Companion Website • xi

Introduction • 1
  How to Use this Book • 3
  A Note on the Musical Examples • 3
  Getting Your Organ Music Performed • 4
  The Organ and Religion • 5
  Accessing an Organ • 6
  Software Instruments • 7
  Extra Resources • 7

1 Introduction to the Organ • 9
  Overview • 9
  Organ Building Trends • 16
    Historic Organs • 17
  Common Mistakes • 18
    Writing Outside the Written Range • 19
    Unidiomatic Textures • 19
    Not Enough Use of the Pedals • 21
    Misuse of Double Pedalling • 21
    Misunderstanding the Relationship between Registration and Dynamics • 21
    Balance • 22
  Extended Techniques • 22
    Clusters • 23
    Half-Drawn Stops/Half-Depressed Notes • 24
    Removing/'Preparing' Pipes • 24
    'Stuck' Notes • 24
    'Registration' Trill • 25
    Altering the Organ Wind Pressure • 25
    Turning the Organ On/Off Mid-Chord • 25
    Electronic Amplification/Audio Effects • 25

2 Registration • 27
  Overview • 27
  Main Stop Categories • 36
    Principals • 36
    Flutes • 37
    Strings • 39
    Reeds • 40
  Other Categories • 50
    Foundations • 50
    Mixtures • 51

Contents

    Mutations · 52
    Miscellaneous Stops · 54
  Couplers · 55
  Registration Aids · 58
    General Pistons · 58
    Divisional Pistons · 61
    Crescendo Pedal · 63

3 The Manuals · 65

  Overview · 65
  Idiomatic Writing · 68
    Non-Chordal Techniques · 70
    Chordal Techniques · 77
  Playing on Multiple Manuals · 86

4 The Pedals · 92

  Overview · 92
  Idiomatic Writing · 98
  Double/Multi-Pedalling · 105
  The Pedals in Context · 112

5 Other Types of Organ · 123

  Overview · 123
  Chamber Organ · 123
  Harmonium · 126
  Theatre Organ · 132
  Hammond Organ · 135

6 The Organ in Ensemble · 139

  Overview · 139
  Organ and Choir · 139
  Organ and Orchestra · 145
    Concertos · 151
  Organ and Chamber Ensembles · 153
  Organ and Electronics · 161

Appendix: National Organ Styles · 163

Glossary · 169

Index · 175

Index of Composers · 181

Foreword by John Rutter

One of the many reasons for giving this book a resounding welcome is that nothing like it has appeared in print before. How to write for the organ is something every composer should know, but too many of us do not. We may think we do, but blunder into ineffectiveness or unplayability; we may fail to take advantage of the infinite resources of the instrument; or be so intimidated by its technicalities that we never write any organ music at all. A modern organ console looks as complex as an aircraft cockpit, but its mysteries are unravelled as you read the pages that follow. As with the harp and the classical guitar, most solo organ literature down the ages has been written by those who play the instrument, but in this concise and readable manual James Mitchell has shown us that this need not be so. He provides us, organists or not, with a practical and comprehensive guide to good organ writing in any style, explaining as much of the technique and workings of the instrument as is helpful to the composer—and enlightening to all who take an interest in the organ and its music. He is refreshingly clear but open-minded about what works on the organ and what does not, and the range of music he points us to is astounding: I expected Bach, Messiaen, and the French organist-composers—I did not expect Jimmy Smith, Bob Dylan, Hans Zimmer, or the Indian harmonium.

    With this invaluable book at hand, no composer need ever again write badly for the organ. Many will find their repertoire knowledge greatly enlarged, and it is clearly the author's aim to encourage and inspire *all* composers to create new organ music, whether for the organ as a solo instrument, as part of an ensemble, or even in a concerto role—how sad that, as he points out, scarcely an organ concerto since Francis Poulenc's (1938) has gained a firm place in the repertoire. With so many talented organists and fine instruments available for composers to write for, the appearance of *The Pipe Organ: A Composer's Guide* could not be more timely. I have read it with pleasure and profit.

John Rutter

Acknowledgements

This book would never have been possible without the love and support of my parents Lynette and Stephen. They have helped me through all the stages of this book, back from when it was just an idea conceived during the coronavirus pandemic lockdown through to proofreading the final manuscript. I hope this book makes you proud.

I am grateful to Michelle Chen, Sean Decker, Laura Santo, and the team at Oxford University Press for helping this book see the light of day. Stephen Farr and Pia Rose Scattergood, as an organist and composer, respectively, gave indispensable advice during the preparation of the manuscript. Anne Page kindly assisted with the section on the harmonium (as well as letting me record on her own instrument) and Tom Horton's guidance on the theatre organ was invaluable. Tiny Evans kindly allowed me to record one of his Hammond organs at the Hammond Hire Company. I must also thank Adrian Partington, Andrew Kirk, and Byron Jones for allowing me to photograph/record the organs at Gloucester Cathedral, St. Mary Redcliffe Church, and Eden Grove Methodist Church, respectively.

Finally, I would like to thank all the musicians, both teachers and collaborators, who have helped me develop into the person I am today. I am very lucky to be nurtured by such creativity and musicianship from the extraordinary performers and composers around me. Even having written this book, my entire perception of the organ continues to change as other people push the instrument beyond what I thought was possible. My wish is that, through this book, I may inspire people in the same way.

About the Companion Website

www.oup.com/us/ThePipeOrgan

The companion website contains many resources to supplement this book, including but not limited to:

- Print-off summaries of each chapter
- Video demonstrations of various instruments, stops, and playing techniques, complete with sheet music transcriptions and brief commentaries
- Sample organ specifications for each of the main national styles listed in the Appendix, including commentaries and links to recordings
- Extended case studies about adapting Howells's *Like as the Hart* and Messiaen's 'Joie et clarté' from *Les Corps Glorieux* for larger and smaller organs, respectively
- A list of major composers who have written for the organ, with a brief commentary about each one

It is generally recommended to start with the book first and refer to the companion website at the relevant points, although the chapter summaries can usefully be consulted at any time. The discussions for the video demonstrations are in-depth and rely on having read and understood the main concepts in the book first. The book also has a greater focus on the existing organ repertoire, while the video demonstrations aim to show the contemporary possibilities of the organ.

The reader can find connected material on the companion website when prompted by this icon: ▶

INTRODUCTION

In the third century BCE, a Greek named Ctesibius invented what he named the 'hydraulis', an instrument where a set of pipes were fed by a mechanical water-powered wind supply. This instrument was the world's first documented pipe organ, and over the past two millennia the organ has evolved into one of the most remarkable instruments in Western music. Organs are living history of past musical cultures: the organ at the Basilica of Valère in Switzerland, built in 1435, is still playable today. No other musical instrument is as connected to architecture as the organ: each organ is custom built for the building where it is situated, with the organ design exploiting the architecture to fill the building with sound. Anyone who has experienced the raw power of a large organ in a big church or cathedral is rarely left unaffected. Consequently, almost every major composer has required the organ in at least one of their most large-scale pieces, including works as diverse as Vaughan Williams's *Sinfonia Antarctica*, Stephen Sondheim's musical *Sweeney Todd*, and Hans Zimmer's soundtrack to *Interstellar*.

Sadly, however, the organ is also one of regularly misunderstood instruments, even by other musicians. The poor quality of many organ keyboard patches and notation software playback makes the instrument appear more limited than it actually is. The traditional orchestration textbooks have been of little help when it comes to the organ. Walter Piston, notably conservative by modern-day standards, describes the organ as "too self-sufficient an instrument to become part of the symphony orchestra," a dismissive attitude that is unfortunately still prevalent today. Samuel Adler's account is better than Piston's, dedicating three pages to the instrument and even providing musical excerpts. However, the advice Adler actually offers is limited, unhelpful, and sometimes even just straight-out wrong (for example, Adler is incorrect about higher-pitched stops being range extensions; see the Chapter 2 for more info). Blatter's orchestration textbook, by contrast, has the reverse problem. It is the most extensive of the three, with twelve pages dedicated to the organ, and the information provided is the most accurate and best written by far when compared to Piston and Adler. However, the technical information Blatter provides is difficult to parse and, combined with a lack of musical examples, his advice is not especially useful in practice. This unhelpful situation has no doubt had a detrimental effect on organ writing, with composers therefore choosing to avoid the organ due to the perceived learning curve in understanding and writing for the instrument.

By contrast, the organ is currently both at its most accessible, and with a higher standard of performance, than at any previous point in history. Pieces considered unplayable a century ago are now a part of the standard repertoire. Digital organs are gradually becoming more commonplace and now can have incredibly realistic sounds, bringing the instrument into many more venues beyond just churches or concert halls. The organ offers abundant performance opportunities for composers: organists are frequently looking for new repertoire, and many commissions for new music come from church, cathedral, or chapel choirs. In addition, software such as Hauptwerk brings the full capabilities of the organ not only to live performance but also as a plugin to digital audio workstations (DAWs for short), offering new possibilities in music production. There has never been a better time for new organ music, yet to many composers the instrument feels difficult to understand and limited in timbral options.

This book therefore aims to fix this situation. It provides all of the information needed to write good organ music, focussing on the practical side as much as possible. Technical jargon is kept to a minimum; not much terminology is needed to write good organ music, although more niche terms are explained in the Glossary should composers require them. Strong emphasis is also placed on reading and listening to the organ repertoire in all its diverse forms, and the music examples should help composers see exactly what good organ music looks and sounds like.

The first chapter provides a general introduction to the organ for those with limited or no experience of the instrument. This chapter will introduce the most common terminology associated with the organ, as well as going into detail about various important organ building trends, the most common mistakes composers make when writing for organ, and various extended techniques. For composers who do not know where to begin when writing for the organ, this chapter is the place to start.

The second chapter deals with the complex art of registration (i.e., controlling the organ timbre). Organ layouts are often more standardised than may be expected and so, with some experience and by consulting Table 2.1, it is possible to be surprisingly specific with registrations without hindering the performability of the work. This chapter therefore explains the typical layout of the organ and function of each sound, as well as how to best specify registrations in a score.

Chapters 3 and 4 deal with writing for the manuals (the keyboards) and pedals respectively. Both chapters focus on the practical performance aspects, using numerous annotated musical examples to immerse composers in idiomatic organ writing. Standard playing techniques and organ textures up to a virtuoso level are all covered, providing composers with a technical idiomatic grounding from which they can innovate.

Chapter 5 covers four instruments related to the pipe organ: the chamber organ, the harmonium, the theatre organ, and the Hammond organ. These instruments have been rather neglected in contemporary classical music. However, they each have their own unique sound and style, potentially offering valuable compositional resources. The foundation established in the previous chapters should provide a solid basis for understanding and writing for these instruments; this chapter therefore deals with the particularities and intricacies of each instrument individually.

Finally, many composers will want to use the organ as part of a larger ensemble, requiring a slightly different approach compared to solo organ music. The sixth chapter, therefore, will cover the various specifics of ensemble organ writing, addressing issues such as balance with other instrumentalists or singers. It draws on examples spanning the whole history of organ music, providing a historical overview of the instrument in ensemble, as well as a jumping-off point for further exploration and listening.

In summary, this book intends to show just how underrated the organ has previously been. The instrument has so much to offer composers, with the instrument being ripe for exploration and with easy scope for original textures and timbres. This guide will therefore hopefully demonstrate exactly why the 'king of instruments' continues to deserve its famous reputation.

How to Use this Book

This book is intended to be an introduction and a reference guide to the organ for composers. It does not purport to be comprehensive, nor to replace collaboration with players. Score study is also incredibly beneficial, and even experienced organists can have their eyes opened by playing the music of Olivier Messiaen or Thierry Escaich, for example. Composers are therefore recommended to fully immerse themselves in as much organ music as possible, through analysing scores, watching and listening to organ performances either live or recorded, and surveying the vast range of educational resources about the organ; the 'Extra Resources' section provides more information about what is available. Where possible, experiment on a real organ, as there is no other substitute for truly understanding the instrument; see 'Accessing an Organ' for further advice.

As a reference guide, the book need not be read from start to finish. The reader should feel free to dip in and out, consulting the sections most relevant to the specific needs. Nevertheless, the book is structured so that any unfamiliar concepts or terminology are always introduced and defined before being used more regularly. Many topics also overlap with each other, so revisiting prior chapters is encouraged as later knowledge gained may offer new insights into old topics.

This book is written in relation to organs in the UK. By and large, however, most of the advice presented should be applicable to organs from every country. The 'eclectic' organ, capable of performing every kind of music equally well, is very common and largely standardised even internationally; a typical specification (i.e., list of stops) is given in Table 2.1. However, different countries tend to have slightly differing organ layouts, as well as specific features not always present on organs from other countries. A brief survey of these differences can be found in the Appendix.

A Note on the Musical Examples

The author believes that the fastest way for composers to learn about organ music is to immerse themselves in as much good organ music as possible. As mentioned earlier, however, much of this music is unknown to non-organists. The musical excerpts in this book, therefore, are intended to not only back up each point but introduce the standard organ repertoire.

The excerpts come from the whole history of notated organ music, from the seventeenth through to the twenty-first centuries, and feature a mix of both well-known and more obscure examples. In all cases, while musical quality is an important factor, idiomatic writing, clarity of notation and relevance to the specific point have been the primary criteria for choosing the excerpts quoted. This book therefore does not apologise for featuring 'organ' composers, such as Vierne and Widor, as prominently as some of the more mainstream names. Registrations, when provided, are usually given as found in the score and in their original language (i.e., how an organist would encounter them).

It is highly recommended to listen to and closely study as many of the excerpts as possible, preferably comparing multiple recordings on different organs. As mentioned earlier, notation software playback is often a poor indicator of how the organ actually sounds and so listening to real organs as much as possible is strongly encouraged. The pieces mentioned in-text should be similarly studied, as they all offer interesting ways to think about the organ. This book hopes to highlight the best organ writing (and that which organists play most regularly) in order to raise the standard, quality and ambition of organ music more generally.

Getting Your Organ Music Performed

Organists are always looking for new music. Not only is the organ repertoire much smaller than for many other instruments, but organists perform more frequently than most other musicians (some cathedral organists perform every day of the week) so consequently always need new pieces. It can therefore be much easier to secure public performances of works on the organ compared to other instruments. Given this situation, the following advice will aim to help composers guarantee their music is played as much as possible.

Most solo organ music is played in the context of a church service. For recitals, organists tend to reuse pieces learned for services in order to economise practice time. Organists are therefore more likely to learn/play pieces which are appropriate for service use (see 'The Organ and Religion') over those which are not. Designating an organ piece for a specific liturgical season such as Christmas or Easter (by quoting a seasonally appropriate hymn/chorale/chant melody, for example) can make a piece more attractive to organists looking for liturgically-appropriate repertoire, although it can limit performances to a particular time of year.

More generally, pieces which are technically less demanding or which have simpler registration are more likely to get a wide transmission. It is true that requiring virtuoso-level technique and complex registrations is sometimes not only unavoidable but even desirable, pushing the organ to new forms of musical expression, and such complex pieces can become very popular or even infamous if executed well (such as Dupré's *Trois Préludes et Fugues*). However, simpler pieces are useful not only for amateur organists but also professionals who need to learn/sight-read a piece quickly for a service or recital. The faster a piece can be learned and the registration set up, the more likely it will be performed in general. Conversely, the harder the piece or the more complex the registration preparation, the greater the musical payoff has to be to justify the time spent learning it.

Many commissions and organ composition competitions request composers to "take the specifics of the organ into account" or words to that effect. What this request means in practice is rather wide-ranging but essentially comes down to making the specific organ sound as good as possible. Make sure, if indicating specific stops, that the particular organ does have the requested ones available in some form. It is also important to know what registration aids are available (see 'Registration Aids' in Chapter 2 for a breakdown of the most common ones). Taking advantage of any particularities of design (see 'Organ Building Trends' in Chapter 1 as well as the guide to national styles in the Appendix) can make a composition really stand out from its competitors. Finally, there is the acoustic in the venue to consider: much traditional organ music is written with a large acoustic in mind, but a dryer acoustic allows for rhythmic precision and clarity at fast tempos unavailable in more reverberant spaces.

Otherwise, as with other types of new music, networking and visibility are crucial in making organists aware of any new compositions. Building a relationship with a specific organist will increase trust and respect between both parties and so increase the likelihood of performance, as well as often guaranteeing a specific organ to write for and explore. Many composers have had their reputations and even legacies established through their organ music; the organ therefore presents exciting opportunities, excelling those for other instruments and potentially guaranteeing a place in the canon for many years to come.

The Organ and Religion

More than any other instrument, the organ commonly bears connotations of religion and spirituality. While organs can be found in venues ranging from concert halls to private houses, they are most commonly located in churches or cathedrals. Since at least the time of St Augustine, organs have been an important part of Christian worship, and today the public perception of the organ is as a religious instrument, particularly associated with high church forms of Christian liturgy. Many of the most successful organ pieces make use of the instrument's spiritual nature, even if the piece is not explicitly Christian. By taking into accounts the requirements of Christian liturgy, composers can ensure that their organ music is performed as frequently as possible.

Solo organ music for church services fills a very functional role. Different denominations of Christianity feature the organ to differing extents. Typically, organists have to play just before a service (normally quiet reflective music of up to about 5 mins) and directly after the service as a 'voluntary' as people leave (a piece generally lasting up to 7 mins, typically louder and more exuberant than pre-service music). Service music is usually relatively limited in dynamic range: music for before the service should not be too loud in case it disrupts the contemplative atmosphere; on the other hand, if the post-service music is too quiet, the organ may be drowned out by the congregation chatting. For longer works, consider splitting the music into multiple movements. Organists commonly excerpt single movements as voluntaries while performing the complete work in recitals, therefore making the music suitable for both service and concert performance.

Much of the organ repertoire is also based around Christian hymns, chorales, and plainchant. For composers wishing to follow suit or to analyse repertoire examples, there are a wide variety of hymnbooks and suchlike in circulation. The *New English Hymnal* is the traditional Anglican hymnbook; other common examples include *Hymns Ancient and Modern* and *Common Praise*. For plainchant, the *Liber Usualis* is still the standard reference resource and can be found online, although it has not been in practical use since Vatican II in 1961. The *Graduale Romanum* and *Graduale Triplex* have a smaller selection of chants but are more up to date and contain the post-1961 revisions. For German chorales, the main hymnbook in circulation is the *Evangelisches Gesangbuch*. Different regions of Germany have different editions with minor variations between them, although all share a core repertory of 535 chorales. Bachian harmonisations of older chorales can also be found (without lyrics) in the *371 Harmonized Chorales* edited by Albert Riemenschneider.

Accessing an Organ

As with any other instrument, practical playing experience is invaluable for learning the ins and outs of the organ. The easiest way to get access to an organ is to find an organ teacher and start taking lessons. This route is typical for many beginning organists, with teachers (who are usually organists at a local church or institution) often letting students practice on 'their' organ. Even just one or two lessons can transform one's knowledge of the instrument and will help contextualise the concepts introduced in this book.

Without teacher connections, finding an organ to play can be more challenging. Some institutions can be unwilling to let anybody practice on their instrument, even other organists. On the other hand, some places can be very friendly and willing to lend access to the organ. In all cases, there is no harm with making a general enquiry to the church or organist in question. There are also many self-teaching resources for the organ; Anne Marsden Thomas's and Frederick Stocken's excellent book *The New Oxford Organ Method* is particularly recommended, focussing on organ technique in the context of proper organ pieces.

There are also alternatives for those not lucky enough to have easy access to an organ. High-quality MIDI-compatible virtual instruments do exist, allowing people to explore the full resources of an organ with just a MIDI keyboard; see 'Software Instruments' for more information. A piano or digital keyboard with an organ patch is a good substitute when learning about keyboard technique. Much can be learned from playing organ parts on a piano without using the sustain pedal; see Chapter 3 for some practical examples. There are many online organ forums if composers have any queries about organ writing. Organists are friendly people and are often willing to help out if asked, especially if it leads to better organ music. Offering services as a page-turner is a non-invasive way to get close to an organ, potentially including large cathedral organs, as well as experiencing the organ repertoire (and its performance) up close. The rise in music live-streaming and virtual recitals among other things makes it easier than ever to find online videos of organists performing. Many recitals film both the hands and feet simultaneously, enabling analysis of all aspects of organ playing in practice.

Software Instruments

As noted above, not all composers will be able to access a real organ. Additionally, beyond classical music, some composers and producers will want virtual instruments for use with DAWs or similar. In the past, organ patches have been very poor quality, giving a very distorted impression of the instrument (notation software playback still has this problem). However, there are an increasing number of high-quality sampled and software organs available in every price range. These virtual instruments can therefore offer much to both classical and non-classical composers and so are worth briefly discussing.

Hauptwerk is currently the best virtual organ software available. As it is primarily aimed at organists, it may not be straightforwardly intuitive to use for composers/producers. However, it offers the user complete control of every aspect of the organ and the sampled instruments often sound indistinguishable from their real counterparts. While it is a standalone program, it can also be integrated into DAWs as a plugin. Hauptwerk also offers a wide range of instruments in a variety of styles, from German Baroque to French Romantic to theatre organs, allowing composers/producers to choose the right organ for their needs. The main drawback is that the software is relatively expensive; individual organ sound sets also need to be bought separately from the main program (although Hauptwerk does include one free instrument by default). There are a range of prices and subscription models available, however, and for a professional composer/producer looking for total control there is no better option. For composers on a budget, GrandOrgue is a free alternative software that, while not having the range of organs or quite the level of sound quality of Hauptwerk, similarly offers total control of registration and the organs available can sound remarkably realistic.

Other companies also offer high-quality organ samples, such as Spitfire Audio's 'Symphonic Organ'. These are typically easier to set up and integrate into DAWs than Hauptwerk, as well as often being cheaper. They also usually offer inbuilt digital effects, making it easy to electronically modulate the sound. The common trade-off, however, is substantially less control of individual stops (see Chapter 1), instead having pre-set combinations such as 'All Stops Out'. In many situations, these presets may be all that is needed. Some of these libraries offer complete lists of stops of each preset, so these can be useful to see whether a certain sound is available.

In short, there is a wide range of organ software available, each with its own advantages and disadvantages. Composers/producers are urged to explore all the options and discover what would work best for them. The availability of sampled organs is greater than ever before, and so there is no better time to search around.

Extra Resources

Beyond this book, many resources have been created specifically to help demystify the organ, with specialist institutions dedicated to the instrument. The Royal College of Organists (RCO) in the UK, American Guild of Organists (AGO) in the USA and the Royal College of Canadian Organists (RCCO) in Canada each have dedicated websites with an extensive range of online videos and resources (although some of the content from these organisations requires paid subscription to access). There are also many smaller societies such as the British

Institute of Organ Studies (BIOS) and the American Theater Organ Society (ATOS). These not only offer online and print resources, but also put on many events throughout their respective countries.

Composers writing for a specific organ may want to consult the instrument's stop-list ('specification' in organ terminology). There are many dedicated websites which offer up-to-date organ catalogues, specifications and photos of the instruments. The main UK resource is the National Pipe Organ Register (https://www.npor.org.uk/); for the USA there is the Pipe Organ Database (https://pipeorgandatabase.org/); and for Australia there is the database provided by the Organ Historical Trust of Australia (https://ohta.org.au/organs-ofaustralia/). Specifications can also be found on the websites for individual churches/institutions, particularly if the instrument is well-known. Other more general websites such as Wikipedia may also contain organ specifications, but these are more infrequent and unreliable than the main databases.

Scores and recordings are plentiful online. IMSLP is the standard resource for sheet music of out-of-copyright composers. For composers still in copyright, digital platforms such as Nkoda offer a wide selection of scores, including some sheet music unavailable for purchase (e.g., large modern choral/orchestral works). While there is often a subscription fee for these platforms, many places own institutional licences allowing students/composers to access them for free. YouTube and Spotify both feature many classic CD recordings and live performances. YouTube in particular has many 'score-videos', displaying the score whilst playing a recording; these cover many of the major organ composers from Bach to Messiaen, as well as a wide range of composers in between.

There are many other resources available both in print and online, covering every aspect of organ design, historical performance practice and every piece of organ terminology conceivable. With technology changing and new books, websites, and videos becoming available all the time, it is easier than ever to access these resources and learn about the organ. The Further Resources section of the Online Resources provides a non-comprehensive but regularly updated list of resources that may be of interest to composers in particular.

INTRODUCTION TO THE ORGAN

Overview

Writing for organ may seem very intimidating at first. However, with some basic knowledge, writing idiomatic organ music is no more difficult than composing for any other instrument. While no two organs are exactly the same, there is a remarkable degree of consistency in organ design even across different centuries and nationalities. The modern 'eclectic' organ, designed to play all parts of the organ repertoire equally well, is the most common type of organ available internationally today and is relatively standardised in design and layout. In addition, there is also surprisingly little technical information that the composer *absolutely* needs to know to write idiomatic music. All the composer fundamentally needs to get started is a basic understanding of the organ and its written range.

The organ is essentially a keyboard wind instrument. Sound is produced through organ pipes, each tuned to a distinct note of the scale, which resonate at their specific pitch when wind is sent through them. Pressing a key opens a valve below the relevant pipes, letting the wind travel into them and creating a constant tone until the key is released. The organ is given a perpetual supply of wind through a set of bellows; this wind is often stored in various reservoirs to ensure a steady stream of air to the pipes (although many pre-Romantic instruments had no such reservoirs, creating a more breathy sound). On modern instruments the bellows are usually operated electronically, but historically they had to be pumped manually, often by an assistant. Pipes are generally made from wood or metal depending on the timbre desired, with most organs having multiple chromatic sets allowing for a wide range of colours and textures.

Figure 1.1 shows the player's control hub for the organ (known as a **console** in organ terminology). An annotated version of this picture is available in the Online Resources.

The Pipe Organ

FIGURE 1.1 A typical organ console

As can be seen in Figure 1.1, there are usually multiple keyboards stacked on top of each other. There is also a pedal keyboard, shown at the bottom of Figure 1.1 (and in focus in Figure 4.1) which is played with the feet; unlike for the hands, the feet can only play one or two notes at a time. The hands have a grand-stave pair like a piano does, one stave for each hand, while the pedals typically have their own separate stave. The written range of these keyboards and pedals is illustrated in Figure 1.2. White noteheads indicate standard range, black noteheads indicate common extensions and brackets indicate rare extensions; Chapters 3 and 4 explain these extensions in more detail for the manuals and pedals, respectively.

FIGURE 1.2 Organ compass

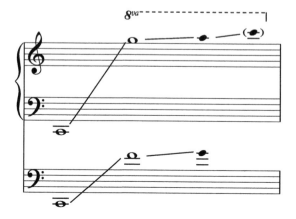

Believe it or not, this is all you need to know about organ notation to start writing idiomatic music. The other thing to bear in mind is that, while the organ is a keyboard instrument, idiomatic organ music is very different from idiomatic piano music; Chapter 3 explains the differences between organ and piano writing more comprehensively. Even the traditional masters of orchestration get this fact wrong, as the following unfortunate example by Strauss shown in Figure 1.3 demonstrates:

FIGURE 1.3 Richard Strauss, *Festliches Präludium* op. 61

Here, Strauss has essentially written for the organ as though it were a piano. It is not clear which notes the pedals should play and which should be taken by the left hand. Strauss goes beyond the lowest note of both the keyboard and the pedals; any attempts to fix it require distorting Strauss' musical intentions. The mid-range is also very sparse, and the gap between top and bottom would sound 'empty'. This example is all the more disappointing because the intention is actually very good, with Strauss' musical ideas being sound (the piece is for organ and orchestra, and Strauss combines the two very effectively). Unfortunately, the execution is poor and requires considerable adaption for actual performance. Figure 1.4 shows what such an adaption may look like.

FIGURE 1.4 Richard Strauss, *Festliches Präludium* op. 61, adapted

Such issues of poor notation are fortunately considerably rarer with modern composers. Even when basic notation has been grasped, however, the organ still offers many untapped possibilities for creativity. The rest of this book is dedicated to the nuances of organ writing, showing the full potential of the instrument. In order to do that, however, it is necessary to start introducing some of the more specific organ terminology. Much of it is not strictly needed to write good organ music, as not very much of it is found in the sheet music itself, but these terms form the basis of discussing the organ in general and so are important to know.

The mushroom-like knobs to the side of the keyboards in Figure 1.1 are called **stops** (sometimes they take the form of tabs; see Figure 5.9). Stops control which pipe valves are opened when a key is pressed, therefore controlling the timbre of the organ. With no stops pulled out, no sound is produced even when the keys are pressed. Each keyboard has different stops available to it. The art of choosing which stops to use and when to change them is known as **registration**. Composers do not necessarily need to know much about registration to write effective organ music; nevertheless, the topic is covered fully in Chapter 2.

The keyboards, in organ parlance, are called **manuals**. The standard number of manuals is two or three; four manuals is typical for cathedral/large concert hall instruments, and some of the largest organs have five or sometimes even more (although in practice these manuals are rarely used). Manuals can also be connected (or 'coupled') to each other by drawing specific stops; these stops are known as **couplers** and are discussed more fully in the 'Couplers' section of Chapter 2.

The **Great** manual (Ger. *Hauptwerk*, Fr. *Grand-Orgue*) is the 'hub' of the organ. It is the middle manual on typical UK/US three-manual organs and the bottom manual for two-manual instruments. Every other manual can be coupled to it and, by extension, every stop on the organ aside from the pedal stops can be played from it. The stops specifically assigned to the Great are usually designed to provide a full, rich sound. It is the loudest manual on the organ unless a Tuba or other solo reed is available on the Choir or fourth manual (see Chapter 2).

The **Swell** (Ger. *Schwellwerk*, Fr. *Récit.*) is the 'expressive' manual. It is usually the top manual for two- or three-manual instruments, although very large organs may have fourth or fifth manuals above it. The pipes on the Swell are voiced softer than the Great and so, generally, the Swell is used for quieter passages than the Great (although there are exceptions). The pipes for the Swell are enclosed by shutters which can be gradually opened or shut with an expression pedal, allowing for a fine control of the Swell dynamics as well as 'true' crescendos and diminuendos. This feature, known as the 'Swell box', is critical for ensuring the organ balances with singers/instrumentalists. The more Swell stops that are out, the more effect the Swell box can have. A good Swell box can make the Swell, with all stops drawn, sound anywhere from *pp* to *ff*.

The **Choir** (Ger. *Rückpositiv*, Fr. *Positif*) is generally only found on three-manual organs, although it can replace the Swell on some two-manual Baroque-inspired instruments. It is often the bottom manual on UK/US organs, although it can be the middle manual particularly on European Romantic instruments. 'Choir' itself is rather a catch-all term, encompassing a wide variety of design principles. A true Choir section is a Romantic invention used for its solo colours as well as for accompanying the choir and which is often enclosed (i.e., it has its own shutters and expression pedal; see Figure 2.36). Modern eclectic organs, however, often instead have a 'Positive' section inspired by Baroque organ design which acts more as a softer secondary Great (although still can be used for solo colours), is unenclosed, and is usually located away from the main case such as in Figure 1.5. In practice, the designation 'Choir' on a stop-list can indicate either a Choir or Positive, particularly in the UK, so it is best to just specify 'Choir' in the score and let the organist adapt to the instrument as necessary.

FIGURE 1.5 Example of a separate Positive case (bottom, on rail) contrasting to main case (middle/top) at Selwyn College, Cambridge, UK. The console is directly behind the Positive case. © Cambridge Filmworks

Much standard repertoire calls for all three manuals and it is often possible to adapt three-manual registrations to two-manual organs. When writing for the manuals, the standard

contractions 'Gt.', 'Sw.', and 'Ch.' are used to save space. Some composers use Roman numerals to indicate manuals, with III, II, and I indicating them in descending keyboard order (III indicating the Swell, etc.). However, this system can lead to ambiguity since the ordering of manuals varies between organs (e.g., 'I' can indicate either the Great or Choir depending on context) and so using the standard contractions is preferable for clarity.

In practice, composers should almost never write for more than three manuals. The fourth manual (known variously as the **Solo, Bombarde, Antiphonal, Echo, Orchestral**, or even other names depending on function; see the Glossary for more detail on the main terms) is uncommon and rarely contains any stops a large three-manual organ would not already have. In addition, balance can also be an issue. For the large venues where most four-manual organs are found, different parts of the instrument are designed to cover different parts of the building, with often only three of the manuals balancing with each other for any particular area. Writing for the standard three manuals alone would not prevent the organist using all the manuals and stops available to them, and they often use the fourth manual where the Swell or Choir is indicated in the score.

Finally, there are some common myths about the instrument which it is important to debunk:

- **"Organs are only available in churches/large concert halls."** With the advent of digital technology, organs are more accessible than ever. The sound quality of digital organs is ever increasing. Software like Hauptwerk also offers sampled instruments and full-scale virtual organ consoles which can be played through MIDI keyboards. It is even possible to hire digital organs; in fact, many UK cathedrals hire in electronic instruments when the main organ is out of action. The fact that some congregations cannot tell the difference between the main organ and the electronic replacement attests to the ever-growing quality of these instruments.
- **"Requesting specific stops will make your music unperformable."** Messiaen, arguably the most internationally performed twentieth-century organ composer, writes incredibly precise registrations that cannot be reproduced exactly on many organs. Organ layouts and stop availability are less varied than may be expected. Organists may have to alter the given registrations for specific organs, but even in this situation precise indications can give a helpful blueprint to work from. Table 2.1 shows which stops are typically found where on a generic organ. The practical aspects of specific registrations are discussed more fully in the 'Overview' of Chapter 2.
- **"The organ is incapable of crescendos/diminuendos."** The Swell box allows 'true' crescendos/diminuendos and is virtually ubiquitous aside from on occasional smaller organs or historic/historically-inspired instruments. In addition, adding or removing stops, when well-timed, can be done so subtly as to be almost undetectable. Mastering smooth crescendos/diminuendos involving stop changes is a fundamental skill to the organist, particularly when playing nineteenth-century organ music and beyond. However, not all crescendos and diminuendos are equally idiomatic. The rapid and wide-ranging crescendos and diminuendos of German Romanticism are manageable with a 'crescendo pedal' (see Chapter 2) but can be virtually impossible without one. When in doubt, slower and smaller-scale hairpins are usually easier to manage than faster and larger ones.
- **"The organ keys are not touch-sensitive."** While the volume is always the same when a key is depressed, subtleties of articulation and phrasing are incredibly dependent on touch.

This sensitivity is particularly noticeable on tracker-action organs (see 'Organ Building Trends'): slowly depressing the key opens the pipe valve slower and so produces a softer attack, while quick presses and releases create a more marcato sound. Articulation is considerably more important on the organ than on the piano, and the nuances of touch are very crucial for expression and musicality on the instrument. Some extended techniques also make use of touch sensitivity; see 'Extended Techniques' for more information.

- **"The larger the organ, the better it will be."** A bigger stop-list does not indicate a better instrument. There are many very fine two-manual or even one-manual organs which sound rich and vibrant with just a handful of stops, while equally there are many poorly designed four-manual instruments with large specifications which sound weaker and are less flexible than the huge stop-list may suggest. Moreover, small organs in small venues can offer a unique character their larger cousins cannot replicate and so are particularly useful for composers looking to get away from stereotypical organ usage.

Organ Building Trends

Across the centuries, various organ building trends have come in and out of fashion, with certain trends being particularly popular in certain countries. The influence of these trends on the instrument's evolution has led to organs which can share a similar stop-list yet both sound and feel very different to play. Even on modern eclectic organs, there are subtle design choices which make each instrument better suited to playing certain types of repertoire. While composers should not worry too much about these variations (the author has heard Messiaen played on historic German Baroque organs!), taking these trends into account when writing for a specific organ can make the instrument (and, by extension, the composer's music) sound at its best. A list of the most common organ styles and their features, with representative builders and composers, can be found in the Appendix. Where possible, composers should also spend as much time at the specific organ in question. Below, however, are some of the most important variations.

Firstly, there is the touch or 'action'. **Mechanical action** (commonly known as **tracker action**) is when depressing the key mechanically opens the pipe valve. This contrasts with **electric action**, where depressing the key connects a circuit which opens the pipe valve. With tracker action, it is possible to control the speed of opening the pipe, allowing for a much greater range of articulation and expressive possibilities; however, the touch can become very heavy with many couplers and stops drawn, making fast figuration and chordal passages harder to play particularly at loud volumes. With electric action, the reverse is true: while the expressive possibilities are limited for individual notes, the keys can have a springiness which makes loud virtuosic passagework and thick chordal textures much easier to play. Tracker action is often preferred by modern organists owing to its expressive potential, but both types have their strengths and weaknesses which composers should seek to exploit.

The tonal design of the organ is also an important consideration. On Baroque and neoclassical instruments, the sound of each stop is more incisive and penetrating, with fewer possibilities for smoothly graded dynamics. On Romantic instruments, however, the stops are designed to blend together to produce a symphonic sound, allowing the organ to transition from *pp* to *ff* with any stop changes being almost imperceptible. Modern eclectic instruments typically fall halfway between these two extremes, with some degree of both independence and blend. A fuller breakdown of the standard organ tonal designs can be found in the Appendix.

Finally, there are the registration aids. The devices available vary considerably from organ to organ: some instruments have none available at all, while others have sophisticated electronic systems with a whole range of programmable buttons. Most eclectic organs will have 'general pistons' which can change all of the stops instantly (see Chapter 2), but other registration aids often depend on the country and style the organ was built in (see the Appendix). While it is ultimately the performer's responsibility to decide which registration aids to use for any given situation, taking account of what is available can help make the composition suit the organ, leading to a better performance. The standard registration aids are covered fully in 'Registration Aids' in Chapter 2.

Historic Organs

On occasion, composers may have the opportunity to write for very old organs. While many have been rebuilt or substantially altered at least every century, some have been preserved unaltered for half a millennium, sometimes longer. The twentieth-century interest in neoclassicism has also seen some modern organs built to replicate historic designs. For non-classical composers, an increasing number of sampled historic instruments are available through Hauptwerk or similar software. Historic organs can present unique compositional challenges compared to the modern organ, but equally they can offer extraordinary sound-worlds of which modern instruments are incapable (Anna von Hauswolff's album *All Thoughts Fly* demonstrates just how modern sounding these historic instruments can be), and so a few of the unique aspects of these instruments are listed here.

Historic organs generally have a more limited manual and pedal compasses than their modern counterparts. It is not uncommon to see an upper limit of C_6 in the manuals and D_4 in the pedals on historic instruments. Even different manuals on the same organ can have different compasses (see, e.g., 'French Classical—Chapelle royale, Versailles' in the Online Resources). Some historic organs only have one manual, like most modern chamber organs. The pedals may also be 'pull-downs', coupled permanently to the manuals rather and not always having a separate set of pedal stops. Registration aids either do not exist or are very limited on true historical organs; however, modern organ builders sometimes add a few 'anachronistic' registration aids as a compromise to modern players. The specifics naturally vary from organ to organ, and so closer study of the particular historic instrument in question is more important than when dealing with more modern organs.

Tuning and temperament must also be taken into account. A = 440hz was only universally standardised in 1953, although A = 435hz was very common from 1859 onwards (and many organs built since the nineteenth century have been retuned to modern concert pitch). Consequently, the pitch of some historic organs can vary significantly, both higher as well as lower than modern pitch. Arguably more crucial for composers, however, is temperament. Equal temperament (where the octave is divided into twelve equal parts) has been widespread since the nineteenth century and is the modern standard. Many historic organs, however, are tuned to unequal temperaments such as meantone. In these unequal temperaments, certain chords can sound more perfectly in tune than in equal temperament, while others (typically those involving accidentals) can sound considerably more dissonant. Some historic organs (mostly from Italy) even have divided sharp keys, as, for example, G♯ and A♭ are different notes in meantone temperaments; see 'Italian Renaissance—Basilica di Santa Barbara, Mantua' in the Online Resources for one example.

Some one-manual organs have 'split keyboards', with different stops for the treble and the bass ranges (see, e.g., 'Spanish Baroque—Capilla de San Enrique, Burgos Cathedral' in the Online Resources). This splitting allows a wider range of textures than non-split, one-manual keyboards: it is possible to have, for example, a solo registration in the treble with accompaniment in the bass or vice versa. A split keyboard can normally be easily adapted to two-manual instruments, although this is not always the case. Split keyboards can also be found on some chamber organs and are a standard feature of harmoniums; see Chapter 5 for more information.

Finally, there is also the so-called 'short octave' which is found on some Renaissance and Baroque organs as well as older harpsichords, clavichords, and so forth. With the short octave, the lowest octave of the keyboard is mostly commonly compacted as shown in Figure 1.6 (this arrangement is usually written as C/E or CDEFGA when describing organ compasses).

FIGURE 1.6 Short octave

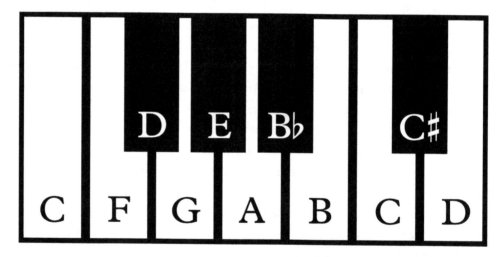

In practice, this short octave means that the lowest octave of accidentals is largely unavailable; however, the compact layout also makes different chord shapes possible in this lowest octave. Fast passagework in the low octave can also be very difficult for modern organists owing to the unfamiliar key layout. Some organs do have extra low accidentals in the form of split D/F♯ and E/B♭ keys (the 'broken octave' layout) or sometimes even more complex layouts. However, Figure 1.6 shows the most common, and most limiting, scenario and so provides a useful reference which can be expanded upon for specific instruments.

Common Mistakes

When writing for organ, there are a number of common 'mistakes' non-organist composers often make. These will be examined in more detail in their relevant chapters, but a brief overview of each is provided here.

Writing Outside the Written Range

Composers who do not understand organ registration frequently write higher or lower than the given ranges to try and capture the extreme high/low sounds of the organ. This was common even for famous composers of the past, as Figure 1.3 shows. These days, many composers have a greater understanding of the organ and so this problem is rarer than it used to be. However, notating high-lying passages in particular still causes problems, especially since the highest note available depends on the specific organ (see Figure 1.2). For practical purposes, it is usually best to not go above a high A_6 except in special circumstances. Chapters 3 and 4 go into more detail on the manual and pedal compasses respectively.

Unidiomatic Textures

Understanding what defines idiomatic textures on the organ can be very difficult without physically experimenting on an instrument. As mentioned earlier, idiomatic organ writing is often very different even compared to other keyboard instruments such as the piano. When handled well, the organ can produce an almost symphonic range of textures that rival orchestras or electronic music in their breadth and variety.

'Overwritten' textures are a common problem even in canonical organ repertoire: the German Romantic school, and in particular the composer Max Reger, is often criticised for very dense organ writing (see, e.g., Figure 3.7). In practice, registration often does much of the work of thickening the chords. Take for example the standard Anglican or Catholic hymn. Organists typically play from the four-part choir score such as in Figure 1.7, the pedals taking the bass part. Through registration, this texture sounds very full and is loud enough to support a full congregation (see also Howells's *Like as the Hart* in the Online Resources for Chapter 2 for a more sophisticated example of this hymn-like texture).

FIGURE 1.7 Hymn-tune 'Caswall'

Additionally, one common textural error is to write too low for the left hand, particularly for loud passages. This is another area where the organ is very different from other keyboard instruments. Low-lying chords project less well on an organ than on a piano, and the organ's indefinite sustain makes these chords sound more 'muddy' than on other keyboard instruments. Registration can add lower as well as upper octaves which can help fill out the mid-range of harmonies, with the pedals providing a solid bass foundation. The most brilliant and full sounds of the organ are therefore in the mid to upper register in both hands. The famous opening of Messiaen's 'Dieu parmi nous' from *La Nativité du Seigneur* offers one example of how effective this upper register can be, with Messiaen achieving a cataclysmic sound despite using only four-note chords (two notes per hand) and single pedal notes. In Figure 1.8, the high register and clever use of counterpoint suits the organ perfectly, being eminently playable and idiomatic while still achieving a rich and full sound.

FIGURE 1.8 Ben Levin, *Small Animal PNG Attachment Open Wide From My Star's New Hand*
© Ben Levin

Conversely, there is no need to be unnecessarily reticent about thicker textures. As numerous French and English Romantic examples show, chordal writing can be as idiomatic as sparser textures if handled well. There is a balance to strike between the two extremes. Chapter 3 in particular will offer a more in-depth consideration of this aspect of organ writing. However, the following techniques (many of which are demonstrated in Figure 1.8) can help to achieve this balance:

- *Chord Voicing*: A well-voiced chord achieves the maximum effect through the minimum number of notes. Careful attention to voicing will yield dividends regarding both playability and effectiveness.
- *Broken chords*: Broken chords (and more general broken figuration) minimise the number of notes sounding simultaneously, often easing execution considerably. With a generous acoustic, the individual notes can blend together into shimmering chords, particularly at faster tempi.
- *Close hand positions between chords*: With no sustain pedal, the hand cannot release chords early like on a piano. Keeping chords close in terms of hand position therefore makes them easier to play, no matter the articulation. Tied notes between chords are very idiomatic.
- *Articulation*: Breaks between chords, through articulation and phrasing, give the hands time to reposition themselves. Organists are trained to follow articulations and phrase marks to the letter; the end of a slur implies a break before the next chord. Well-chosen articulation is what shows that a composer truly understands the organ.

Not Enough Use of the Pedals

The pedals as a unit are often undervalued and underused. The lack of percussive upper partials in the organ sound, combined with the organ's indefinite sustain, means that manuals-only passages have a very different effect compared to being played on a piano. The pedals' main function is to strengthen the bass, making up for the lack of these upper partials and giving support to the rest of the organ sound as well as reinforcing (or contrasting with) articulation in the manuals. Every manual can be coupled to the pedals, and so the pedals can be used as a completely independent extension of the hands. Note that the pedals do not always have to be used in their lowest octave. Just like for double basses, the middle and upper register of the pedals are often under-utilised yet have lots of potential. As Chapter 4 will show, the pedals can also fill a variety of non-bass roles and so can open up a whole range of compositional possibilities.

Misuse of Double Pedalling

In contrast to the previous point, double pedalling is so regularly misunderstood that using it at all has become a worryingly good indicator for inexperience with the organ. Not only is double pedalling technically challenging (especially so with straight pedalboards; see the 'Overview' to Chapter 4 on straight vs. concave pedalboards) but it also limits control of dynamics: smooth crescendos/diminuendos are virtually impossible since neither foot is free to operate the Swell box. Double pedalling can also inadvertently weaken the clarity of the bass line, particularly with small intervals between the feet. Many double-pedalled passages can be made more idiomatic simply by assigning the upper pedal note to the left hand. However, in the right context, double pedalling can be incredibly effective and lead to entirely new soundworlds. A full discussion of double pedalling is provided in Chapter 4.

Misunderstanding the Relationship between Registration and Dynamics

Registration and dynamics are fundamentally intertwined. To change dynamics, stops must be added or removed unless the Swell box is used, with the box only able to cover a limited dynamic range unless many Swell stops are drawn. Stop changes therefore *must* be taken into account when thinking about dynamics, even if no specific registrations are given in the score (so for example timing stops changes to happen in phrase breaks; see Figure 2.6). In addition, when specific registrations are given, the dynamics should reflect the relative volume the stops drawn produce. Registrations and dynamics which do not match (e.g., crescendoing from *p* to *ff* while requesting 8′ stops alone; see Chapter 2) are confusing and can lead to the organist misunderstanding and/or compromising the composer's intentions. This issue is explored in more detail in the 'Overview' to Chapter 2.

Balance

One common issue when composers request specific stops is balance. It is not uncommon to see registrations which do not balance with themselves (e.g., loud stops such as reeds overpowering other quieter stops, louder manuals inadvertently drowning out the softer ones, etc.) or with other instruments/singers. The organist may have to substantially compromise these given registrations to make the balance work, therefore distorting the composer's vision. Difficulties with balance are most acute when dealing either with uncoupled manuals or with very soft registrations (e.g., Swell Flute 4′ alone). Balancing gets harder the larger the organ (and the venue) becomes, with softer stops often inaudible and loud stops often overwhelming. Successful balance can even depend on exactly where the audience/congregation will be sitting, as well as where any other instrumentalists or singers will be positioned. Such issues of balance are often minimal where registration is left entirely to the performer, who can then adapt to the given situation. Precise registrations can be equally valid in this regard, however, as long as the composer takes due care.

While issues of balance are best solved in collaboration with an organist, there are some general practices that can help minimise risk of imbalance. The more couplers that can be out, the easier precise balance will be to control overall as the organist will effectively have more stops per manual to work with. The Swell box, usually available on all but historic or historically-inspired instruments, is indispensable for fine gradations of volume; coupling the Swell (or any other enclosed manual) to other manuals can therefore give more leeway for flexibility. When in doubt, it is also advisable to make the Swell registration itself louder and let the box do the rest of the work, as the Swell box has more effect the more stops are drawn. Chapter 2 examines the specifics of registration in more detail; Chapter 6 looks at how to balance the organ in an ensemble.

Extended Techniques

Extended techniques on the organ are a controversial topic. On the one hand, many such techniques are now fairly standard in organ music. On the other, many organists (and organ-builders) are still nervous about these techniques and may even refuse to program works which include them. 'Preparing' the organ will usually require employing an organ tuner to avoid long-term damage, which can be costly and time-consuming. Nevertheless, such techniques do have the potential to be used successfully; as such, a variety of the most common extended techniques are listed here. Chamber organs (see Chapter 5) are often better suited for extended techniques than regular instruments, with the effects being more audible, reliable, practical, and less prone to inadvertent damage on these smaller instruments. Note that there is no standardised notation for most of these techniques, so any symbols should be explained where necessary. A full interview with an organ builder about extended techniques is provided in the Online Resources.

Clusters

Cluster chords have become a mainstay and even cliché technique in contemporary organ music (see, e.g., Ligeti *Volumina*, Rautavaara *Annunciations*, Ginastera *Turbae ad Passionem Gregorianum*, Gubaidulina *In Croce*, Xenakis *Gmeeorh*). However, clusters can also be problematic to perform. Organ manuals are delicate and using anything other than the hands for clusters can potentially damage the instrument. An organ's wind supply may not be able to cope with a large number of notes held down, particularly if the organ has no reservoirs to store wind beforehand. Clusters are generally more awkward to execute on the organ than on a piano, given the physical position of the manuals relative to the player. Very large clusters have even caused organs to break down on occasion as the notorious performance history of Ligeti's *Volumina* attests. However, if treated with care, clusters can be a very useful compositional tool with minimal risk to the instrument.

Effective cluster chord writing on the organ is essentially just an extension of effective chordal writing more generally. Smaller clusters are more idiomatic, easier to play, will not damage the instrument and can sound as loud and dissonant as larger clusters through well-chosen registration and tessitura. Staccato cluster chords are also easier to execute than legato ones as the hand has time to reposition. Figure 1.9 demonstrates these principles excellently. The clusters are saved for the climax of the piece, maximising their impact. Their small size and detached articulation makes them easily manageable by the flat part of the left hand alone, with no risk of harm to the organ. Escaich's very musical use of these clusters (copying the opening motif of the piece, the plainchant tune Ave Maris Stella) also elevates them from just being a gimmick to being an integral development of the musical material.

FIGURE 1.9 Thierry Escaich, *Récit* © Éditions Billaudot

Half-Drawn Stops/Half-Depressed Notes

On organs with mechanical stop action (where drawing the stops mechanically controls whether air reaches the pipes), the stops need not be drawn out fully. By only half-drawing the stops, the wind to the pipe is weakened, thus changing the sound quality. A similar effect can be achieved by depressing the key only halfway, although this can be very difficult to control. Note that mechanical stop action is relatively rare, even on tracker-action organs, and many older organs have been retrofitted with electric stop action where the stops and keys are either 'on' or 'off'. These techniques can also sound like an organ fault rather than an intended musical effect, so take care to make sure it sounds deliberate. Kit Downes provides an excellent example of these techniques in 'Rat Catcher' from his album *WEDDING MUSIC*.

Removing/'Preparing' Pipes

Some composers request for some pipes to be removed (see, e.g., Bauckholt *Gegenwind*) or otherwise 'prepared' by, for example, taping coins or other objects to them. Such preparation normally requires a specialist in order to avoid damage. Preparation is also a time-consuming process, meaning that pipes generally cannot be removed (or replaced) during a piece or even a full recital/service/concert. For large organs especially, the pipes will often be so far from the listener that the effect of preparation will be inaudible. Preparation is generally however both easier and more audible on smaller instruments, chamber organs in particular (see 'Chamber Organ' in Chapter 5), and so these instruments offer more potential in this regard.

Microtonal tuning is a more practical application of this type of preparation. Once again, such tuning must be used for an entire programme, and the pipes must obviously be tuned back to normal afterwards thus incurring additional costs. Organists *might* occasionally be able to tune certain pipes on organs themselves without requiring a specialist, saving time and money, but this is very context-dependent (most types of organ pipe require specialist tools to tune, and individual pipes can be incredibly difficult to access on some organs) and the organist should always be consulted in this instance.

'Stuck' Notes

As notes on the organ last until the key is released, they can be held indefinitely through the use of small weights or other contraptions. The device is called 'stuck' notes because it physically replicates a common organ fault, called a 'cipher', where notes keep sounding even though a key is not depressed. It is possible to change the registration around the stuck note, even cancelling it entirely for the appropriate manual. White keys are easier to 'stick' than black keys.

This technique has a surprisingly long history. Theodor Dubois employs it in his 'Marche de Rois Mages' from his *12 Pièces pour orgue*; the piece has become a novelty classic and is frequently performed for Epiphany services (see also Grainger *The Immovable Do* for the same technique in a similar novelty piece). This technique is less invasive and more practical than many others listed in this section and, given that it combines well with the organ's indefinite sustain, can prove a useful resource for exploring new textures.

'Registration' Trill

It is possible to rapidly add and remove a single stop to produce a type of 'registration' trill. More wide-scale changes can be achieved through trilling on registration aids. This is one of the few extended techniques which works better on electric-action over mechanical-action instruments. Obviously, the organist will either need a hand free to operate the stops/registration aids or a registrant (see Chapter 2) will need to be present. The speed of this trill is also limited by how fast the specific organ responds to stops being added/removed or registration aids being used. Trills involving fewer stops are often able to be performed more quickly than those requiring more stops. The organ's wind supply may also struggle to cope with the constant changes of registration. This technique is very rarely requested so its true practical value has yet to be fully determined.

Altering the Organ Wind Pressure

Some composers such as Ligeti (see, e.g., *Two Etudes for Organ*) request reducing the wind pressure of the organ in order to achieve a more 'pale' sound. Such a request would require hiring a specialist organ builder or tuner to make this alteration. In addition, it could essentially prevent the organ being used for other pieces in the same programme. Organ winding and wind pressure is very carefully calibrated, and so altering this wind-flow could upset the fundamental tonal unity of the instrument. Requesting this technique, while not unviable, would therefore inevitably hinder further performances.

Turning the Organ On/Off Mid-Chord

Different instruments turn on and off in different ways: for some, the wind slowly tails off leading to sagging chords, while for others the electric relays turn off instantly causing the sound to stop abruptly. While some composers have made use of this technique (e.g., Pärt *Annum per Annum*; Frances-Hoad *Psalm 1*), the effect is especially inconsistent and unreliable even compared to other extended techniques. However, this technique is very effective (and non-damaging) on older mechanical and bellow-operated organs.

Electronic Amplification/Audio Effects

Traditional amplification has mixed effectiveness on an organ. The organ is notoriously difficult to mic: a large instrument can have thousands of pipes, with different sections of pipes spaced very far apart, so close micing is often impractical. Furthermore, the wide dynamic range of the organ makes balancing and levelling the audio input very difficult. However, amplification can be useful in certain situations such as bringing out quieter extended techniques (e.g., blower noise, stop action). An increasing number of institutions these days also have PA systems, enabling easy incorporation of amplification without much extra equipment needed.

It is with digital organs, however, where the future really lies in this regard. Most digital organs, and even a few modern 'real' instruments, have MIDI in/out ports. This feature allows for radical reconceptions of the organ, for example, using the organ console as a synth controller (or mixing synth sounds in with traditional organ stops) or controlling the organ through a DAW (with the potential for incredibly complex looping setups and videogame-like dynamic and adaptive music). Such options have been largely unexplored either by organists or composers, yet these features can offer an exciting and very modern way of thinking about the organ.

While extended techniques can offer new timbral and colouristic options, composers should also explore the full possibilities of registration. There is much unexplored potential in registration, offering composers novel sounds without the inconvenience necessary for preparing extended techniques. The art of registration and its nuances is therefore the topic for the next chapter.

REGISTRATION 2

Overview

Registration is perhaps the most important yet misunderstood aspect of organ playing. Many books on the subject jump straight into technical registration terminology; however, this approach rarely helps with knowing what to actually write in the score. Yet registration is less complicated, and more standardised across organs, than it initially may seem. Once the basic principles are understood, it is possible to exploit the full range of colours from any size of organ and show how versatile the instrument can truly be.

Firstly, there is no 'wrong' way to go about notating registration. Different styles of music will need different approaches, with personal preference as important a factor as any other. Inventive approaches to notation can also lead to very effective and innovative uses of the organ (see, e.g., Nishimura *Vision in Flames*). In practice, most approaches fall between two extremes:

- The composer leaves the registration and manual distribution entirely to the organist, using dynamics as guidance. There are many advantages to this approach, the main one being that organists can easily adapt registrations to any instrument they play. The trade-off is that the composer themselves has less control over specific registrations, hindering compositional exploration of more complex organ colours.
- The composer specifies every single stop used at every point. Dynamics and hairpins indicate the Swell box position alone and give a rough outline of relative volume; they do not indicate stop changes. This approach is common to twentieth-century French composers such as Messiaen and Duruflé. The main advantage is that the composer can explore the full timbral potential of the instrument rather than just relying on the organists to choose the stops. However, performers may have to make compromises if certain stops are unavailable.

There is also a 'half-way' approach, where composers indicate some specific registrations while leaving other decisions (e.g., which stops to add in crescendos) up to the performer. This compromise allows for both precise colours and flexible adaption to each organ, but the drawback is potential confusion. Does *pp* indicate a quiet registration or possibly a loud registration but with the Swell box shut? Does a hairpin from *p* to *f* indicate adding stops or just opening the box? Being wary of such ambiguities can help ensure the composer's vision is accurately realised.

The Pipe Organ

⏵ All of these approaches to registration can be equally viable and idiomatic. Minimal registration instructions can allow organists to adapt the music to any instrument, with composers including Paul Hindemith and Kenneth Leighton writing very idiomatic music with a minimum of registrations. It is still possible to access the whole range of organ colours, potentially even beyond what can be achieved with more precise registrations, while keeping the music suitable for smaller organs. Video 2.1 in the Online Resources show how Howells's *Like as the Hart*, a piece easily playable on most two-manual organs, may be adapted to utilise the full resources of a four-manual English Romantic organ.

Bear in mind also that registrations can be implied through musical features such as texture, dynamics and articulation. In Figure 2.1, Parry's slow tempo, homophonic chordal texture and use of tenuto marks indicate a very specific character (majestic, rich, and stately) for which organists can select an appropriate registration (e.g., Foundations 8′; see 'Foundations' later in this chapter). Manual indications such as 'Sw.' in Figure 2.1 are incredibly useful to the organist, as they can help indicate dynamic contrast better than dynamics alone can (Parry indicates manual changes later in the piece). It is always clear to the organist if the composer understands organ registration, even when no registration indications are given, by how the composer uses these features to guide the performer's approach to organ sonority.

FIGURE 2.1 Charles H. H. Parry, *Elegy*

⏵ At the other end of the spectrum, extremely precise registrations are equally viable and performable, even if the requested stops are not always available. Specific registrations need not be a barrier to performance; in fact, traditional organ repertoire requiring specific stops (e.g., French Romanticism, Messiaen) is performed as frequently, if not more so, than the music where registration is left more to the performer (e.g., German Romanticism). Organists are used to adapting specific registrations to different organs, either by substituting similar-sounding stops or even making do without certain stops. Precise stop indications can give organists a clear blueprint to work from so that, even if the exact stops are not available, they know the composer's envisaged sound and so can find the most suitable alternative. The Online Resources contain an explanation of how

Messiaen's 'Joie et clarté' from *Les Corps Glorieux* (a work with extremely complex and specific registrations) could be adapted for a typical eclectic organ and how organists go about such adaption more generally.

Moreover, such compromises can be minimised and even avoided through well thought-out registrations. While the names and precise sounds of stops vary from organ to organ (including across organs built by the same builder), the general type and placement of stops is surprisingly consistent even across organs of different time periods and nationalities. With some experience, it is possible to predict roughly what stops will be available where on any given size of organ and, consequently, plan registrations that will fit on as many organs as possible. Table 2.1 later in this chapter provides a sample stop-list for the average organ, showing the typical stops available and their location.

To explore registration further, and to talk about notating for specific stops in more detail, we first need to understand the fundamental principles of how organ stops work. A typical organ stop is shown in Figure 2.2.

FIGURE 2.2 A typical organ stop

As can be seen, there are typically three pieces of information indicated, given here from top to bottom:

1. The stop number ('23' in Figure 2.2). This number is used in stop-lists and is useful for registrants (console assistants who pull stops in and out) but is largely irrelevant for composers.
2. The name ('Salicional' in Figure 2.2). This indicates the timbre of the stop. For practical purposes, most of these timbres can be grouped into four distinct and universal families: principals, flutes, strings, and reeds. Specific stop names and spellings vary markedly from organ to organ and so organists use prior experience, as well as common sense, to work out how a stop will sound from its name alone (see the sample stop-lists in the Appendix section of the Online Resources; patterns should quickly emerge even across this small selection of organs). In Figure 2.2, 'Salicional' indicates a type of string stop. The main families, along with common stop names, will be discussed in more detail in the 'Main Stop Categories' section.
3. The sounding octave ('8″' in Figure 2.2.). In organ terminology, pitch is described in feet, that is, 8′ is 'eight foot', 4′ is 'four foot', etc. 8′ indicates written pitch (the number comes from the length of a low C_2 pipe). Halving the number raises the pitch one

octave, while doubling the number lowers it one octave. Figure 2.3 provides a practical illustration (see also Video 2.2 on the companion website for a visual demonstration).

FIGURE 2.3 Written vs sounding pitches

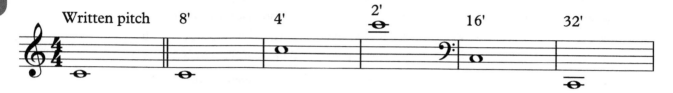

The two main outliers in this numbering system are the mixtures (which sound multiple pipes at once, the exact number being indicated by Roman numerals, e.g., III, IV) and mutation stops (which sound at non-octave harmonics and so contain fractions, e.g., 2 2/3). Both of these stop types are discussed fully in 'Mixtures' and 'Mutations' respectively later in this chapter.

8′, 4′, 2′ are very common across all manuals. 1′ are only found on the very largest organs, typically as a flute on the Swell or Choir. Mixtures are also very common on all manuals although they are not always available on the Choir. 16′ are relatively common on the Great, less common on the Swell and very rare on the Choir. For the pedals, everything is an octave lower (i.e., 16′ stops are the most common, followed by 8′, 4′, and rarely 32′); this 16′ basis is why the pedals sound lower than their written range may suggest.

These upper and lower octaves are *not* primarily range extensions, unlike what Samuel Adler implies in his *Study of Orchestration*, for example. Instead, these stops are designed to reinforce and blend with the 8′ (or 16′ in the pedals' case), thus strengthening the overtones of the fundamental pitch, forming a so-called 'chorus'. Adding/removing these higher-pitched pipes is therefore *essential* to controlling dynamics. Single stops can make all the difference on whether a registration does or does not balance in practice.

Higher and lower-pitched stops can also be used without the 8′, although audibility and balance must be carefully considered. Figure 2.4 provides one successful modern example (see also Liszt arr. Saint-Saëns *Deux légendes*, 'St. François d'Assise' and Escaich *Evocation IV*). Gubaidulina 'doubles' the 2′ and 4′ with the 1′ and 2′, respectively, helping make sure the organ is audible in the orchestral texture (this technique is especially useful on enclosed manuals such as the Swell). Note also that Gubaidulina could have written both hands an octave higher but chose not to. This decision gives the organist considerably more flexibility regarding registration, with multiple alternatives available if a 1′ stop is not present (e.g., playing the right hand an octave higher with 4′ and 2′).

FIGURE 2.4 Sofia Gubaidulina, *The Rider on the White Horse* © Sikorski Music Publishers

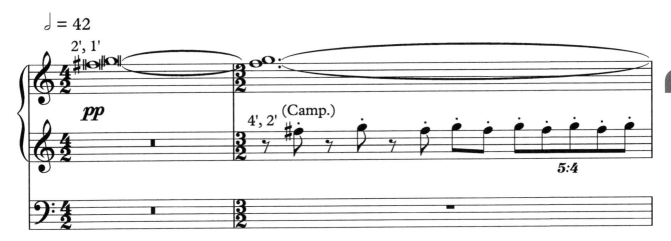

'Gapped' registrations are when either the 8′ or 4′ is absent but both octaves either side are present, most commonly using flute stops (e.g., Flutes 8′, 2′). The resulting effect sounds modern (traditional registration practices avoid such gaps) and can be very effective, particularly in quieter contexts. Messiaen provides a beautiful example, with the 16′, 4′, and 2′ flutes, in 'Le Dieu caché' from the *Livre du Saint Sacrament*. The pairing of Flutes 8′ and 2′ (or 8′ plus a mutation) is relatively common for a light, sparkling sound; Figure 2.5 by Escaich demonstrates the filigree yet uncanny nature of this sound excellently (see also McDowall *A Prayer of St Columba*, Litaize *Prélude et danse fuguée*).

FIGURE 2.5 Thierry Escaich, *Cinq Versets sur le Victimae Paschali*, III © Éditions Henry Lemoine

To indicate specific stops in a piece, standard practice is to provide its name (or category) and octave, for example, Bourdon 8′; Founds 8′, 4′. Terms such as 'Tutti', 'Full Swell' or similar indicate that most stops should be drawn aside from the quietest stops (which would be inaudible and might cause phase cancellation) and/or the Choir solo reed (which would overly dominate the tutti sound). In ensemble situations, the organist may also leave out some stops for better balance with other instruments/singers (see Chapter 6). Consolidate information wherever possible: it is clearer and more efficient to write 'Founds 8′, 4′, 2′' than 'Principals

8′, 4′, 2′, Flutes 8′, 4′, and so forth. It is normal to include the starting registration setup at the head of the piece, for example,

Sw.: Full Swell
Gt.: Founds 8′, 4′, Sw. to Gt.
Ped.: Founds 16′, 8′, Sw. to Ped., Gt. to Ped.

Later in the piece, any indications can be much shorter (for example, Sw. + 2′, – Gt. to Ped). If just one stop needs to be added or removed, use a plus/minus sign respectively. If a manual's registration needs to be substantially changed, write the new registration out in full (see, e.g., Figure 2.34). Experience will help determine how much/little information is needed.

Some composers include a full organ specification in the prefactory notes (e.g., Adès *Fool's Rhymes*, Moussa *A Globe Itself Infolding*). However, this information is usually unnecessary: not only does a stop-list give remarkably little information about how an organ will sound, the stops actually needed will be clear in the score itself. It is more efficient to just include the name of the venue and, where applicable, the national style of the organ (see the Appendix); organists can then look up the exact organ specification online if necessary.

A sample specification is provided in Table 2.1, showing a standard stop layout for an average eclectic modern organ. This stop-list is useful if writing without a specific instrument in mind and, even if writing for a particular instrument, it can help ensure the piece can be adapted to other organs. For two-manual instruments, just remove the Choir stops/couplers and the specification should otherwise work unchanged. (fl), (pr), (str), and (rd) indicate flutes, principals, strings, and reeds, respectively for clarity and need not be written in scores.

Table 2.1 Sample specification

Great	*Swell*
[Flute 16′/Principal 16′]	[Flute 16′]
Principal 8′	[Principal 8′]
Flute 8′	Flute 8′
Solo Flute 8′	[Flute Celeste 8′]
Principal 4′	Gamba 8′ (str)
Flute 4′	Voix Céléste 8′ (str)
Twelfth 2 2/3′ (pr)	Principal 4′
Principal 2′	Flute 4′
Mixture	Principal 2′/Flute 2′
[Cornet]	Mixture
[Reed 16′]	Oboe 8′ (rd)
Reed 8′	[Vox Humana 8′ (rd)]
[Reed 4′]	[Bassoon 16′ (rd)]
	Trumpet 8′ (rd)
Swell to Great	[Clarion 4′ (rd)]
Choir to Great	

Table 2.1 Continued

Choir	Pedals
[Principal 8′]	[Principal 32′/Flute 32′]
Flute 8′	Principal 16′
Principal 4′	Flute 16′
Flute 4′	Principal 8′
Nazard 2 2/3′ (fl)*	Flute 8′
Flute 2′/Principal 2′	[Flute 4′]
Tierce 1 3/5′ (fl)*	[Mixture]
Larigot 1 1/3′ (fl)	[Reed 32′]
[Mixture]	Reed 16′
Clarinet 8′/Cromorne 8′ (rd)	[Reed 8′]
[Tuba 8′/Solo Reed 8′ (rd)]	
	Great to Pedal
Swell to Choir	Swell to Pedal
	Choir to Pedal

Square brackets indicate stops which, while less commonly available, can still be reasonably requested (although composers should check if they are available before asking for them when writing for specific organs). Slashes (/) indicate where an organ usually has one stop or the other; very large organs will sometimes have both. The two stops indicated by an asterisk (*) are often found on the Swell in the US; see 'Mutations' later in this chapter for more information. The Flute Celeste is virtually non-existent in the UK but is relatively common in the US. A printable version of Table 2.1 is available in the Online Resources.

Unfortunately, it is very difficult for composers to explore practical registration outside of physically experimenting on an organ. Software such as Hauptwerk or GrandOrgue (see 'Software Instruments' in the Introduction) can be a useful substitute, but not all composers will have the budget or necessary hardware to use them. There are online videos and resources on registration, although these are typically very general and aimed at organists rather than composers. Otherwise, the best way to understand registration in practice is by doing as much score-study and critical listening to organ performances as possible. Bear in mind that organists will often adapt registrations from the written score (e.g., substituting an Oboe for a Clarinet) as was discussed earlier in this chapter. With enough listening and analysis, however, composers can nevertheless form a fairly comprehensive picture of how each stop sounds.

Finally, a few specific points:

- **Always check the stop-list when writing for a specific instrument**. The specification in Table 2.1 provides a useful template when writing without a specific organ in mind. However, even some large instruments will not necessarily have all of the stops listed there, particularly those marked with square brackets. Therefore, when writing for a particular instrument, it is a good idea to check if the requested stops are available so that the organist does not need to make any unnecessary compromises.

- **Avoid unintentional ambiguity.** Ambiguity can arise when registration intentions are unclear or do not work in practice. Note that an absence of indications can still clearly express intent, with Kenneth Leighton, Herbert Howells and William Mathias among others implying a clear sonority despite using minimal registrations. Some common causes of ambiguity:
  - *Lack of stop names/categories for 16′, 8′, and 4′ stops.* Indications such as '+4″ are vague and can mean a wide range of very different-sounding options (e.g., adding 4′ principals, flutes, reeds, or any combination of these groups), so stop names or categories here are helpful for clarifying intentions.
  - *Inconsistency in approach.* When opting for a middle-ground approach to notating registration, make sure this approach is applied consistently. One common question organists may have is whether to add stops in crescendos/diminuendos or whether to just use the Swell box. As long as the approach is clear and consistent, there is no need for other verbal explanations aside from maybe a brief prefatory note.
  - *Mismatching dynamics and registration.* Having dynamics and registrations which are incongruent with each other (e.g., a general crescendo from *pp* to *ff* while requesting 8′ stops alone) can be awkward for the organist, who may have to compromise on either the dynamic or the specific registration. Make sure the written dynamics roughly match the actual loudness of the given registration on all manuals but the Swell (where dynamics indicate how open the Swell box should be). See also the final point in this section about the dynamic range of individual stops.
- **Plan stop changes carefully.** Stop changes must be timed carefully, even taking modern registration aids into account. Requiring external help from page turners or registrants can limit performance opportunities. With proper usage, however, music with multiple stop changes can be as idiomatic as that without. Figure 2.6 shows varying situations the organist may find themselves in (the starting registration for each example here is always Founds 8′, 4′ on the manuals and Founds 16′, 8′ in the pedals with all couplers drawn): (a) is the ideal situation; with one hand free, registrations can be changed completely, easily and whenever necessary; (b) is also excellent organ writing: timing registration changes with natural phrase breaks, either in the manuals or in the pedals, makes them easy to execute and sounds very idiomatic. In (c), the pedals can operate the generals/sequencer and pedal divisionals (see 'Registration Aids' later in this chapter) but the hands are likely to be too busy even to operate divisionals. The reverse is true for (d): using the divisionals is possible, but the pedals are too busy to operate the generals. For (e), any form of registration change is a challenge; avoid writing any changes here if possible.

FIGURE 2.6 Registration changes

- **Take account of couplers.** Couplers are an essential part of organ registration and can be critical for ensuring different manuals balance and blend with each other (see 'Common Mistakes' in Chapter 1). Modern organists commonly draw the Swell to Great and Swell to Pedal (and Great to Pedal depending on context) by default unless otherwise requested or if the Swell is being used for solo colours. When asking for specific registrations, it is therefore important to factor in and request the couplers if appropriate. See 'Couplers' later in this chapter for more information.
- **Do not require a wide dynamic range from individual stops.** Different stops have varying degrees of loudness. The principal and reed stops are comparatively louder than the flute and string stops. It is unreasonable to expect, for example, the Swell strings to play *ff* or the Tuba to sound *pp*. Stops are designed to be used in combination and adding/removing stops, particularly of a higher pitch (e.g., 4′, 2′) is the main way to modulate dynamics on the organ as mentioned earlier.

Main Stop Categories

Principals

Common stop names: Open Diapason (or just Diapason), Montre, Geigen, Principal [4′], Prestant [4′], Octave [4′], Fifteenth [2′], Doublette [2′]

The principals (Ger. *Prinzipalen*, Fr. *Principaux*) are the prototypical 'church' organ sound. Most default organ keyboard patches are a type of principal chorus, and the principal stops regularly define the organ sound in pop music contexts (e.g., Muse, 'Megalomania'; The Irrepressibles, 'In This Shirt'). Principals 8′, 4′, 2′, and mixtures on both the Swell and the Great are available on all but the smallest organs. On the Choir, principals are not as ubiquitous, although 4′ and 2′ principals are still relatively common. A 16′ principal on the Great and 32′ principal in the pedals are common on large English Romantic organs, although the former in particular has been gradually replaced by an equivalent flute stop.

The principals have a wide range of uses. The principal chorus (i.e., 8′, 4′, 2 2/3′, 2′, and mixtures, sometimes with a 16′) is the standard sound of the Baroque full organ (known as a 'plenum'). For quieter volumes, the higher-pitched stops are successively removed. The pedal principal chorus is registered similarly (i.e., 16′, 8′, 4′, mixtures and a 16′ reed, sometimes also with a 32′). Figure 2.7 shows a typical situation where this principal chorus would be used (see also Figures 4.41 and 4.49).

FIGURE 2.7 Johann Sebastian Bach, *Fantasia and Fugue in G minor* BWV 542

In Romantic music, the principals are often combined with the flutes as part of the foundation stops (see the 'Foundations' section) to provide a rich sound. For standard crescendos, the principals are usually added after the equivalent flutes and strings; a typical stop crescendo would be 'Flute, Gambe 8'; + Principal 8'; + Flute 4', + Principal 4'', and so forth. The pedal Principal 32' is the quintessential sound of Romantic orchestral organ parts, even at quiet dynamics such as in the famous example in Figure 2.8.

FIGURE 2.8 Gustav Holst, *The Planets* op. 32, 'Saturn, the Bringer of Old Age'

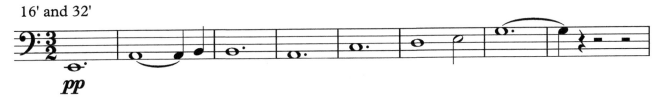

Bear in mind that the principals are noticeably louder and more prominent than flutes or strings, and so their use at quieter dynamics must be carefully considered (although a solo Principal 8', for example, can be an effective solo colour with delicate backing). Additionally, the principals on the Great are usually more substantial than those on other manuals. Because of this, the common request for two manuals of equal volume (in, e.g., the music of Mendelssohn and Leighton) can be difficult to achieve above about *mp*.

Flutes

Common stop names: Flute, Stopped Diapason, Bourdon, Piccolo [2'], Flageolet [2'], Octavin [2']

The flutes (Ger. *Flöten*, Fr. *Flûtes*) are the quieter counterparts of the principals. As the name suggests, the sound is flutelike and delicate, providing a clear and luminescent sound. 8' and 4' flutes are common across all manuals; 2' flutes can sometimes be found on the Swell or, more commonly, the Choir. The Great 16' is normally a flute, although some instruments (e.g., traditional English Romantic organs) may have it as a principal stop. The 16' Swell flute is technically a standard resource, but the stop is surprisingly rare even on medium-sized instruments. While the Pedal 32' is usually a principal stop in the UK, the Flute 32' is very important to composers such as Messiaen and so has seen some spread abroad. Flute Celeste stops (see the 'Strings' section) are relatively common on the Swell in the US but almost non-existent outside of North America; however, their effect can sometimes be roughly replicated with a tremulant (see the 'Miscellaneous Stops' section).

The 8' flute on the Swell can be very quiet on some organs, particularly with the Swell box shut, and should only be used alone with great care (see, e.g., Duruflé *Scherzo*). The Choir and Great flutes, however, have better projection and so can be used more successfully as solo colours. As shown in Table 2.1, the Great may have two 8' flutes: a softer one, usually named 'Bourdon', 'Stopped Diapason', and so forth, designed to blend easily into the foundations and useful for more muted effects (see Figure 2.9); and a more soloistic flute, often named 'Hohl Flute', 'Flute Harmonique', and so forth, which is better suited for expressive melodic lines (see, e.g., Figure 2.34).

The Pipe Organ

In Romantic music, the flutes are often combined with the principals to form the 'foundation' stops (see 'Foundations' later in this chapter). However, unlike the principals, the flutes are commonly requested by themselves as well. They typically lend a delicate, floating colour to scherzo-like passages (see, e.g., Figure 4.51). In Figure 2.9, Judith Weir uses the 8′ flute on the Great alone to simulate the playfulness of water fountains. The alternating chords are easy to play and very effective with the registration.

FIGURE 2.9 Judith Weir, *Ettrick Banks* © Novello & Co Ltd

The pairing of 8′ and 4′ flutes on the Choir is one of the stock sounds of post-Impressionist French organ music, the 4′ helping bolster the soft sound of the 8′ flute while not adding any heaviness. This pairing is frequently used for transparent filigree passagework, with Dupré's 'Prelude in G minor' being a prototypical example. Figure 2.10 provides one of many examples of flute filigree by Duruflé (here, he specifies the 2′ flute should only be used if the Choir is 'enclosed', i.e., has its own Swell box). Notice how the left hand is essentially just playing broken chords, allowing the hand to stay in the same position and so making rapid execution very easy. A Cornet on the Swell is rarely available on English organs; see the 'Mutations' section for more detail.

FIGURE 2.10 Maurice Duruflé, *Prélude et Fugue sur le nom d'Alain* op. 7 © Éditions Durand

The flutes are capable of more than just fleeting passagework, however. A more tender and introverted use of the flutes can be found in pieces as diverse as 'Flûtes' from Clerambault's *Suite du deuxième ton* and 'S.T.A.Y.' from Hans Zimmer's soundtrack to *Interstellar*. Figure 2.11 shows the playful nature of the 8′ and 4′ flutes used in a darkly ironic way, contrasting with the horrific incident the piece depicts.

FIGURE 2.11 Thomas Kerr, *Anguished American Easter, 1968* © GIA Publications

Be aware that the sound of the solo flutes is easily covered by other stops. The Choir flutes in particular often sound deceptively prominent in isolation but can be overwhelmed even by an *mp* Swell registration. As ever, practical experimentation is the best way to find out what balances; the music of the French Romantics, particularly Duruflé, is exemplary in how to manage the flutes alone against the rest of the organ.

Strings

Common stop names: Gamba, Salicional, Violin, Voix Céléste, Vox Angelica

While flutes and principals are by far the most common types of stop available, there is also a small category of string sounds. These are typically found on the Swell alone, although larger Romantic organs may contain a second set of String stops on the Choir or even on a fourth manual. The string stops are normally very quiet, rarely able to go louder than about *mp* even with the Swell box open.

The normal Gamba 8′ is frequently paired with a special string stop called the **Voix Céléste**. All of the pipes on this stop are slightly detuned. When drawn with the Gamba, it produces an undulating, lush sound (see, e.g., Figure 2.34). Similar celeste stops for flutes and principals do exist but are considerably rarer; see 'Flutes' later in this chapter as well as 'Italian Renaissance—Basilica di Santa Barbara, Mantua' in the Online Resources. Note that the Voix Céléste does not have any pipes in the lowest octave, instead substituting the Gamba pipes for these bottom notes; other types of celeste stop also share this facet. It is standard practice to indicate either 'Strings' or 'Gamba, Voix Céléste' (the latter *without* octave designation) when this celeste sound is desired.

This string pair is one of the 'stock' sounds of French Romanticism to the point where it became clichéd even in the nineteenth century. Nevertheless, this combination has value to modern composers. Pieces like Messiaen's *Verset pour la fête de la Dedicace* shows how the sound need not have a saccharine quality. Figure 2.12 demonstrates a standard yet exceptionally well written example, achieving a very rich sound through clever chord voicing. Note that most organs do not have dedicated string or celeste stops at 4′ pitch; in this instance, the organist would either use Sub/Super Octave couplers (see 'Couplers' later in this chapter), use a Flute 16′/Flute 4′ (the former played an octave higher than written) or just use the 8′ strings and celestes alone.

FIGURE 2.12 Thomas Kerr, *Suite Sebastienne*, 'Reverie (for Celestes)' © MorningStar Music Publishers

Man.: Strings and Celestes 8', 4'
Ped.: Soft 16', Man. to Ped.

The Gamba 8′ is more rarely used on its own, although it can be useful for certain very quiet effects (see, e.g., Duruflé *Suite*, 'Sicilienne'). The strings are less suited for fleeting passagework than the flutes and principals. Not that they cannot be used in this way, however; James MacMillan's *A New Song* provides an innovative and effective example which, while not printed here, is well worth examination.

Reeds

Common stop names: Oboe, Trumpet, Clarinet, Cromorne, Tuba, Vox Humana, Bassoon [16′], Trombone [16′], Ophicleide [16′], Clarion [4′]

The reeds (Ger. *Zungen*, Fr. *Anches*) are the most idiosyncratic set of stops on the organ. Unlike with the other families, the reeds can produce widely different sounds from each other, often emulating orchestral instruments. The stop-list in Table 2.1 shows the standard reeds and where they are typically found. On small instruments, the most common reeds are an Oboe (or Trumpet) 8′ on the Swell and a Trumpet 8′ on the Great. Normally, specifying Reed(s) 8′ (4′, 16′, 32′, etc.) indicates using the Trumpet/Tuba/Trombone stops for each manual, possibly the Swell Oboe and Choir Clarinet at softer dynamics. To indicate the other reeds, it is necessary to use the specific names.

The reeds are generally the loudest type of stop on the organ. The distinct reedy character of each is often most pronounced at the lower end of the compass, while at the extreme upper end the reeds can blend almost seamlessly with other stops. While these stops may imitate orchestral wind and brass instruments, they are best considered on their own terms with timbres distinct from their orchestral counterparts. Because the reed stops each have such distinct characters and usage, each stop will be explored in turn.

Swell

Oboe: The Swell Oboe is often the softest reed on the organ. On English and German Romantic organs, the Oboe is commonly designed to blend into the foundations (with trumpets used for the full 'reed' sound); composers often specify a 'soft reed' on the Swell in this context. Figure 2.13 shows a typical example of this usage.

FIGURE 2.13 Edward Elgar arr. George Martin, *Imperial March* op. 32

It is equally common for the Oboe to be used as a solo stop, especially in French music. The solo Oboe is very effective for plaintive melodies (e.g., Whitlock *Five Short Pieces*, 'Folk Tune') although it can work equally well for more joyous solos. Figure 2.14 gives a standard example of solo use from French Romanticism.

The Pipe Organ

FIGURE 2.14 Charles-Marie Widor, *Organ Symphony No. 6 op. 42 no. 2*, Cantabile

R: Hautbois
G: Flûte 8'
Ped.: Basses 8' et 16'

Many oboe stops on modern eclectic instruments are designed to fulfil both chorus and solo functions, so composers shouldn't worry about having to choose one or the other. Large instruments may have both types available, with the 'solo' Oboe often found on the fourth Solo manual on English Romantic and American Classic organs.

Trumpet 8′ (Bassoon 16′, Clarion 4′): These Swell reeds are the softest trumpet stops on the organ. They are a crucial part of the 'Full Swell' sound where most of the stops on the Swell are drawn (aside from celestes, the Vox Humana, and some of the softer stops) and which is commonly requested by English and French Romantic composers in particular.

Although the 16′ and 4′ are not always present on smaller organs (the 16′ is more likely to be present than the 4′), specifying all three together is incredibly common and organists can usually 'fake' a Full Swell on small instruments without these outer reeds, such as by coupling the Swell to the Great 16′ flute. The resulting sound is monumental even with the Swell box shut. The Full Swell is typically used for slow, grandiose statements (see, e.g., Vierne *Pièces de Fantaisie*, 'Cathédrales' and 'Sur le Rhin'), or for loud passagework (see virtually any French toccata) but this sound can also be very useful in more nuanced contexts. Figure 2.15 shows one example where the Swell trumpets with the box shut, while not requested by name, perfectly capture the 'menacing' yet hushed sound Wallen desires.

FIGURE 2.15 Errollyn Wallen, *Tiger* © Faber Music

The Swell reeds are significantly louder than other Swell stops, and so their addition needs to be timed carefully. In many loud French solo organ works, the Swell reeds are kept permanently drawn even when the dynamics go down to *pp*. This approach has many advantages, allowing a wide dynamic range yet with consistency of timbre across the whole spectrum. Inventive composers have found ways to innovate even here, however. In the famous opening shown in Figure 2.16, the absence of the 16′ reed (which is added halfway through the piece) gives this section a brighter, more sparkling quality adding to the effect of a peal of bells.

FIGURE 2.16 Louis Vierne, *Pièces de Fantaisie*, Suite III op. 54, 'Carillon de Westminster'

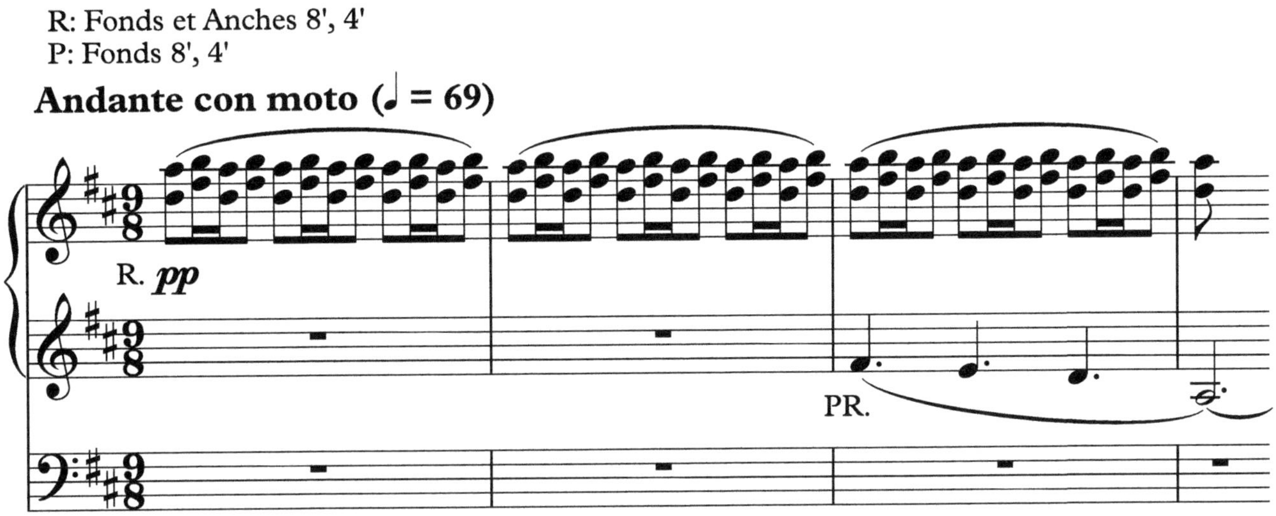

The trumpets are occasionally used as solo stops, such as shown in Figure 2.17. In such cases, it is usually accompanied by the Great or Choir flutes alone (as here), where the reed stands out clearly against the accompaniment. The separation in pitch register between melody and accompaniment in Figure 2.17 also helps with such balance; McDowall intelligently suggests the Oboe as an option in case the Trumpet is too prominent for this texture in this case.

FIGURE 2.17 Cecilia McDowall, *O Antiphon Sequence*, 'O Sapientia' © Oxford University Press

The 16′ and 4′ reeds are used much more rarely in solos, although sporadic examples do exist (e.g., Weir *Ettrick Banks*). These stops can provide unique and interesting reed colours even when used in the middle of the compass and so are worth exploring more.

Vox Humana: The Vox Humana is perhaps the most idiosyncratic reed stop. Its sound is indescribable, best being approximated by calling it a type of string-reed hybrid. Vox Humanas are fairly rare in the UK and US, although they are a relatively common resource on larger organs and are more common in Europe. While initially created as a solo stop for French and German Baroque organs, the modern Vox Humana is mostly associated with the French Romantic school. It is virtually always used in conjunction with the Swell Tremulant (see 'Miscellaneous Stops' later in this chapter), to the point where composers often specify if they do *not* want the tremulant on with the Vox Humana (see, e.g., Messiaen *Les Corps Glorieux*, 'Joie et clarté').

The sound of the Vox Humana with Tremulant was said to resemble the human voice, hence the name. As such, it was commonly used as an 'angelic' sound in French Romanticism, most notably in the music of César Franck (see, e.g., the *Trois chorals pour orgue*). Such a usage may sound bizarre or even comical to modern listeners, especially since these days the stop is strongly associated with the theatre organ. Nevertheless, some modern composers have successfully modified this vocal approach: in Figure 2.18, the stop helps create an ethereal, almost unsettling sound, an effect enhanced by the octatonicism and quasi-choral texture.

FIGURE 2.18 Kerensa Briggs, *Light in Darkness*

The stop's unique sound can also be very useful for novel effects. Vierne ingeniously exploits its uncanny sound to evoke the sinister, phantasmal will-o'-the-wisp (see Figure 4.50). Aside from the Briggs example quoted in Figure 2.18, other effective modern examples include

Langlais *Suite médiévale*, 'Tiento' (where the stop is used for its Baroque connotations) and Hakim *Toccata*. The stop has a strong modern connection to the theatre organ and can do a surprisingly good emulation of the sound of a talk box, therefore giving it a clear role in secular as well as sacred music. As such, the Vox Humana offers much potential for composers looking to break away from the traditional organ sound.

Great

Reeds 16′, 8′, 4′: Unlike the other two manuals, the Great normally only has one set of reeds. They are virtually always trumpet stops (normally, e.g., Trumpet 8′, Double Trumpet 16′, and Clarion 4′, or similar) and, outside of the Tuba, are generally the loudest stops on the organ. Unlike the Tuba, they are 'chorus' reeds, designed to blend with the principal chorus rather than being used in isolation. Typically organs either have all three Great reeds or just the 8′, but the Reed 4′ is marginally more common than the 16′.

These reeds are most often used as part of the full tutti (see again any French Romantic organ toccata, e.g., Figure 2.25). In this role, they provide a brassy edge to the organ sound, boosting it for the loudest moments while being removed for the softer sections. In the French Classical period (see the Appendix), the Great reeds formed part of the 'Grand Jeux' along with the Great Cornet (see 'Mutations' later in this chapter) and coupled Choir reeds, providing a very strident sound such as demonstrated in Figure 2.19 (note that in this example there is no separate pedal part, the bass being played on the Great by the left hand).

FIGURE 2.19 Pierre du Mage, *Livre d'orgue*, Grand Jeu

It is much rarer for the Great trumpets to be explicitly used as solo stops. On some smaller organs, the trumpets are designed to work as a stand-in for the Choir solo reed as well as being a chorus reed stop. Nevertheless, the Great Trumpet can be effective even when a Choir solo reed is also available; the Great reeds offer a slightly less protuberant sound with a subtly different timbre from the Choir solo reed, therefore providing composers another possible colouristic resource. Figure 2.20 shows an effective example of soloistic usage, where the slightly softer edge of the Great Trumpet compared to the Choir solo reed suits the lyrical character of the melodic line and complements the subtle accompaniment on the Swell.

The Pipe Organ

FIGURE 2.20 Chelsea Chen, *Taiwanese Suite*, 'Mountain of Youth' © Wayne Leupold Editions

Choir

Clarinet/Cromorne: Where there is a Choir manual, there is often a clarinet stop, occasionally also called a Corno di Bassetto. There are two common types of this stop, depending on whether the Choir is enclosed or not. If it is enclosed, the stop is softer and more expressive and is commonly used as a solo stop in Romantic music such as in Figure 2.21. In this passage, taken from the organ introduction, the Clarinet provides a useful soft solo colour, contrasting nicely with the Swell accompaniment and with the Choir box helping providing shape and musicality.

FIGURE 2.21 Gerald Finzi, *Lo, the Full Final Sacrifice* op. 26 © Boosey and Hawkes

When the Choir is not enclosed, the stop is typically called a **Cromorne** and is both more powerful and considerably more pungent than the enclosed Clarinet. This stop is primarily associated with the French Classical school, with Figure 2.22 providing a traditional example of its usage. Its uniqueness is perhaps most striking at the low end of its range, such as in Figure 2.22, where it gains a snarling quality; Messiaen also provides striking examples in both his *Verset pour la fête de la Dedicace* and his *Les Corps Glorieux* ('Joie et clarté'). An explanation of the 'Jeu doux' in Figure 2.22 is provided in the Appendix.

FIGURE 2.22 Louis-Nicolas Clérambault, *Suite du deuxième ton*, Basse de Cromorne

The stop is traditionally associated with the French Classical organ style (see the Appendix) and many later uses call back to this Baroque heritage (see, e.g., Alain *Variations sur un thème de Clément Jannequin*, Duruflé *Prélude et Fugue sur le nom d'Alain* and Litaize *Reges Tharsis*). Nevertheless, the stop's brazen quality can be useful in its own right as works such as Litaize's *Prélude et Danse Fuguée* attest. Its common availability on organs yet surprising rarity in scores therefore gives composers an interesting timbre to innovate with and explore.

Tuba/Solo Reed: The Choir solo reed is the loudest stop on the organ yet is *not* usually used as part of the organ tutti; instead, it is designed to balance *against* the full organ. This stop is mainly associated with English Romanticism, where it is commonly known a Tuba and has a round, warm sound. Many large non-English organs instead have an 'en chamade' trumpet stop (i.e., with the pipes outside the case pointing directly at the listener) which fills the same role as the Tuba but is more piercing and bombastic. Some composers just specify 'Solo Reed' with an *ff* dynamic, which is also clear and unambiguous. These solo reeds are rare even on organs with three manuals; however, they are a standard resource on four-manual instruments and are common enough otherwise to be reasonably requested (although an alternative should be supplied where possible, e.g., playing the solo reed passage on the Great).

Typically, the Choir solo reed is used to contrast with the full Swell/Great, often to provide a fanfare such as in Figure 2.23:

The Pipe Organ

FIGURE 2.23 James Mitchell, *Festival Toccata* © The Royal School of Church Music

The rich sound of the Tuba is also well suited for louder lyrical solo lines with a thick-sounding accompaniment on the Great, such as shown in Figure 2.24:

FIGURE 2.24 Percy Whitlock, *Five Short Pieces*, 'Paean' © Oxford University Press

While the Tuba is typically used for slower fanfares or melodies, it is equally suited to rapid passagework (e.g., Walton *The Twelve*). More rarely, the Tuba may be available at other octaves (most commonly 4′) or with the Sub/Super Octave couplers (see, e.g., Grainger *Marching Song of Democracy*; the 'Couplers' section has more information on Sub/Super Octave couplers) but these extra octaves are not a standard resource. All in all, as one of the few solo stops that can compete with the full organ, the Tuba provides a valuable solo colour for louder dynamics.

Pedals

Reeds 16′, 32′, 8′: The pedal reeds go by a variety of names; among the more common are Trombone, Posaune, Ophicleide, and Bombarde. The 8′ and 32′ pedal reeds, while rarer than the 16′ and 4′ reeds on the Great and Swell, are not especially uncommon on large instruments. Typically, the reeds are used to fill out the pedal chorus, particularly at climactic moments or for dramatic pedal solos. In the famous example in Figure 2.25, the pedal reeds help make the pedal melody stand out against the toccata figuration in the manuals.

FIGURE 2.25 Louis Vierne, *Organ Symphony No. 1* op. 14, Finale

Use of the pedal reeds in isolation is less common. The 16′ reed is almost never used by itself except in exceptional situations (e.g., Messiaen *La Nativité du Seigneur*, 'Jésus Accepte la Souffrance', MacMillan *A Scotch Bestiary*, '2. Reptiles and Big Fish (in a small pond)'). The pedal Trumpet 8′ however is an important sound for Baroque organ music, particularly for the French Classical school (see Figure 2.26 for one example). As such, while relatively uncommon on small and medium-size instruments, this reed is a standard resource on large modern organs.

FIGURE 2.26 Nicolas de Grigny, *Veni Creator Spiritus*, Plein Jeu

Adding the 16′ (or 32′) reed on the final chord in music from the Romantic period onwards, while rarely written in the score, is a standard technique in both solo and choral music. In the latter, balance must be considered. Both 16′ and 32′ together usually overwhelm the choir, so choosing one or the other is often most effective.

Other Categories

In addition to the four main stop families, there are special groups of stops commonly requested in scores that either combine the families (foundations) or are unique in terms of pitch (mixtures, mutations). These groups are described in the following sections.

Foundations

- The foundations (shortened to 'Founds' or 'Fonds') describe the combination of every stop except the reeds, mixtures, mutations, and Voix Céléste, although the Swell Oboe may also be added if it is relatively soft. As such, when specifying foundations, there is no need to also specify flutes or principals the same octave as they would be drawn anyway. One of the staple sounds of Romantic organ music, no matter the nationality, the foundations provide a rich and balanced sound. They are therefore the default registration for Romantic music and are used when composers do not specify otherwise. The Parry example in Figure 2.1, for example, is often played with the Founds 8′ (and sometimes 4′) on the Swell; when the hands move onto the Great later in the piece, it would also likely be registered with Founds 8′ and with the Swell coupled.

As would be expected, the Great foundations are louder and more full-sounding than those of the Swell or Choir. In fact, the Swell reeds are typically necessary to couple/balance with just the 8′, 4′, and 2′ foundations on the Great. This setup, with reeds on the Swell and just foundations on the other two manuals, is standard in the French toccata repertoire; see Figure 2.15 for one of many examples.

Mixtures

Common stop names: Mixture, Fourniture, Plein-jeu, Cymbale, Sesquialtera [often 2 2/3′ + 1 3/5′; see 'Mutations' later in this chapter]

Mixtures (Ger. *Mixturen*) are typically made up of principals, more rarely of flutes and strings. On specifications, they are recognisable by the roman numerals (e.g., III, IV) in place of the octave designation and are described in terms of ranks (i.e., Mixture IV would be a 'four-rank' mixture; see the Glossary for an explanation of a 'rank'). What makes the mixtures unique is that, when a key is pressed, it sounds multiple pipes at once. The number of pipes is indicated by the roman numeral: as an example, 'IV' would mean four pipes sound simultaneously. Different types of mixtures may use lower or higher pitched pipes respectively: Fournitures tend to be lower-pitched mixtures, while Cymbales tend to be higher pitched. Some mixtures also label each constituent harmonic, e.g., '19,21,25'. In most cases, the fundamental written note is typically clear except at the extreme bottom end of the compass. The exact number of ranks and constituent harmonics are unpredictable and vary from mixture to mixture. For practical purposes therefore, composers should just indicate 'Mixtures' or 'Mixt.' despite multiple variants of mixture often being available. The one exception is for the mixture known as the Cornet; this is a lower-pitched mixture which is associated with the mutations and so is described in the 'Mutations' section.

The most common function of the mixtures by far is to add the high-pitch 'shine' to choruses. Historically, mixtures have been used in isolation only very rarely (see, e.g., Figure 3.14 as well as Messiaen *Livre du Saint Sacrement*, 'La manne et le Pain de Vie'). This lack of independence is partly because of the mixtures' variability and partly because they 'break back': at certain points in the compass, as the written pitch ascends, higher-pitched pipes are gradually replaced by lower-pitched ones, making distinct octaves for mixtures hard to discern. This unique trait, far from being a defect, gives mixtures incredible possibilities for creating novel sounds and textures yet has been barely explored in the repertoire. The mixtures' variability (which in practice is less extreme than may be imagined) has led to their full potential being largely overlooked. However, the unique characteristics and common availability of the mixtures offer a very exciting timbral resource to modern composers looking to reinvent the traditional organ sound.

Mutations

Common stop names: Nazard, Twelfth, Quint, Tierce, Larigot

Mutations, like mixtures, are normally either flute or principal stops. Also like mixtures, the octave identification on the stop may seem at first strange, mutations being the only stops to use fractions as they are the only ones which do not sound distinctly at written pitch. As with the reed stops, their unique character is most distinct in the low range while blending with other stops best in the high range. The mutations are arguably the most useful stops for producing original modern registrations, perhaps more so than any other type of stop, with the music of Messiaen and Escaich among others showing just how much potential these stops have.

The mutations are primarily designed to sound at and reinforce the non-octave harmonics. This fact explains their octave designation, produced by dividing 8′ by the relevant partial number of the harmonic series. Applying this theory for partials 3, 5, and 6, the most common choices for mutations, produces 2 2/3′ (the **Nazard**, or **Twelfth** if on the Great, sounding at the octave and a perfect fifth), 1 3/5′ (the **Tierce**, sounding at two octaves and a major third), and 1 1/3′ (the **Larigot**, sounding at two octaves and a perfect fifth) respectively. Figure 2.27 illustrates the written versus sounding pitches for these mutations; pitches are approximate since mutations are tuned in pure intervals relative to the fundamental.

FIGURE 2.27 Written vs sounding pitches (mutations)

The availability and placement of mutations is notoriously inconsistent and unpredictable, more so than for any other type of organ stop. Many older English and German Romantic organs have no mutations at all, aside from maybe a 2 2/3′ on the Great. UK eclectic organs typically have the Nazard and Tierce on the Choir, whilst in the US they are usually on the Swell. French organs often have mutations on all three manuals owing to their abundance in the French Classical style, hence why Messiaen requests them so regularly (see 'French Romantic (b)—Église de la Sainte-Trinité, Paris' in the Online Resources). Some instruments even have mutations not listed above, such as the Septième 1 1/7′ or the Gros Nazard 5 1/3′. Where possible, check what mutation stops are available on each specific organ before requesting them.

One of the most common uses of mutations is combining the Nazard with the 8′ and 4′ flutes, a popular combination in French scherzo-like movements. Vierne's 'Feux follets' from his *Pièces de fantaisie* is an excellent example, exploiting the uncanny sound of 8′, 4′, and 2 2/3′ to unsettling effect (see Figure 4.50). Figure 2.28 shows an interesting modern example, with the

8′, 4′, and 2 2/3′ providing an innovative accompaniment to a soft 4′ melody (i.e., a Flute 4′) in the pedals.

FIGURE 2.28 Nathan James Dearden, *storms don't last forever* © Nathan James Dearden

Used creatively, mutations are capable of incredibly unnatural and even un-organlike sounds. In Figure 2.29, the Nazard and Tierce are used without any 8′ or 4′ stops to root the sound. The medium-low range causes the mutations to sound less blended together than they would do in a higher range. The total sound is luminous and ethereal, with the resultant tone sounding distinctly at written pitch but without the heaviness of an 8′ or 4′ foundation (see also Kit Downes's track 'Optics' from *WEDDING MUSIC* for an extraordinary example of the low-register Nazard and Tierce alone).

FIGURE 2.29 Mikhail Johnson, *Si Di Staar Deh* © Johno Muzik (ASCAP). International Copyright Secured. All Rights Reserved

The **Cornet** (pronounced as in French, i.e., 'cor-nay') is a special type of low-pitched mixture normally comprising the 8′, 4′, 2 2/3′, 2′, and 1 3/5′ flutes. While there is often a specific Cornet stop (usually on the Great), it is equally common for organists to 'build' one from the five constituent stops on the Choir or Swell. Be aware that the Great Cornet stop often does not sound below middle C (the specific stopping point depends on the organ), although the 'built' Cornet has no such limitations.

The Cornet is traditionally associated with the French Classical school. While often used to strengthen the loud reed stops in the Grand Jeux, the Cornet is also used as a solo stop in its own right. Figure 2.30 shows a typical example (note again that, as for much French Classical music, there is no independent pedal part in this example).

FIGURE 2.30 François Couperin, *Pièces d'orgue*, 'Messe pour les couvents' (Récit de Cornet)

With the twentieth-century resurgence of interest in this period, the stop's use was increasingly specified by Dupré, Duruflé (see, e.g., Figure 2.11) and Messiaen among others. These days, the stop is a common solo colour in any type of music and so forms a valuable part of the registration 'arsenal' at a composer's disposal.

Miscellaneous Stops

There are a few other important stops which are not so easy to classify; these are outlined in this section.

> **Tremulant**: The tremulant is a stop that is both virtually ubiquitous on organs yet almost never requested in scores. Drawing the tremulant stop causes the wind supply to the pipes to fluctuate, producing a tremolo rather like the wind equivalent of a vibraphone motor. The rate of fluctuation varies wildly depending on the organ, although some large instruments have options to control the tremulant speed. Tremulants are most common on the Swell, although they can be found on all three manuals (being relatively rare on the Great). In traditional pipe organ music, the tremulant is normally only specified in conjunction with the Vox Humana (see, e.g., Figure 2.18). However, tremulants can be very useful for

a more modern organ sound, taking the cold edge off the straight organ tone. Both the theatre organ and Hammond organ traditions also make excellent use of the tremulant for dynamic and expressive purposes, and their usage of the stop should be studied regarding the traditional organ. Note that the loud reed stops are often designed to be unaffected by the tremulant.

Zimbelstern: One of the most common 'toy' stops, the Zimbelstern consists of a set of small bells mounted on a mechanised rotatable stand outside the organ case. Drawing the stop causes the stand to start rotating, producing an unpitched and arhythmic carillon. Most typically used to add a sparkle to the end of festive pieces, they are very rare and so should only be specified with an 'ad lib'.

Chimes/Glockenspiel/Celesta/Harp: These are the only stops of definite pitch on the organ that don't involve pipes. Instead, the wind operates a set of mallets which hit tubular bells/glockenspiel bars. While very common for theatre organs, they are very rare for organs outside of North America (and even in North America they are not ubiquitous). The Chimes are the most common of these stops on church instruments, being found on the Great. The Glockenspiel is rarer and is usually found on the Choir, as are the Celesta and Harp. Leo Sowerby's *Carillon* is a good showcase piece for these stops.

Couplers

'Couplers' are stops that allow various manuals to be connected together. For instance, when the Swell to Great coupler is drawn, playing a note on the Great will cause the same note to be played simultaneously on the Swell (on mechanical organs, it is possible to see the keys on coupled manuals physically depress). Coupler stops can also be activated by pistons, that is, buttons under the manuals and on the pedalboard; see Figure 2.35.

For three-manual organs, the typical couplers available are as follows:

- Swell to Great
- Swell to Choir
- Choir to Great
- Great to Pedal
- Swell to Pedal
- Choir to Pedal

Couplers are indicated using their full name with abbreviations as appropriate, for example, 'Sw. to Gt.', 'Gt. to Ped.'. Plus/minus signs (e.g., '+ Sw. to Ch.') should be used as for other stops, although they are not universally found in scores (see, e.g., Figure 2.31). In Romantic music, all the couplers are typically drawn even when not indicated unless any manuals are being used for solo colours (e.g., the Choir Flutes 8′, 4′). As mentioned earlier, French composers tend to indicate coupling through consecutive manual indications; for example, 'GPR' indicates the Choir and Swell are coupled to the Great (the first letter indicates the manual to be played on).

Couplers are an essential part of the organ. It is the coupled manuals which give the richness of sound to Romantic organ music, and even in Baroque music modern organists will often draw couplers to help fill out the sound or finely gradate the dynamics. Coupling to the Swell is particularly useful as it makes the Swell box, and its fine control of dynamics, available to other manuals. Coupling is particularly important at louder dynamics: the couplers are a crucial part of 'full organ' registrations and should normally be drawn from at least *mf* upwards. Even in softer solo passages on the Great and Choir with Swell accompaniment, coupling the Swell can often help create a more blended, symphonic sound.

The Gt. to Ped. coupler is by far the easiest coupler to operate, with a dedicated piston under the Great manual (see the centre left of Figure 2.35) as well as with a large 'Gt. to Ped.' toe piston commonly located next to the Swell pedal (see Figure 4.1). Being able to operate this coupler smoothly, in a wide variety of contexts, is a standard requirement for diploma-level sightreading. Figure 2.31 provides a typical example.

FIGURE 2.31 Percy Fletcher, *Festival Toccata*

Some couplers occasionally have dedicated foot pistons, most commonly the Swell to Great and/or Swell to Pedal couplers, but the other couplers generally have pistons only under the manuals if at all. If the hands are busy, it may be necessary to allocate a general piston for changing these couplers instead of altering them on the fly (see the following 'Registration Aids' section for more on general pistons).

In Romantic music, the Swell is virtually always coupled to the Great, even at quieter dynamics, unless either the Swell or Great are being used for solo colours. This coupling allows for better balance on the Great, with the Swell box allowing the organist to control the exact shade of dynamic. It is also common to have all couplers drawn, creating a three-tier system of dynamics with the Swell, Choir, and Great. Figure 2.32 shows a standard repertoire example of how, by having the couplers drawn, it is possible to create a very symphonic crescendo (see also Figure 3.37 and the related discussion).

FIGURE 2.32 Louis Vierne, *Organ Symphony No. 3* op. 28, Finale

Couplers do come with minor drawbacks, however. Drawing all manual couplers to the Great on mechanical-action instruments can make playing on the Great feel considerably 'heavier', requiring more physical effort to depress the keys and therefore making loud virtuosic passagework harder (although not impossible) to execute. Such physical difficulties are particularly acute when playing repeated chords (see 'Idiomatic Writing' in Chapter 3 for more information). In practice, the Choir to Great coupler is sometimes not drawn for *ff* passages on three-manual tracker-action organs as the small gain in volume does not compensate for the increased action weight and consequent difficulty of playing. Electric-action instruments, however, have no such issue, and it is very common to see all three manuals coupled together in most of the louder standard French and German Romantic repertoire.

There is also certainly a place for isolating manuals without using couplers. The most common situations for such isolation tend to involve solos on the various reeds such as the Swell Oboe (see, e.g., Figure 2.14) and Choir Tuba (see, e.g., Figure 2.24; note in that example that the Swell and Great are still coupled together). As noted in

Chapter 1, the Choir in particular is often designed to be both physically and tonally independent from the main Swell/Great pair, and so it is frequently very effective to use the uncoupled Choir for solo colours; such a usage is also easy to adapt to two-manual organs. However, it is difficult to balance uncoupled manuals beyond quieter dynamics. Complex registrations on uncoupled manuals can be effective (see, e.g., Figure 3.40 and the related discussion) but are very risky without, and sometimes even with, extensive practical experience.

It is briefly worth mentioning the **Sub Octave** and **Super Octave** couplers. Most commonly found on the Swell, they add the octave below and octave above respectively. These couplers almost never extend the normal range of the instrument, usually taking an octave off the lower and upper ends respectively. They are less rare than may be expected on Romantic organs and are most often found on either very small or very large instruments, helping fill out the Swell choruses on the former or adding extra octaves to solo stops on the latter. Indications for these couplers can be found very occasionally in organ scores (e.g., Vierne *Pièces de fantaisie*, 'Les cloches de Hinckley'). However, composers should always provide alternate options where possible when specifying these couplers so that organists can easily adapt them to the average mid-sized instrument.

Registration Aids

Traditionally, stops were drawn entirely by hand (often known as 'hand registering'), with organists sometimes eliciting the help of a registrant. Gradually, however, various mechanical and electronic aids have come into use, allowing organists to change stops with the press of a button. Availability of registration aids varies from organ to organ, with some organs lacking any such aids. Additionally, registration aids are an extension of hand registration rather than a replacement of it. The most idiomatic registration schemes treat registration aids in exactly the same way as hand registration (leaving the same amount of time to operate, etc.; see Figure 2.6).

The composer should *not* normally indicate the use of registration aids in the score. Instead, just give the desired registration changes (see, e.g., Figure 2.34) and the organist will figure out the most appropriate registration aid to use for each given situation. However, understanding how registration aids work can help the composer incorporate these stop changes idiomatically and effectively.

General Pistons

The **general pistons**, typically shortened to '**generals**', are the main way to change registration across the entire organ. They are a row of typically six to ten numbered buttons, most commonly lying on the left-hand side below the top two manuals, split under the far left and far right of the top manual, or in a row above the top manual. Figure 2.33 shows this first arrangement.

FIGURE 2.33 General pistons

Pressing a general piston changes the registration of the entire organ, including the couplers, to a combination pre-programmed by the organist. It is therefore possible to change the sound instantly and completely. In practice, generals are not only used for large-scale stop changes but also adding or removing individual stops when inconvenient to do so otherwise. Most organs with generals also have multiple electronic memory channels, allowing multiple sets of generals to be stored and prepared in advance. Video 2.1 in the Online Resources shows how generals are used in practice.

There are a few practical points composers can draw from this system:

- It is arguably more idiomatic to change a larger number of stops across multiple manuals at one time rather than a smaller number in succession unless divisional pistons are intended. In Figure 2.34, the new registration can be set on a single general, allowing the extreme shift in registration and dynamics to happen virtually instantaneously. Even though Messiaen permits enough time for the registration to be changed entirely by hand if needed, using generals makes the change considerably quicker and easier, allowing the organist to focus on musical considerations instead of just which stops to add or remove.

FIGURE 2.34 Olivier Messiaen, *Les Corps Glorieux*, 'Combat de Mort et de la Vie' © Alphonse Leduc Editions Musicales

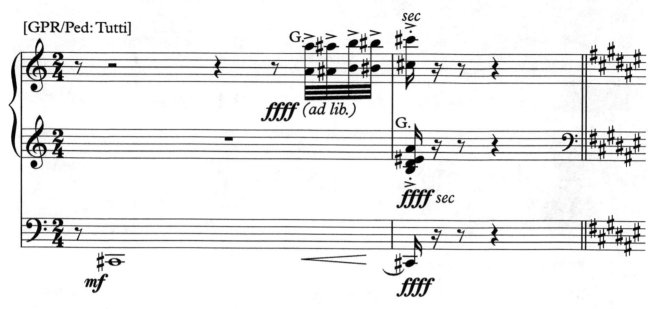

R: unda maris et salic. [i.e. Gambe, Voix Celeste]
P: flûte harm.
G: flûte harm.
Ped.: bourdons 16 et 32, tir. R

Extrêmement lent, tendre, serein (dans la Paix ensoleillée du Divin Amour)

- Consider if manuals can be 'prepared' in advance, such as having a solo Clarinet ready on the Choir while the Great/Swell are doing other things. Check also if generals can be re-used; Messiaen is a paragon in this regard, with many of his pieces only requiring two or three generals and so being easy to set up despite requiring some exotic registrations (see, e.g., 'Joie et clarté' from *Les Corps Glorieux*, 'Le Dieu caché' from *Livre du Saint Sacrament*).

The **stepper** is a device on some modern organs which scrolls through consecutive generals, allowing the organist to control all of their registration needs with a single button. A **sequencer** is similar but works independently of the generals. These devices are common on continental organs which do not have divisional pistons. However, while they are becoming increasingly prevalent on English instruments, they are still relatively rare and considered 'unidiomatic' compared to the traditional system of generals and divisionals. These devices are essentially an extension of the generals system and so writing as if for generals in any case is recommended.

Divisional Pistons

The **divisional pistons**, commonly shortened to '**divisionals**', were originally exclusive to English and American organs but are gradually becoming increasingly common internationally, particularly on organs in concert halls. They are a row of numbered buttons which bring out pre-set stop combinations, just as the generals, but they operate on the level of individual manuals and so each manual has its own set as shown in Figure 2.35. They commonly number between six and eight per manual. In the UK, the Great and Pedal divisionals can often be 'coupled' together so that pressing one of the Great divisional pistons will also operate the same numbered Pedal divisional and vice versa.

FIGURE 2.35 Divisional pistons (centre) located under the Swell (top), Great (middle) and Choir (bottom)

Management of divisionals is a fundamental skill for organists in the English organ tradition. The divisionals are the main way for adding stops in Romantic music where registration is not specified. By combining divisionals with skilful usage of the Swell box, organists can create a seamless crescendo from *pp* to *ff*. They also obviate part of the need for generals, allowing generals to be saved for more large-scale registration changes. Divisionals can be easily replicated by a stepper/sequencer or even hand registration by a registrant, and so writing as if for divisionals is a very idiomatic way to compose for the organ. Again, Video 2.1 in the Online Resources shows how divisionals would typically be used in a real case study.

The specific stops pre-set to each divisional are based on personal preference and the specifics of the organ and venue; while they can usually be changed easily if needed, they are rarely altered outside of exceptional situations. Divisionals may also have their own memory channels, allowing different settings of divisionals to be stored and quickly retrieved. The specifics of the standard divisional setup are surprisingly easy to predict with experience. To give a theoretical example of a generic setup for eight divisionals on the Swell:

1. Flute, Gambe 8′ (or Gambe, Voix Céléste)
2. Flutes 8′, 4′, Gambe 8′
3. Founds 8′, 4′ (- Oboe)
4. Founds 8′, 4′ (+ Oboe)
5. Founds 8, 4′, 2′
6. Founds 8′, 4′, 2′, Mixt.
7. Founds 8′, 4′, 2′, Mixt., Reeds 8′
8. Founds 8′, 4′, 2′, Mixt., Reeds 16′, 8′, 4′

This type of setup, essentially crescendoing as the divisionals get higher, is also standard for the Great and pedals. For the Choir (and/or fourth manual) which tends to be used for solo colours, the higher divisionals are often set to allow easy switches to these colours (in Figure 2.35, the final Choir divisionals are actually named 'Clarinet' and 'Tuba'). A generic eight-divisional setup for the Choir would perhaps be as follows:

1. Flute 8′
2. Flutes 8′, 4′
3. Founds 8′, 4′
4. Founds 8′, 4′, 2′
5. Founds 8′, 4′, 2′, Mixt.
6. Cornet (i.e., Flutes 8′, 4′, 2 2/3′, 2′, 1 3/5′)
7. Clarinet
8. Tuba

The same advice given about generals also applies broadly to divisionals. As the divisional pistons lie in the middle of the manuals' compass, they are typically closer to the organists' fingers and so can be pushed more quickly, and reliably, than the generals (note that higher-numbered divisionals are more easily pressed when the hands are higher up the keyboard and vice versa for lower-numbered divisionals; see Figure 2.35). Divisionals therefore provide a convenient way to change registrations for a single manual, and taking them into account can make for interesting, idiomatic, and effective organ music.

Crescendo Pedal

The crescendo pedal is similar to a regular Swell or Choir pedal. However, instead of opening shutters, it gradually adds stops across all manuals in a pre-programmed sequence. This order is usually set by the organ builder or technician and cannot be altered by the organist. The crescendo pedal is usually found to the right of the other expression pedals, such as in Figure 2.36. Sometimes, the pedal is designed as a treadmill roller which the organist rolls back and forth with the foot, in which case it is known as a 'Rollschweller' (this is the most common form of crescendo pedal in Germany).

FIGURE 2.36 Example of a crescendo pedal (right) alongside those for the Swell box (centre) and Choir box (left)

The crescendo pedal is only rarely called for in scores. Messiaen specifies individual levels of the crescendo pedal in works such as *Meditations sur le mystère de la Sainte Trinité*, a practice which virtually no other composer has adopted and which it is not recommended to follow. More usually, the crescendo pedal is implied rather than directly requested. Reger's music is full of such implied usage, for instance in Figure 2.37. Reger generally uses hairpins for the Swell box but the terms 'crescendo'/'diminuendo' to indicate the crescendo pedal:

The Pipe Organ

FIGURE 2.37 Max Reger, *12 Stücke* op. 65, 'Te Deum'

For traditional classical music, it is recommended to avoid explicitly writing for the crescendo pedal unless a very particular effect is required. Even in North America and Germany where the pedal is most common, it is not universally available and is virtually non-existent on all but the largest organs in other countries. The effect of the crescendo pedal is extremely difficult to replicate otherwise, even with divisionals. Leaving registrations entirely to the organist or writing as if for divisionals/hand registration, possibly requesting the crescendo pedal in a footnote or explanatory note, would allow the organist to use the crescendo pedal when available without compromising on playability if not.

Nevertheless, the crescendo pedal still has much potential, particularly in non-classical contexts. Larger digital organs often have a crescendo pedal (the organ in Figure 2.36 is a digital instrument) as do a number of sampled organs for Hauptwerk. The crescendo sequence in Hauptwerk is also programmable, allowing for endless novel registration palettes inaccessible on most traditional instruments. Side-chaining effects with the crescendo pedal (or even with a regular Swell pedal) offer much undiscovered potential, particularly when merged with electronica. While the full possibilities of crescendo pedal have so far been unexplored, the pedal may well eventually become a crucial aspect of the modern organ sound.

THE MANUALS 3

Overview

Composers frequently assume that writing for the manuals is like writing for the piano. However, while piano textures can inspire innovative organ writing, the two instruments have largely separate idioms: what works well on a piano may be unidiomatic on an organ and vice versa. This chapter therefore aims to explain the idiosyncrasies of the manuals and so how to exploit them to their fullest.

There are three main differences between the piano and organ which fundamentally shape their different idioms. Firstly, held notes on the organ do not fade out as they on the piano. Instead, they continue at the same volume until the key is released. As such, they can be sustained for a theoretically infinite amount of time. Secondly, the organ has no sustaining pedal. Once a key has been released, the note stops instantaneously with no way to prolong it. Finally, the organ sound is naturally much less percussive than a piano's, since wind is being blown through pipes rather than strings being struck by hammers. This lack of transient makes successive notes blend together, leading to a generally smoother sound than for most other keyboard instruments.

These differences have important consequences, leading to very different ways of thinking about the keyboard. Consider the passage shown in Figure 3.1:

The Pipe Organ. James Mitchell, Oxford University Press. © Oxford University Press 2023. DOI: 10.1093/oso/9780197645284.003.0004

The Pipe Organ

FIGURE 3.1 Johann Sebastian Bach, *Nun komm, der Heiden Heiland* BWV 599

On a piano, it would be easy to depress the sustaining pedal and not pay attention to the precise note duration. On the organ, however, each note must be held for its full value. Organists therefore have to develop an eye for exactly how long each note lasts. In Figure 3.1, the first note must be physically held for the full minim. The crotchets on the third beat also have to be held down for their full duration.

Try playing the manual parts in Figure 3.1 on a keyboard, observing the note lengths and rests carefully and without using the sustaining pedal. It is best to use a keyboard patch with indefinite sustain (e.g., organ, strings, etc.) but this exercise will also work on a regular piano. In Baroque music such as in Figure 3.1, each note is usually given a distinct articulation so legato techniques such as finger substitution (see Figure 3.2) are not needed here (legato becomes the default organ touch from the Romantic period onwards). It may feel physically awkward to play the first time, but with some practice it should start to become more natural.

As should be obvious from this experiment, precisely notating note lengths is of the utmost importance. When a note is released is just as important as when it begins. The best organ writing always takes into account what is held over and what is released. Holding notes also has important physical connotations, limiting what the rest of the hand can reach. Finally, as notes do not decay, voice leading is very clear, even in denser textures. Linear counterpoint is therefore much more important to the organ than other keyboard instruments, hence why fugues are such a staple of the organ repertoire.

Organists also employ some legato techniques which pianists rarely use. One such technique is finger substitution: by changing fingers on a single key, organists can reposition their hand to ensure a perfect legato. Figure 3.2 shows finger substitution in a typical chordal context.

FIGURE 3.2 Finger substitution

There is also the technique is known as 'thumb legato', shown Figure 3.3 (a). Unlike the other fingers, the thumb can slide to take adjacent notes legato. Additionally, any finger can slide from a black note onto an adjacent white note, although not vice versa, as demonstrated in Figure 3.3 (b).

FIGURE 3.3 Thumb legato and finger sliding

Finally, when playing on a single manual, it is possible to share individual contrapuntal lines or even single sustained notes between both hands. In Figure 3.4 (a), the ear hears three unbroken contrapuntal voices, while in (b) the sharing makes the chordal textures easier to navigate. This technique can minimise many difficulties in thicker textures and is commonly used by the best organ composers including Bach (see, e.g., Figure 3.20) and Messiaen (see, e.g., *Livre du Saint Sacrement*, 'Adoro te').

FIGURE 3.4 Distributing across hands

It is strongly recommended to test manuals' parts out on a keyboard as for Figure 3.1 wherever possible. There is no substitute for tactile experience and playing manuals' parts in this manner is the fastest way to learn what idiomatic writing feels like. The composer is also strongly urged to similarly play through all the examples in this chapter (and, indeed, in the other chapters). If no keyboard is available, critical score study and watching organists perform, either live or recorded, is the best approach.

With clever manuals' writing, it is possible to control dynamics to an extent without needing to alter registration. The organ is governed much more by acoustic physics than the piano. The more notes there are in a chord, the louder it will sound. Similarly, higher pitches often sound louder than lower ones, as low frequencies do not 'carry' as well (which is partly why the pedals are so important, being designed to counterbalance this phenomenon). Ascending into the higher range and increasing the note density will naturally increase the volume even when all the stops have already been pulled out; the manual 16′ can fill out the mid-range of frequencies so there is no audible gap between the manuals and the pedals. Many of the great traditional organ composers take both of these facts into account, allowing for subtle changes of dynamics through texture alone. Figure 3.5 shows one of these climaxes in practice.

The Pipe Organ

FIGURE 3.5 Eugène Gigout, *10 Pièces pour orgue*, Toccata

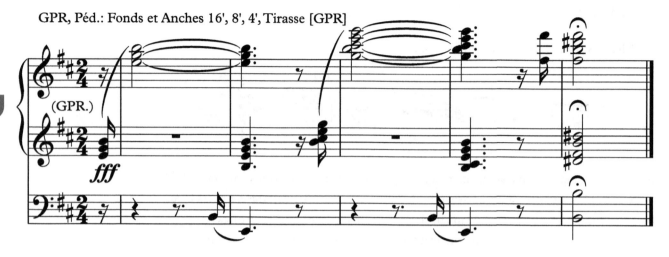

Precisely notating articulation is extremely helpful to the performer and in extreme cases can determine whether or not a passage is physically playable. Touch and articulation are the main ways to make the organ expressive. In modern times, the default articulation for unfamiliar pieces is generally legato. However, organists will seize on any articulations given by composers, even if just a verbal 'non legato' at the start of the piece. The organ is capable of a whole spectrum of legato, non legato and staccato textures and careful attention to articulation is one factor which defines truly great organ music.

Idiomatic Writing

On paper, idiomatic manuals' writing can initially look strange to those accustomed to piano composition. For example, simple gestures can be incredibly impactful on an organ compared to on other keyboard instruments. The example in Figure 3.6 sounds sparse and weak played as written on a piano. On full organ, however, it sounds very dramatic and is justly one of the most recognisable organ introductions of all time.

FIGURE 3.6 Johann Sebastian Bach, *Toccata and Fugue in D minor* BWV 565

Effective chordal writing is also very different for the organ. The lack of a sustain pedal can make thick chords harder to grapple through than on a piano, as the hands cannot release early to reposition themselves. Figure 3.7 shows a standard situation. This example may look idiomatic at first, and the contrapuntal ideas at least are well suited to the organ. However, the sheer density of notes in the chords make finger substitution difficult and legato hard to achieve, making the passage awkward to play. This type of writing is very common in German and English Romantic music and so is perhaps why organists are so keen to warn composers about 'overwriting'.

FIGURE 3.7 Max Reger, *7 Stücke* op. 145, 'Siegesfeier'

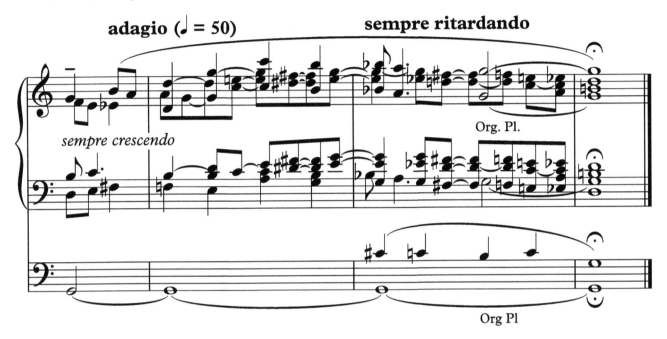

On the other hand, thick chordal textures on the organ can actually be very idiomatic when written carefully. In Figure 3.8, Widor uses thick chords just like Reger does in the previous example. However, through the articulation and higher register, the organ writing this time is brilliant, very effective and satisfying to play.

FIGURE 3.8 Charles-Marie Widor, *Organ Symphony No. 6* op. 42 no. 2, Finale

As can be seen, idiomatic organ writing can be hard to pin down and relies on a combination of many small factors. The rest of this chapter aims to help composers discover what works and what does not. Chordal and non-chordal techniques are presented in separate sections; although there is often overlap between both aspects, chordal writing poses unique challenges (particularly in comparison to piano chordal writing) that are best addressed separately.

Non-Chordal Techniques

Non-chordal techniques have been used very effectively across the whole history of organ music: the doubled monophonic approach seen in Figure 3.6 has been put to good effect in more modern contexts, for example, the opening to Langlais's 'Te Deum' from *Trois Paraphrases Gregoriennes*, Messiaen's 'Force et agilité des Corps Glorieux' from *Les Corps Glorieux* and Jacques Charpentier's 'Sortie' from his *Messe pour tous les temps*. Fleeting passagework can also be very effective in softer contexts, as Dupré's *Prelude and Fugue in G Minor* attests among others. With well-chosen registration, even the simplest gesture can have a decisive impact.

Scales are rarer in organ music than in piano music, although they are arguably more effective on the organ and are often used for special effects. Vierne's 'Naïades' from his *Pièces de Fantaisie* is an effective if rather technically challenging example, creating the image of sparkling water jets (see Figure 4.51; see also Jenkins *6000 Pipes*, 'Secret Orchids' for a similar effect combining organ and orchestra). In 'Les Cloches de Hinckley' from the same collection, Vierne uses right-hand scales in the final section to simulate the peal of bells. Most commonly, however, scales are used as an ornament, and in this form can be found in styles as diverse as German Baroque (e.g., Buxtehude *Prelude in C major* BuxWV 137), French Classical (e.g., du Mage *Suite du Premier Ton*, Tierce en taille) and English Romanticism (e.g., Elgar arr. Sinclair *Pomp and Circumstance March No. 4*; Bairstow *Blessed City, Heavenly Salem*). In Figure 3.9, the scale is doubled by both hands, creating a very full sound just like in Figure 3.6.

FIGURE 3.9 Max Reger, *2 Choralfantasien* op. 40, 'Wie schön leucht't uns der Morgenstern'

Baroque scales often use a cross-handed 'passaggio' fingering as shown in Figure 3.10.

FIGURE 3.10 Passaggio fingering

This fingering allows scales to be played rapidly yet easily. Consequently, it is a popular technique found in many Baroque cadenzas as well as the more 'showy' works of the period (e.g., Bach *Prelude and Fugue in D major* BWV 532, Buxtehude *Toccata in F major* BuxWV 157). This fingering is also very useful in post-Baroque music. The example by Karg-Elert shown in Figure 3.11 is very effective, creating a virtuosic-sounding line that is relatively easy to play. Modern applications (e.g., Martin *Ut Unum Sint*) show how much potential this technique still has.

FIGURE 3.11 Sigfrid Karg-Elert, *Choral-Improvisationen für Orgel* op. 65, 'Ein Feste Burg'

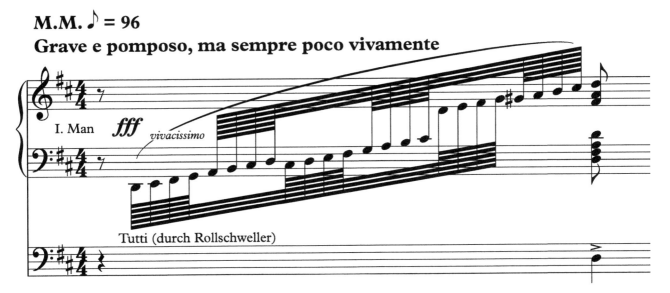

Scales in thirds and other intervals are generally less effective on the organ than the piano, with the lack of sustaining pedal making them harder to execute cleanly (the major exceptions are double chromatic scales, which are remarkably effective on organ). Legato passages such as in Finzi *God is Gone Up*, while playable, cannot be said to be truly idiomatic. Even staccato thirds can be very technically challenging, with those in the Magnificat from Stanford's *Morning, Evening and Communion Service in A major* being an infamously difficult example. Figure 3.12 shows an effective use of such scales; the fact that both hands are always going in the same direction, as well as the small turns at the start of the first three bars, both greatly ease execution.

FIGURE 3.12 Adolphus Hailstork, *Toccata on 'Veni Emmanuel'* © E. C. Schirmer Publishing

Arpeggio figurations on the organ have a very different effect than on the piano, yet they can be equally as idiomatic if used properly. Organ arpeggios are generally most effective where the hand does not have to move, in contrast to the wide-ranging piano arpeggios such as used by Rachmaninoff, for example. In Figure 3.13, from Widor's very famous toccata, the right hand does not have to move at all, therefore making the passage easy to play. Figure 3.14 shows a more involved example: although the hand has to shift between each group of four semiquavers, the short duration of each arpeggio helps make the passage more manageable to play. Passagework such as in Figure 3.14 is undeservedly rare in the organ repertoire and is an extraordinary example of how effective arpeggios can be at softer dynamics.

FIGURE 3.13 Charles-Marie Widor, *Organ Symphony No. 5* op. 42 no. 1, Toccata

FIGURE 3.14 Jeanne Demessieux, *Sept Méditations sur le Saint-Esprit* op.6, 'Lumière' ©
Alphonse Leduc Editions Musicales

Just like for cross-hand scales, cross-hand arpeggio figures can be very effective, lying easily under the fingers. In Figure 3.15, the sustained melody and bass line clearly contrast with the accompanimental cross-hand arpeggios, creating a passage that both sounds very symphonic yet is idiomatic and easy to play (see also Koechlin *La course de printemps*, 'Flûte de Krishna' for an extraordinary usage of these arpeggios in an orchestral context).

FIGURE 3.15 Albert Renaud, *Deux Toccatas* op. 108 no. 1

Single-hand octaves passages have their place but are much less useful than on a piano. Legato octaves are common in Romantic organ music, usually written with spongey electric-action organs in mind. These octaves are usually played only semi-legato and cannot be said to be truly idiomatic; in practice, organists may even cut out the lower note to achieve a better legato. In Figure 3.16, Respighi uses octaves to highlight the plainchant melody, the 'Gloria' from the *Missa De Angelis*. While Respighi's organ writing is normally very effective, it would be more idiomatic if the octaves were marcato/tenuto, which would help to emphasise the melody, and possibly played on a Choir solo reed (the Kyrie of Duruflé's *Requiem* demonstrates these principles in action).

FIGURE 3.16 Ottorino Respighi, *Vetrate di Chiesa*, 'S. Gregorio Magno' © Ricordi

Sustaining a melody above an animated accompaniment is incredibly effective and can be found in all types of organ music, particularly French toccatas. This technique can also be applied in a more nuanced way to accompaniments: sustaining individual accompaniment notes in filigree textures can create a very symphonic sound. Duruflé's music in particular should be studied in this regard, as his careful use of sustained notes in fleeting passagework creates some of the most truly symphonic organ music ever written (see especially his *Scherzo* and *Suite*). Figure 3.17 by Langlais provides a compact example: the left hand provides both sustained note and elaborate fingerwork, the right hand plays the melodic line in thirds and the pedals play the main theme staccato in augmentation, thus creating an elaborate multi-layered texture.

FIGURE 3.17 Jean Langlais, *Trois paraphrases grégoriennes* op. 5, 'Hymne d'actions des grâces "Te Deum"' © Éditions Combre

Repeated notes are more common on the Hammond organ than in traditional church organ music, the Hammond having a more incisive attack and often played in dryer acoustics. The speed of repetitions on a pipe organ will also depend on the action, with much faster speeds often possible on electric-action over tracker-action organs (see 'Building Trends' in Chapter 1). Figure 3.18 is an exceptional example, pushing the concept of repeated notes to a pianistic level of virtuosity. In this case, the loud registration helps make each repetition clearer, therefore minimising the risk of 'blurriness'.

FIGURE 3.18 Marcel Dupré, *Evocation* op. 37, Allegro deciso © Alphonse Leduc Editions Musicales

Glissandi are relatively rare in the organ literature (although examples do exist, notably Holst *The Planets*, 'Uranus') and are much easier to perform on electric-action rather than mechanical-action instruments. Trills and tremolos are similarly less important on the organ than on other keyboard instruments in terms of pure functionality, given the organ's indefinite sustain. However, trills can still usefully add movement to otherwise static lines, creating a more mutable and dynamic texture than if they were not present. The value of this application is perhaps best seen in Baroque music, where ornaments still figure very prominently and can add much expressive weight such as in the famous example shown in Figure 3.19 (in this example, the right hand is usually played on a solo manual).

FIGURE 3.19 Johann Sebastian Bach, *O Mensch, bewein 'dein' Sünde groß* BWV 622

The Pipe Organ

Finally, before moving onto a full discussion of chordal techniques, it is worth briefly talking about strict linear contrapuntal writing. As already mentioned, counterpoint is very effective on the organ. Bach is the undisputed master of contrapuntal organ writing, Figure 3.20 being one of many examples. He often keeps the counterpoint relatively thin, cleverly using rests and breaks in voices, which both keeps the texture light and aids with execution considerably. When writing strict counterpoint in his organ music, Bach also rarely exceeds three-part counterpoint in the manuals, with any more parts being difficult to play and so limiting the contrapuntal potential of the lines already present. When he does exceed three manual parts, it is usually a special effect and the counterpoint normally loosens noticeably (see, e.g., Figure 4.49). In his four-part fugues, he often assigns the soprano, tenor and bass voices to the right and left hand and pedals respectively, the alto voice being shared between the two hands (see the discussion around Figure 3.4). All of these features, demonstrated in Figure 3.20, are extremely idiomatic (if occasionally difficult to read), allowing for rich textures while still maintaining full independence of each voice. Try playing through this extract, bearing in mind that the left hand will have to take some of the right-hand notes.

FIGURE 3.20 Johann Sebastian Bach, *Prelude and Fugue in G minor* BWV 535

In the twentieth century, composers such as Hindemith (in his organ sonatas) successfully imported Bachian textures into a more modern idiom. However, some of the most innovative yet idiomatic writing in the past century has merged contrapuntal thinking with more chordal techniques pioneered by the Romantics. Therefore, this chapter will now examine these chordal techniques in more detail.

Chordal Techniques

Many non-organist composers are relatively reticent about writing more chordally for the organ, perhaps worried about 'overwriting' as discussed in Chapter 1. However, chordal organ writing can be just as idiomatic as non-chordal writing if done well. French Romanticism is very good for learning about idiomatic chordal writing, and it is strongly recommended to closely study organ works by Vierne, Dupré, Duruflé and Messiaen in particular.

Chord voicing and voice-leading are crucial to successful chordal writing. Efficient voicing is a feature of a lot of the best organ music, from Bach through to the present day, as it achieves the maximum result from the fewest number of notes. Additionally, a quasi-contrapuntal approach to chordal writing, with clear voice-leading between chords, is incredibly idiomatic. Messiaen is a master of both voicing and voice-leading within a very modern harmonic language; his *Livre du Saint Sacrement* is a masterclass in these aspects and should be studied/played through in full (Messiaen also provides fingerings, illustrating standard organ techniques such as finger substitution and thumb legato in a practical context).

Choral textures, unsurprisingly, can translate very effectively onto the organ. In fact, the earliest published collections of organ music largely contain transcriptions of Renaissance vocal motets (e.g., Ammerbach's 1571 *Orgel oder Instrument Tabulatur*). Four-part SATB writing, either on the manuals alone or with the pedals taking the bass part, sounds very idiomatic and is useful even in solo contexts. Figure 3.21 shows an excellent example of this texture in action. Note that there is no pedal part for this piece, with 'Man. I' applying to both hands in this case (see also Figure 4.51).

FIGURE 3.21 Johannes Brahms, *11 Chorale Preludes for organ* op. 122, 'Es ist ein Ros'

The number of voices also need not be fixed and a freer approach to contrapuntal chordal textures can work very well on the organ. Take Figure 3.22, with chords comprised variously of three to five notes. Try playing the manuals part of the following example with a perfect legato. Finger substitution and thumb legato will help enormously. In bars 5 and 8, start as written then use finger substitution to switch the top left-hand note to the right hand. Notice how Elgar varies chord thickness to help shape the phrase, with larger chords being used almost as accents. As will be apparent, the careful chord voicing and voice-leading make this example easy to play while sounding very effective.

The Pipe Organ

FIGURE 3.22 Edward Elgar, *Variations on an Original Theme 'Enigma'* op. 36, Variation XIV

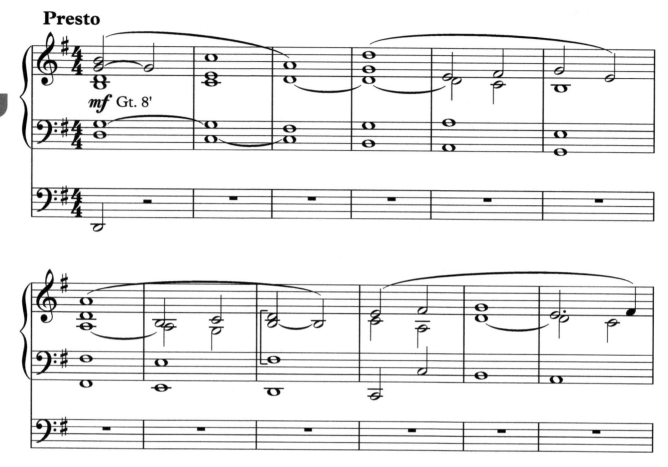

These principles also can be expanded to denser textures. Try playing Figure 3.23, which comes from the first of Ligeti's *Two Etudes for Organ*. Despite the five-note chords in both hands, the passage is very idiomatic since only one note changes at a time and each change is only by a semitone. The overall effect is of ten-part counterpoint, in a very effective synthesis of linear counterpoint and homophonic chordal writing (see again Messiaen *Livre du Saint Sacrement* for a paragon of these principles in action).

FIGURE 3.23 György Ligeti, *Two Etudes for Organ*, 'Harmonies' © Schott Music

Chordal writing in one hand alone requires more care. As the organ has no sustain pedal, the less physical movement needed between chords, the better. Tied notes can help bind chord

progressions together. For more legato textures, finger substitution is essential. In Figure 3.24, from Poulenc's *Organ Concerto*, the two hands are on different manuals and so cannot share notes between them. Note that, in French music from the Romantic period onwards, identical notes in consecutive chords are assumed to be tied together. This practice is known as *notes en commun* (lit. 'shared notes'); modern composers are recommended to use ties for clarity. For the final left-hand chord in bar 4, the perfect legato has to be broken. However, with a good touch and legato right hand, the break is almost indiscernible (such breaks only work for chords very close together such as in this example).

FIGURE 3.24 Francis Poulenc, *Organ Concerto*, Largo © Éditions Salabert

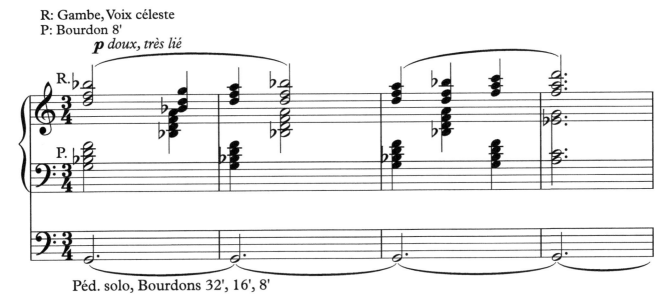

Staccato chords are very effective, particularly when combined with the pedals. At *ff* dynamics, fast repeated staccato chords can have a very dramatic effect as demonstrated in Figure 3.25; in this example, all the chords and pedal notes would be assumed to be played marcato. Such writing can also be very effective at quiet dynamics (see, e.g., Figure 4.44).

FIGURE 3.25 Lili Boulanger, *Psaume XXIV*

Bear in mind that there are also many types of staccato, ranging from very short and sharp to almost legato yet subtly detached. Messiaen, in 'Les Bergers' from *La Nativité du Seigneur*, employs two different types of staccato simultaneously, as shown in Figure 3.26. The right hand plays with a normal staccato, while the left hand plays 'louré', a type of slurred staccato normally indicated for string instruments. This latter staccato makes execution easy whilst bringing out the melodic nature of the left-hand part, contrasting with the twinkling staccato of the right hand. Despite both hands playing staccato chordal lines, therefore, the subtlety of Messiaen's articulation creates an idiomatic and very effective texture.

FIGURE 3.26 Olivier Messiaen, *La Nativité du Seigneur*, 'Les Bergers' © Alphonse Leduc Editions Musicales

Alternating chords between hands is a stock toccata texture (see, e.g., Figure 2.31). Rapid alternation can be difficult on heavy mechanical-action organs, particularly when many couplers are drawn (see 'Couplers' in Chapter 2), but there is essentially no such speed limit on electric-action organs. This technique can be equally as effective at quieter dynamics: Judith Weir's piece *Ettrick Banks* uses alternating chords with just the Great Flute 8' to marvelous effect, creating a shimmering liquescent sound (see Figure 2.9). Her choral-orchestral piece *Stars, Night, Music and Light* similarly employs this texture to great effect in the organ part, adding a sparkle to woodwind staccato chords while lying easily under the hands. Figure 3.27 shows an interesting example where the latter chord of each alternating pair is different from the former. This alternation allows for sophisticated harmonic effects which are still idiomatic to play (see also Escaich *Evocation IV* and *Poèmes pour orgue*, 'Eaux natales' for similar innovative applications of this technique).

FIGURE 3.27 Olivier Messiaen, *L'Ascension*, 'Transports de joie' © Alphonse Leduc Editions Musicales

Rapid successions of (staccato) chords in a single hand require care in approach. They can be very effective on electric-action organs yet fatiguing and even unidiomatic on mechanical-action instruments (see again 'Organ Building Trends' in Chapter 1). In large acoustics, rapidly repeating the same chord can cause the repetitions to blur together and lose their distinct articulation. Such rapid repeated chords tend to work best in short bursts rather than extended passages, where more hand stamina is required. No such issue is present at slower tempi, and there are many effective examples (e.g., Schnittke *Requiem*, 'Tuba Mirum') especially when some of the notes are sustained, linking the chords together (see, e.g., Franck 3 *Pièces pour grand orgue*, 'Pièce héroïque', Price *Adoration*). This issue of blurring is reduced, but not entirely eliminated, when the hand moves between different chords. As on the piano, the closer the chords are to each other in terms of physical hand position, the easier it will be to move between them and so the easier the passage will be to execute.

Figure 3.28 shows a two-bar repeated pattern from Jonathan Dove's *Missa Brevis*. The minimal shifts in hand position make the passage lie under the fingers well. The quaver rest at the end is crucial, giving the right hand a brief but essential moment to recover. Repeating the A_4 in the given rhythm is surprisingly awkward; the passage would be technically easier if the A_4 appeared in every chord (in practice the note also often blurs into itself). Note also the rare but effective use of crossing the hands: playing with the hands the normal way round would make this passage considerably more difficult (and the crossing becomes more important when bass notes are introduced later in the piece).

FIGURE 3.28 Jonathan Dove, *Missa Brevis*, Gloria © Edition Peters

'Double' staccato chords in alternating hands are a standard toccata texture. Figure 3.29 shows a typical example accompanying a pedal melody: the hand movement required between chord changes is minimal, not only easing execution but also creating clear voice leading between chords (which is very idiomatic even in this staccato, 'broken' context). Further examples exploring this technique for interesting effects include Alain *Litanies* (Alain disrupts the regular doubled pattern with extraordinary results), the final toccata section of Messiaen's 'Dieu parmi nous' from *La Nativité du Seigneur*, and the 'Toccata' from Duruflé's *Suite* (Duruflé pushes this technique to its practical limits in the recapitulation).

FIGURE 3.29 Ralph Simpson (arr.), *King of Kings* © GIA Publications

As mentioned in Chapter 1, there are various 'tricks' that can help when trying to write idiomatic chordal textures. Rapid broken chords can be an effective substitute to regular chords. In large resonant venues such as cathedrals, the acoustic will blur the notes together, giving the impression of a 'static' yet shimmering chord. Even in less reverberant spaces, this figuration can give a rich effect while avoiding the heaviness of block chords. Figure 3.30 provides a good example of this technique, breaking up a right-hand C minor chord into individual notes. Note how Boëllman creates a 'melody' using the first note of each semiquaver group, maximising the contrapuntal value gained from the texture (other good examples of this technique include Vierne *Organ Symphony No. 3*, Finale and Duruflé *Suite*, Toccata).

FIGURE 3.30 Léon Boëllman, *Suite Gothique* op. 25, Toccata

'Cascading' chords, where the notes in broken chords are held down instead of being released immediately, can be incredibly effective. While the technique has been used at least since the time of Bach (see Figure 3.1) and was notable in German Romanticism in particular (see, e.g., Karg-Elert *Choral-Improvisationen für Orgel*, 'Ein Feste Burg'), modern composers such as Hans Werner Henze in his *Toccata senza fuga* have discovered the full utility of the technique. In Figure 3.31, Leighton cleverly varies the order of the spread to create a simple motif. He later expands this motif into the left hand and even the pedals in an idiomatic way, creating organ music that is simple yet striking and which has become a repertoire staple for organists of all ages and experience.

FIGURE 3.31 Kenneth Leighton, *Paean* © Oxford University Press

Dividing four-note chords into two-note pairs is a stock technique. Arguably the most well-known example is the Finale from Vierne's First Organ Symphony, reproduced in

Figure 2.25 (note how both hands participate, with the pedals taking the melody; see also Dupré 'Prelude and Fugue in B major' for an idiomatic variation of this pattern). Single-handed tremolos using similar dyad patterns can also be very effective, adding movement to static chords (see, e.g., Finzi *Lo, the Full Final Sacrifice*, Mulet *Carillon-Sortie*). Figure 3.32 shows this technique pushed to its limit in an idiomatic yet technically challenging passage.

FIGURE 3.32 Louis Vierne, *Pièces de fantaisie*, Suite II op. 53, Toccata

Isolating the thumb note from the rest of the chord is also very effective for fast passagework. This technique was much favoured by Messiaen in the toccatas of the *Livre du Saint Sacrement* (e.g., 'Les deux murailles d'eaux', 'Offrandre et Alleluia Final'), showing how effective it can be for creating dissonant toccata textures that are still idiomatic. Figure 3.33 by Vierne demonstrates this technique in an unsettling scherzo, with the passage lying nicely under the fingers since both hands are able to remain largely static.

FIGURE 3.33 Louis Vierne, *Organ Symphony No. 6* op. 59, Scherzo

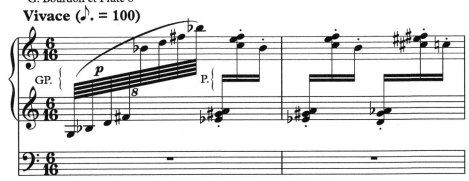

There are also some special chordal techniques that, while more rarely used, can be effective in certain contexts. Harp-like 'spread' chords can be surprisingly useful, being an extension of cascading chords mentioned in relation to Figure 3.31. As such, they often work best in isolated instances rather than repeatedly in rapid succession, given that the organ lacks a sustain pedal. In Figure 3.34, Bairstow makes each chord short and sharp, avoiding the issue of lack of sustain (note that the pedals would play on the beat and not be involved in the spread despite Bairstow's indications).

FIGURE 3.34 Edward Bairstow, *Blessed City, Heavenly Salem*

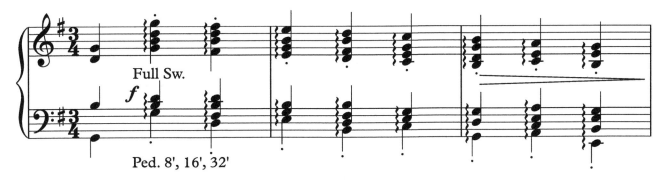

Tremolo chords can also be surprisingly valuable on the organ in the same way as regular trills, adding movement to otherwise static chords. In Figure 3.35, Lili Boulanger ingeniously uses a tremolo in combination with low intervals to produce a soft rumbling tone, exploiting the dissonant, almost percussive sound it produces. All of the lowest stops are drawn, including the 32′ in the pedal and 16′ in the manuals, in order to emphasise this effect. In context, the organ is doubled by a pianissimo bass drum roll (see also Guillou *Jeux d'orgue*, 'Au miroir des flûtes' for an extraordinary example of a high-pitched chordal tremolo).

FIGURE 3.35 Lili Boulanger, *Psaume CXXX*

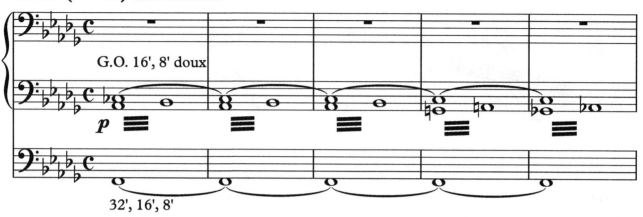

Finally, Hammond organists have developed a technique of 'palm glissando'. By using the flat of the palm for the glissando, the fingers are free to catch full chords. This technique is non-conventional on pipe organs and so no standard notation for it exist; Figure 3.36 offers one possible way to notate it (see also Bolcom *Gospel Preludes*, 'What a Friend We Have in Jesus!' for a rare classical example). Hammond organists typically only palm glissando upwards, the downwards one being performed like regular piano glissandi. This technique is easier on Hammonds than traditional pipe organs owing to the very light electric action and design of the keys. With practice, however, it can work on every kind of organ, and is thus worth experimenting with in any context. Such cross-instrument influence offers many exciting avenues for innovation, and so composers are strongly encouraged to explore these other types of organs (see Chapter 5 for further discussion) and experiment with these types of techniques.

FIGURE 3.36 Palm glissando

Playing on Multiple Manuals

The examples so far have largely been concerned with single-manual technique. Indeed, there is much fine organ music that requires only one manual. However, the use of multiple manuals, either simultaneously or in alternation, has always been an important aspect of organ playing. Composers such as Duruflé exploit multiple-manual technique to its fullest, creating a truly symphonic sound. The following section therefore examines how to combine multiple manuals idiomatically and effectively.

One of the most common situations with multiple manuals is when one manual (normally the Great or Choir) has a solo line while another (normally the Swell) is used for accompaniment. Common stops used for the solo line include the Swell and Choir reeds (see, e.g., Figures 2.14, 2.17 and 2.21), single principal or flute stops (see Figure 2.34) or more extensive registrations on the Great or Choir with as many manuals coupled as possible (see, e.g., Figure 2.16; this last option is very common for registering the main theme of English marches). Quieter passages offer more possibilities for different colours than loud passages. Besides requesting specific registrations, writing 'solo' above a solo line is also clear while being more flexible, allowing the organist can choose an appropriate stop depending on the instrument (see, e.g., Jackson *Evening Service in G*, Leighton *Missa di Gloria*, 'Gloria').

Changing manuals can also be used to aid Romantic crescendos and diminuendos. Organists often move between the Swell, Choir and Great manuals even when not indicated in order to vary the dynamics, the Swell being used as the quietest manual and the Great the loudest. With the Full Swell out but only 8′ and 4′ foundations on the Great and Choir, the manual transitions would blend together seamlessly, providing a symphonic crescendo used frequently by French Romantic composers. Figure 3.37 demonstrates such a crescendo in practice. Note how, by keeping the right hand on a quieter manual, five separate dynamic levels can be achieved with only three manuals and no registration changes.

FIGURE 3.37 Manual changes

Alternating between two or three manuals to create a type of 'echo' is common in the German Romantic school, particularly Mendelssohn and Brahms (see Figure 4.48 in the following chapter). Ideally, the two manuals should be coupled together. Composers sometimes specify alternating 'two manuals of equal volume'; however, achieving balance can be very difficult without substantially different registrations on each manual. Figure 3.38 shows one effective instance of this type of equality between manuals. Part of its success is that the manuals are not intended to be entirely separate but instead blend together to create a rich, almost antiphonal effect. The bright and loud registration of both manuals also helps with balance issues in this instance.

FIGURE 3.38 Vicky Chang, *Suite for Organ*, 'Cloudy Sky' © Wayne Leupold Editions

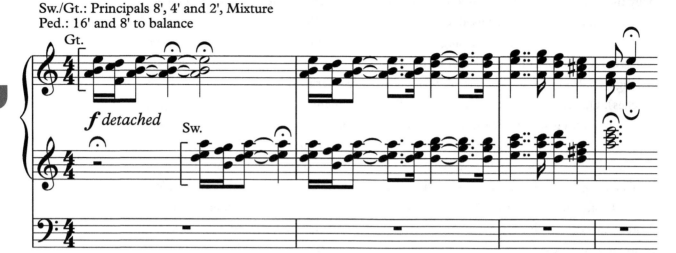

The 'trio sonata' texture, where the two hands and pedals play three independent monophonic lines, have the hands allocated to different manuals with no couplers drawn. The challenge for organists is to choose a registration where the two manuals are distinct but balanced. For this reason, trio sonatas are often played with delicate registrations, for example, Principal 8′ on the Great in the right hand and Principal 4′ on the Choir or Swell in the left hand (the left hand playing an octave lower than written). Figure 3.39 gives a famous traditional example of this trio sonata texture. Incidentally, the three separate parts also require much concentration and coordination to perform successfully; Bach's trio sonatas are often set for exams or job interviews as a test of an organist's competence. For a more modern take see, e.g., both 'Pièces en trio' from Messiaen's *Livre d'orgue*.

FIGURE 3.39 Johann Sebastian Bach, *Trio Sonata No. 1* BWV 525

More complex textures on multiple uncoupled manuals can be difficult to write idiomatically and should be very carefully planned, preferably in consultation with an organist. 'La Transsubstantiation' from Messiaen's *Livre du Saint Sacrement*, shown in Figure 3.40, provides one of the rare complicated yet successful examples. The fingerings are Messiaen's own. The three manuals (and pedals) have contrasting registrations, providing clear timbral differentiation and so allowing each manual to sound completely distinct from the others. The Swell registration of Oboe and mixture is very colourful and enables it to balance with the other two manuals. Messiaen's dynamics indicate the boxes for both Swell and Choir should be open, enabling them to balance better with the Great (which Messiaen marks as slightly quieter than the other two). As such, the total sounding volume would be no more than about *mf* in practice. Despite Messiaen's careful handling of this texture, even these registrations are not guaranteed to balance correctly for every organ.

FIGURE 3.40 Olivier Messiaen, *Livre du Saint Sacrement*, 'La Transsubstantiation' © Alphonse Leduc Editions Musicales

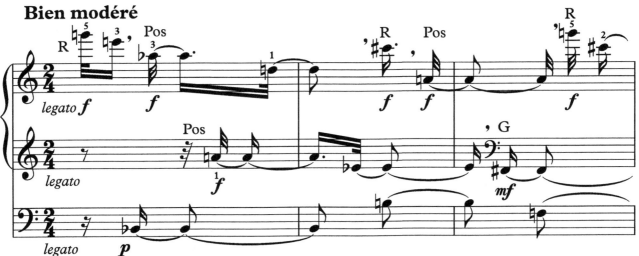

Playing on two manuals with one hand is possible but can only be done with adjacent manuals (e.g., the Great and the Choir), requires a lot of coordination and is very difficult to play legato. Typically, the thumb goes down to a lower manual while the rest of the hand stays on the higher manual. This use of the thumb is often indicated with a plus sign. Figure 3.41 is a well-known example, although it is difficult to execute well.

FIGURE 3.41 Edwin Lemare, *2 Pieces for Organ* op. 83, 'Moonlight and Roses'

Other notable examples of this technique do exist, particularly by French composers. Duruflé requires this technique in both his *Scherzo* and the 'Sicilienne' from his *Suite*. Escaich, in his 'Eaux natales' from the *Poèmes pour orgue*, also employs this technique for an extended period of time, the thumb playing the melody while the other fingers hold down a chord. In many of these cases, execution is difficult and awkward and can verge on being unidiomatic, even in music by experienced organists. This technique therefore should be used very carefully and preferably in consultation with an organist. Nevertheless, it is a viable compositional resource which has yet to be fully explored: Figure 3.42 shows one astonishing modern example where the judicious use of double manuals, staccato articulations (giving the hands time to reposition) and the minimal hand stretch required make this passage remarkably easy to play, just like playing regular staccato chords.

FIGURE 3.42 Zoë Martlew, *Starlude* © Zoë Martlew

As has hopefully been demonstrated, the manuals are capable of more than is often asked of them. Virtually anything that is technically possible on the piano is also possible on the organ, and modern organists often have as proficient a command of the keyboard as virtuoso pianists do (and some are even virtuoso pianists in their own right). Composers are thus encouraged to be ambitious in their manuals' writing. Once again, practical experimentation on the piano, without using the sustain pedal and holding each note for its full value, is the fastest way to discover idiomatic and innovative manuals' textures. Composers such as Dupré and Duruflé show just how idiomatic virtuoso keyboard figurations can be, particularly when merged with symphonic-style counterpoint (just as the great pianist-composers such as Rachmaninoff cleverly incorporated symphonic counterpoint into virtuosic piano writing). There is so much that has not been explored regarding manuals' technique and so, if composers are willing to experiment, many exciting discoveries await.

THE PEDALS

Overview

▶ The pedalboard separates the organ from almost all other modern keyboard instruments. Unsurprisingly, therefore, writing for pedals can be difficult to understand without having actually played an organ before. In addition, many organ keyboard patches do not contain separate pedal samples, therefore making the low end of the organ sound weak and lacking depth and giving a distorted impression of how the organ works. The pedals are fundamental to the organ sound, with the 16′ not only strengthening the bass line but also the organ's projection overall, compensating for the lack of overtones in the initial transient when a key is pressed. As will be seen, creative composers have also explored using the pedals for melody lines and even chords. This chapter will therefore seek to show how to write idiomatically for the pedals, as well as the potential they can bring to innovative organ writing. A video demonstration of basic pedal techniques is provided as Video 4.1 in the Online Resources.

Figure 4.1 shows the pedalboard of a typical modern eclectic organ. In practice, there are many sizes and shapes of pedalboard. The pedal keyboard in Figure 4.1 is 'radiating', that is, the white keys converge towards the organ bench, following the natural angle of the legs when sitting at the centre of the organ bench. While this design is the standard in the UK and US, 'parallel' pedalboards (where each key is parallel to each other) are not uncommon even on new organs. The size and shape of the black keys can also vary significantly, altering how the organist can play them. Taking differences between pedalboards into account can help avoid unduly difficult pedal passages on specific organs, particularly with sections involving double or multi-pedalling (see 'Double/Multi-Pedalling' later in this chapter).

FIGURE 4.1 A typical pedalboard

The pedalboard contains more than just the pedal keyboard, as can be seen in Figure 4.1. Most organs have a Swell pedal (centre) as well as sometimes a Choir pedal and a crescendo pedal; see Figure 2.34. The pedalboard also has various registration aids (the buttons to the side of the Swell pedal in Figure 4.1); the most common are the Great to Pedal coupler and the pedal divisionals. There is also often a duplicate set of general pistons and, more rarely, a stepper piston; see 'Registration Aids' in Chapter 2 for more information. As such, one foot (typically the right foot) will need to be free in order to operate them. When writing a passage calling for these registration aids, simple pedal writing is strongly recommended.

The written range of the pedals, given in Figure 1.2, is provided here again for convenience in Figure 4.2. Note that in practice, as the pedal is based on the 16′ stops, this range typically sounds an octave lower than written.

FIGURE 4.2 Pedals range

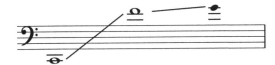

The high F_4 (a 30-note compass) is standard across all except the very smallest organs or historic instruments. The top two semitones (a 32-note compass) are not uncommon; however, there is no way to predict whether an organ will have this extension. Even the largest organs may only have a 30-note compass (see, e.g., 'French Romantic (a)—Église Saint-Sulpice, Paris' in the Online Resources). If the upper two notes are desired, try and make them ad lib if possible (see, e.g., Karg-Elert *Choral-Improvisationen für Orgel*, 'Ein Feste Burg'). Some experienced organist-composers have created incredibly contrived alternatives for the smaller pedal compass (e.g., Duruflé *Prelude, Adagio et Chorale Varié sur le theme du 'Veni Creator'*). Otherwise, the high notes may have to be omitted. For example, many organists will just omit the high $F\#_4$ in the 'Sicilienne' of Duruflé's *Suite*, sustaining the following E_4 a quaver earlier to fill the gap. The simpler the alternative, the more effective it will likely be.

For solo music, the pedals are almost always given their own stave, making the pedal line clear and unambiguous even in complex pedal passages. Much organ music pre-1650, as well as music written for chamber organs (see Chapter 5), has no separate pedal line and so no third stave, the former often being intended to be playable on portable organs or even harpsichords. In some choral and orchestral scores, the pedals are often consolidated into the grand-stave pair to save space such as in Figure 4.3. Here, the pedals take the bottom notes with downward-facing stems; it is usually assumed they take the lowest note if not marked otherwise.

FIGURE 4.3 Camille Saint-Saëns, *Symphony No. 3 'Organ'* op. 78, Maestoso

To play the pedals, two parts of each foot are used: the big toe and the heel. For Baroque music, pedal parts are typically performed with the toes alone (just as in the manuals, the standard Baroque articulation is detached rather than legato). By the early 1800s, however, use of the heels and pedal legato became gradually more and more common, and today are essential for the execution of many pedal passages.

Just as for fingering, there is a relatively standardised system for marking pedalling where necessary. Pedalling indications for the left foot are written below the stave while those for the right foot are written above. There are also independent symbols for the left toe (indicated with a '∧' symbol), the right toe (indicated with a '∨'), and the heels of both feet (here indicated with a circle above the stave for the right foot and below the stave for the left foot). There are occasionally some minor variants, such as the use of horseshoe shapes to indicate heels, but the intention is usually obvious as long as the left and right feet indications stay below and above the stave, respectively. Marking pedalling is largely unnecessary but, like for string bowing, occasional indications can help clarify intent and precise articulation; see Figure 4.29 for one helpful example.

It is strongly recommended to plan where each toe and heel should go in any case, even if it is not then written into the score. Planning the pedalling will invariably lead to more idiomatic pedal writing, as well as steering the composer on what may be more or less technically challenging.

Foot substitution, just like finger substitution, is a fundamental legato technique for organists. Not only can one foot substitute for another (Figure 4.4a), but on the white keys it is possible to switch between toe and heel on a single foot (Figure 4.4b). This technique is very useful for single-foot chromatic passages; however, this substitution can only happen so fast, so the more time that can be allowed for it the better.

FIGURE 4.4 Foot substitution

Pedal passages are easier in the centre of the pedal compass than at the extreme ends. As the pedal board is so wide, the organist has to swivel the entire body if both feet are needed close together. This swivel can only happen so fast, and so care must be exercised in places where the pedals span the whole range of the pedalboard. The size and shape of the pedalboard will also influence how much swivel is needed. In Figure 4.5, (a) is very easy, even though it spans the entire compass, because no swivel is needed; (b), by contrast, is considerably more difficult because the organist has to swivel very fast to reach the other end of the pedal compass in time. To fully understand this swivel, composers should try it themselves sitting on any available flat bench or surface, alongside watching professional organists either in-person or through videos.

FIGURE 4.5 Pedalling across the whole compass

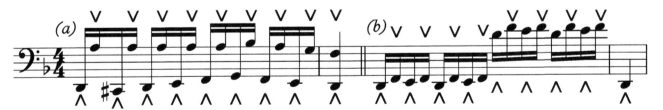

Note also that the span between the toe and heel on each foot is only so wide. The 'safe' maximum legato interval between toe and heel is a major third, although a perfect fourth is sometimes seen (e.g., Franck *3 Pièces pour grand orgue*, 'Pièce Héroïque'); slightly larger intervals can be reached if the articulation is non legato.

Ankle flexibility is also a consideration, particularly for black notes and at the extreme ends of the keyboard. The back part of the foot naturally points to the centre of the pedalboard and twisting the foot in the opposite direction can be extremely awkward. In Figure 4.6, the intervals marked (a) and (b) are at best physically challenging and at worst unplayable owing to how much the ankle needs to be twisted; (c) and (d) are considerably easier, as the feet can follow the line of the leg and so no ankle twisting is required. Once again, physical experimentation is the best way to learn what is possible and what is not.

FIGURE 4.6 Ankle twisting

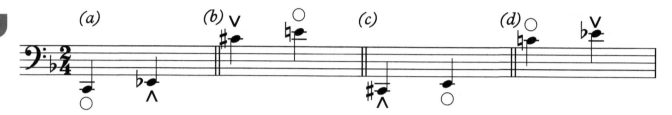

The black notes require particular care. Heels cannot be used on them because the keys are so far back on the pedalboard (see Figure 4.1), making the black notes generally more awkward to navigate than white notes. To take adjacent black notes legato with a single foot, the foot has to 'rock' from the big toe to the little toe (as shown in Figure 4.7). This rocking is physically awkward and very difficult to sustain repeatedly for extended periods (see, e.g., Langlais 7 *Études de Concert*, 'Trilles').

FIGURE 4.7 Rocking the feet

On the other hand, the black keys are physically raised higher than the white keys. Consequently, single-foot legato bass lines, where the toe and heel of one foot have to alternate, are often easier when black keys are mixed in, particularly when these bass lines involve intervals over a major second. In Figure 4.8, (a) is much easier to execute with a single foot than (b), where both feet would be used if possible.

FIGURE 4.8 Pedalling with/without black notes

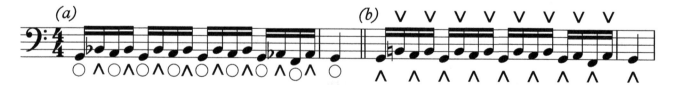

Using the Swell pedal, or any other foot registration aid, can add a complex dimension to pedal technique. In many styles of organ playing, one foot (typically the right foot) is often kept free to operate any expression pedals or foot pistons. It is helpful to have both feet available for more complex pedal passages, so care should be taken if any expression pedal is to be used. Note also that some Swell boxes can only be opened so fast, so rapidly opening or shutting the box may not be possible on some organs.

Figure 4.9 shows a few common situations regarding the Swell pedal. (a) is straightforward, the right foot operating the box while the left foot takes the bass notes. (b) is harder but still doable; this style of writing is common in theatre and Hammond organ playing. (c) is difficult; the right foot has to quickly jump between the box and the pedal notes. (d) is very difficult; the organist may have to postpone using the box until after the right foot is no longer needed. (e) is impossible, requiring three feet to operate both pedal notes and the Swell pedal simultaneously. Despite this, (e) is very commonly seen even in music of experienced organ composers (e.g., Boulanger *Psaume XXIV*); in these cases, the organist will have to sacrifice either the crescendo or the upper pedal note.

FIGURE 4.9 Swell pedal demonstration

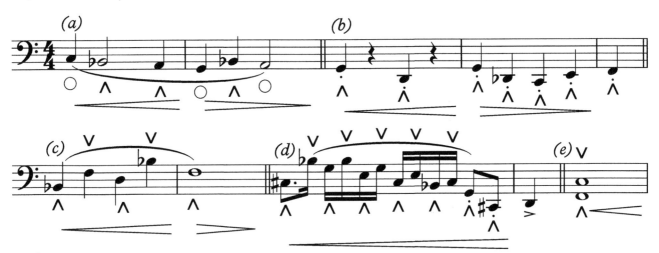

Precision of articulation is perhaps more important for the pedals than for the manuals. Articulation can fundamentally influence the pedalling choices all the way down to which foot to use. Clear phrasing and articulation will help the organist with both technical and expressive choices, leading to better performances. Without any articulations, the pedal line will usually be played as legato as reasonably possible. In any case, organists will always appreciate being told the articulation explicitly.

In most situations, there is no need for the pedals to double notes already in the manuals for extended periods. Every manual can be coupled down to the pedals, and the Swell to Pedal coupler is often drawn as a default when there are no registration indications. Treating the pedals as a distinct line can also free up fingers to take other notes or help create a smoother legato in the manuals.

Virtuosic pedal parts should preferably be balanced by simpler manual parts and vice versa. The physical contortion and shifting centre of gravity when turning the body (as is often necessary for virtuosic pedal footwork) can make even simple passages in the hands much harder to execute. Even infamous virtuoso works such as Dupré's *Trois Préludes et Fugues* rarely involve fast-moving manuals and pedal parts at exactly the same time. While simultaneous virtuosity in hands and feet does have its place, it can make the music inaccessible to all but the best organists and so should be applied carefully.

Composers may have heard of a 'split' pedalboard, where the top and bottom half of the pedal compass can be programmed to have different stops. This device is extremely rare, and even the very largest instruments often do not have this feature. As such, composers should never write for one unless in very special circumstances.

As ever, the fastest way to learn idiomatic pedal writing is to physically experiment with playing on a pedalboard. However, if a composer does not have access to an organ, there are analogies which may help with visualisation. The best one is perhaps comparing pedalling to sticking for mallet percussion; the same principles of single-mallet passagework also broadly apply to pedal writing. Another method for visualising pedal movements on a piano is to play using only the two thumbs, the joints of the thumbs representing the heels. While this approach is unable to do the heels full justice, it does provide a tactile way to explore pedalling without needing an organ.

There are many resources available about pedal technique for composers wishing to explore this area further. The main practical book on the subject is Anne Marsden Thomas's *Pedalling For Organists*, a comprehensive study of pedal technique. While aimed at organists, the book contains all of the main pedal excerpts in the standard repertoire, all fully marked-up. In addition, Marsden Thomas includes many colour photographs to demonstrate pedalling, giving a clear idea of the ergonomics required. Otherwise, watching organ recitals is strongly encouraged as many, both live and digital, have a separate camera feed for the pedals. General immersion in organ music and playing will also help develop an intuitive understanding of the pedals and just how much they have to offer.

Idiomatic Writing

Traditionally, pedal parts pre-1800 were usually played with the toes alone (although the extent to which the heels were used historically is a contentious issue). Alternating the toes was a popular technique, with much of the pedal writing in Bach and Buxtehude carefully written to be easily playable this way. By alternating toes, sophisticated and virtuosic pedal solos such as in Figure 4.10 can be executed accurately and musically. (N.b., all pedal markings in the following excerpts are editorial unless otherwise specified.)

FIGURE 4.10 Johann Sebastian Bach, *Prelude and Fugue in A Minor* BWV 543

This style of pedal writing is still very useful to modern composers, where it allows for easy execution of fast-moving passagework spanning the whole pedal compass. Figure 4.11 gives a sophisticated example from English Romanticism, where alternate toes are mixed into other types of pedalling (see also Figure 4.46 for an effective twenty-first-century example of this type of pedalling).

FIGURE 4.11 Charles H. H. Parry, *Fantasia and Fugue* op. 188

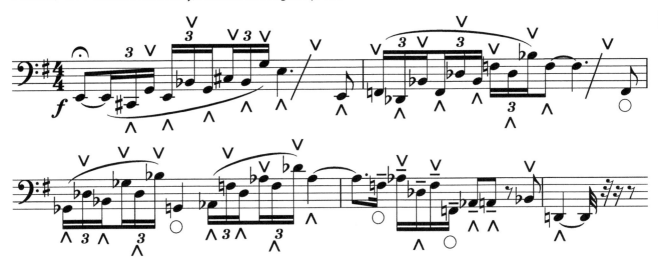

Outside of alternating toes, it was common to use a single foot to take adjacent pedal notes, giving each note a distinct articulation. This was particularly common in traditions with less virtuosic pedal parts such as the French Classical school where, for example, the cantus firmus was played in the pedals (see Figure 2.26). Even scalic 'walking bass' lines are often played using the toes alone, switching feet at accidentals or to help position both legs more generally. In Figure 4.12, the clear articulation for each note gives the pedal line a stately character without the potential heaviness or lugubriousness of true pedal legato. After the widespread adoption of heels in the 1800s, this method of pedalling became increasingly rare. For modern composers, it is necessary to indicate at least "non legato" if they desire passages to be played in this way.

FIGURE 4.12 Johann Sebastian Bach, *Nun komm, der Heiden Heiland* BWV 658

Larger leaps for individual feet are possible but relatively unidiomatic and can be difficult to execute, particularly at faster speeds. Obviously, such leaps cannot be made legato; it is also hard to quickly judge the exact distance the foot needs to travel with wide intervals. Such single-foot leaps are relatively common in Baroque music, mainly in pieces using the aforementioned 'walking bass' technique (as in, e.g., Figure 4.12) but examples can also be found in music of the Romantic period and beyond (e.g., Duruflé *Scherzo*). The situation shown in Figure 4.13 is extreme owing to the double pedalling (see also 'Double/Multi-Pedalling' later in this chapter).

FIGURE 4.13 Johann Sebastian Bach, *Aus Tiefer Not schrei' ich zu dir* BWV 686

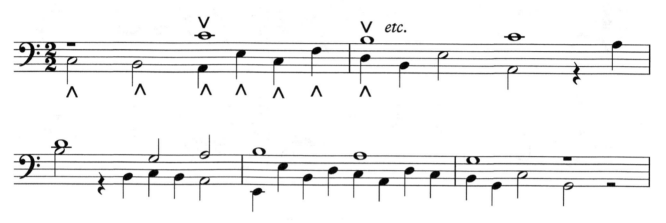

Crossing the feet should usually be avoided if possible but it is often manageable if necessary. It is easiest to do in scalic passages, where the legs do not have to cross far over each other while allowing fast scales to be executed with a distinct articulation on each note. Wider intervals are also possible although even more awkward. Quick lateral shifts, often needed in Baroque music such as in Figure 4.14, are slightly easier to manage than foot crossing. In this example, the right foot would stay further back on the pedalboard to achieve the passage in tempo.

FIGURE 4.14 Johann Sebastian Bach, *Prelude and Fugue in D major* BWV 532

The Pedals

With the introduction of heels, legato became the default articulation in organ repertoire. The specific pedalling depends on the passage, the articulation and on personal preference. However, to help composers understand how organists approach pedalling, some extended marked-up examples are provided in Figures 4.15 to 4.17. Incidentally, these three examples are currently set as pedal solos for the ABRSM Grade 6 and 7 organ exams.

FIGURE 4.15 Alexandre Guilmant, *Organ Sonata No. 1* op. 42, Allegro

FIGURE 4.16 Max Reger, *12 Stücke* op. 59, 'Fugue'

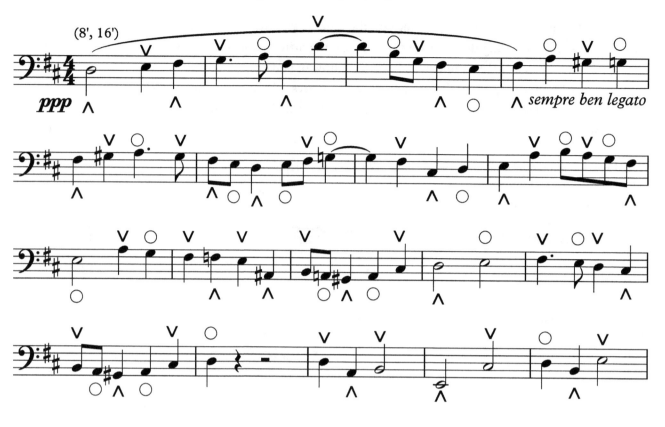

FIGURE 4.17 Felix Mendelssohn, *Organ Sonatas* op. 65 no. 3, Con moto maestoso

The toe and heel of each foot form an independent pair. While the interval coverable between toe and heel is relatively small, the two feet can be as far apart as necessary. Some organ composers have cleverly exploited this aspect of pedalling to make pedal lines that can span wide intervals while being relatively straightforward to play, such as in Figure 4.18.

FIGURE 4.18 Louis Vierne, *Organ Symphony No. 3* op. 28, Finale

While legato pedal lines are the default for Romantic music and beyond, staccato pedal lines can also be very effective. The articulation provides more flexibility in pedalling options. It is easier to play staccatos with the toes rather than the heels; as such, staccato passages are often easier and more effective with the toes alone (although heels can be used if necessary, e.g., in Elgar arr. Sinclair *Pomp and Circumstance March No. 4*). In Figure 4.19, Mendelssohn uses a staccato pedal line to imitate cello and double bass pizzicatos.

FIGURE 4.19 Felix Mendelssohn, *Organ Sonatas* op. 65 no. 5, Andante

Marcato pedal lines can also be effective at louder volumes. In Figure 4.20, the organ doubles the other orchestral bass instruments (cf. also the second movement of his *Vetrate di Chiesa* and 'Modus XII' of his *Metamorphoseon*). Using toes alone in this case helps give a more incisive marcato than mixing toes and heels.

FIGURE 4.20 Ottorino Respighi, *Pini di Roma*, 'I pini presso una catacomba, lento'

Pedal scales in every key are possible, even at quite fast speeds. Typically, the concurrent manual parts are relatively simple given the technical and ergonomic difficulties of these scales. In Figure 4.21, the pedal scale functions as an ostinato, starting alone before being joined by a chorale-like part in the manuals. Note the complex alternation of left and right feet, necessitated by the number of black notes in the scale.

FIGURE 4.21 Undine Smith Moore, *Variations on "There Is a Fountain"* © MorningStar Music Publications

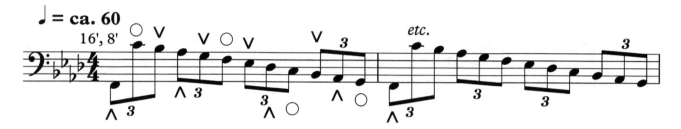

It is possible to trill in the pedals, both with alternating feet and by rocking between the toe and heel on a single foot. Trills with a single foot are naturally much harder than trills where both feet can be used. Trills are generally less effective in the pedals than the manuals because the low pedal pipes require more air and are slower to speak than those in the manuals. Mordents are common in Baroque music, but extended pedal trills are typically only found in German Romanticism (Liszt uses them frequently, e.g., in *Fantasia and Fugue on 'Ad nos ad salutarem undam'*). The following example in Figure 4.22 requires both single-foot and double-foot trills.

FIGURE 4.22 Max Reger, *Choralfantasie über 'Freu dich sehr, o meine Seele'* op. 30

Pedal glissandi along the white keys are possible but very rare in the repertoire. These glissandi are much easier on light pedalboards than on heavy mechanical-action ones. Because of the ergonomics, the accompanying manual passages should ideally be as simple as possible. Figure 4.23 shows an example for solo pedals with no accompaniment in the manuals; the pedalling indications are Langlais' original. Notice how both feet always move in the same direction, aiding execution considerably, as well as the breaks between glissandi allowing the feet to reset.

FIGURE 4.23 Jean Langlais, *7 Études de concert*, 'Alleluia' © Universal Edition

Many composers do not realise the full potential of what the heels and toes can do in combination. By combining alternating toes with heels, a whole range of pedal lines are opened up to the composer. Figure 4.24 is an excellent example of a modern pedal solo: McDowall combines alternate toes with use of the heels to produce a very idiomatic pedal line that sounds very effective and is fun to play.

FIGURE 4.24 Cecilia McDowall, *Sacred and Hallowed Fire* © Oxford University Press

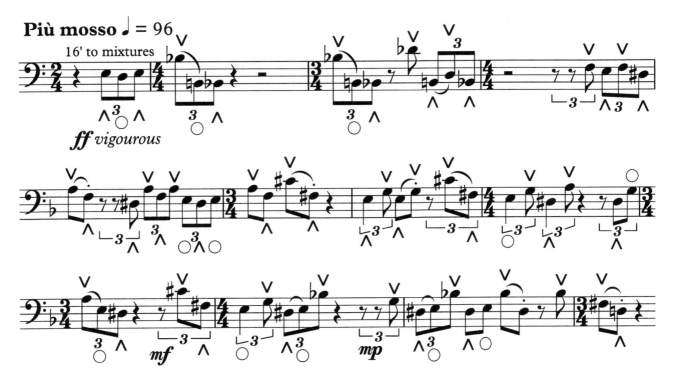

Double/Multi-Pedalling

Most of the previous examples have the pedals playing only one note at a time. However, both feet can play notes simultaneously; this practice is referred to as 'double pedalling'. In addition, both heel and toe can play notes simultaneously, allowing chords to be played in the pedals; this is referred to as 'multi-pedalling'. The former is relatively common, while the latter is unsurprisingly very rare. For two-stave organ parts, square brackets are helpful to clarify any double pedalling such as in Figure 4.25 (multi-pedalling in two-stave format is virtually nonexistent):

FIGURE 4.25 Thomas Walmisley, *Evening Service in D minor*, Magnificat

Firstly, a word of caution. Overuse of double or multi-pedalling is a common sign of inexperience in many contemporary organ compositions. While this technique does offer an extra note to play with, the advantages are often outweighed by both the technical and expressive limitations double pedalling causes. When both feet are in use, it is impossible to use the Swell pedal or any foot pistons, greatly limiting registration options. The shape of a pedalboard can even make certain double/multi-pedalling passages unplayable. It is notable that many organist-composers use double pedalling *very* sparingly and usually only for a special effect.

Nevertheless, there are definite occasions where double and multi-pedalling are effective. Provided care is taken, they can offer new textural and sonic possibilities to composers, making full use of what the organ can offer. The following section suggests some possible approaches to double/multi-pedalling as well as looking at the most successful examples in the repertoire.

The most effective examples of double pedalling are either for isolated notes or for extended passages in parallel intervals. The most common of the latter, and easiest to use effectively, is the octave. Many French toccatas end with octaves in the pedals, providing an easy way to fill out the final chords, particularly if the manuals are high in the compass. Alternatively, the doubled octave can be used to thicken the final quiet chord of a piece (e.g., Rachmaninoff *The Bells*) although the consequent loss of Swell box control makes this usage less practical than at loud dynamics. Figure 4.26 provides an idiomatic example of this technique. Note how each foot only moves in conjunct motion, enabling a smooth legato as the pedalling shows.

FIGURE 4.26 Louis Vierne, *Pièces de fantaisie*, Suite III op. 54, 'Sur le Rhin'

As a side note, do also consider substituting in 'broken' octaves such as in Figure 4.27, which have the same advantages over double pedalling as broken chords do over full chords in the manuals.

FIGURE 4.27 Max Reger, *12 Stücke* op. 65, 'Consolation'

The second-most common interval is the perfect fifth, found in much modern French organ music such as by Messiaen and Langlais. The sound is low and rumbling; it can also be used to 'fake' the 32′ where one is not available. However, even this 'perfect' interval can cause the bass (i.e., the lower note) to lose clarity with 16′ stops drawn. In Figure 4.28, the loud registration helps mitigate this loss of clarity (the 8′s, 4′s, and upperwork coupled from the manuals adding definition to both notes). Both pedal voices again move stepwise, easing technical execution considerably, with the crotchet rest giving the feet time to reposition.

FIGURE 4.28 Charles Tournemire, *L'Orgue mystique*, Cycle de Noël op. 55, 'Office No. 7 Epiphania Domini' © Éditions Heugel

Using other intervals smaller than an octave is *not* recommended without careful planning and consideration of all other options. The low pitch of the 16′ pedals can make close intervals sound dissonant and even pitchless. Extended close-interval passages can also be very physically awkward to manage given the angle of the feet, legs, and body required. Even organist-composers can struggle to use them in a non-contrived manner (see, e.g., Demessieux *6 Études* 'Tierces' and 'Sixtes' where, even given the pieces' nature as etudes, Demessieux has to work hard compositionally to justify the pedal thirds and sixths, respectively) and these intervals can inadvertently present many technical and musical problems. However, these intervals can be useful in very specific instances, the feet offering a flexibility the hands are unable to achieve. Figure 4.29 shows one of the very rare successful applications in the standard repertoire. The 8′ registration avoids many of the problems mentioned above. The pedalling is Duruflé's own, indicating some of the upper notes should be taken by the left foot to help with the legato.

FIGURE 4.29 Maurice Duruflé, *Suite* op. 5, 'Sicilienne' © Éditions Durand

Intervals over an octave, by contrast, are surprisingly easy to execute can sound very effective, the wider gap between pedal notes minimising the muddiness found with smaller intervals. Perfect twelfths are by far the most frequently found in the repertoire; essentially a wider-spaced perfect fifth, it can add richness without the heaviness of the smaller interval. Lili Boulanger is a particular fan of this wide spacing, as can be seen in Figure 4.30.

FIGURE 4.30 Lili Boulanger, *Psaume XXIV*

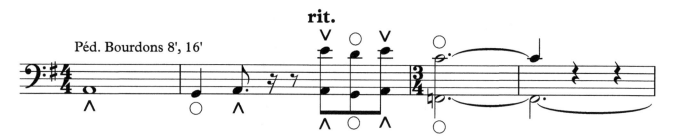

Other compound intervals are also considerably more usable than their smaller counterparts, and there is much potential to use these intervals in innovative and idiomatic ways. The first of the *Poèmes pour orgue* by Thierry Escaich opens with the two feet a major tenth apart, shown in Figure 4.31. Registered with 16′ and 2′ (coupled from the Swell) alone, the pedals take the melody accompanied by string stops in the hands to magical effect.

FIGURE 4.31 Thierry Escaich, *Poèmes pour orgue*, 'Eaux Natales' © Éditions Billaudot

It is also possible for each foot to perform two completely independent lines. This level of separation between feet is particularly taxing ergonomically and mentally and so it is unsurprisingly very rare beyond isolated examples such as in Figure 4.32 (see also Figure 4.13). This example is often registered without 16′, again in order to minimise the dissonance of the low, close intervals.

FIGURE 4.32 Nicolaus Bruhns, *Praeludium in G major*

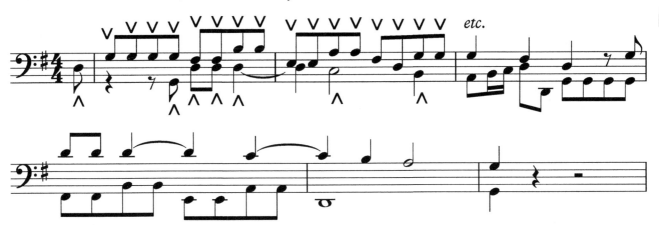

A half-way approach is possible, where there is a small amount of independence without being overly mentally taxing. Such passages should preferably be slow in tempo and with simple manual parts, to give the organist as much processing time as possible. Once again, the interval between the two lines is typically over an octave, easing execution and minimising the muddiness of the clashing 16′ pipes. Figure 4.33 shows an excellent example of this half-way approach by Lili Boulanger.

FIGURE 4.33 Lili Boulanger, *Psaume CXXX*

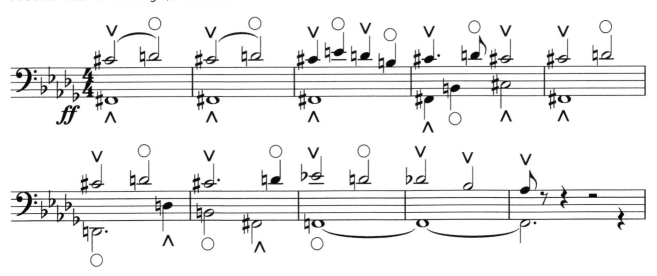

A further simplification is to keep one foot static while the other has a more involved line, allowing the organist to keep their balance more easily. Consequently, both the right foot and the manuals are able to execute more complex passages than if both feet were moving. This texture is very common in all genres of Romantic music, with Figure 4.34 showing a very idiomatic usage of this technique.

The Pipe Organ

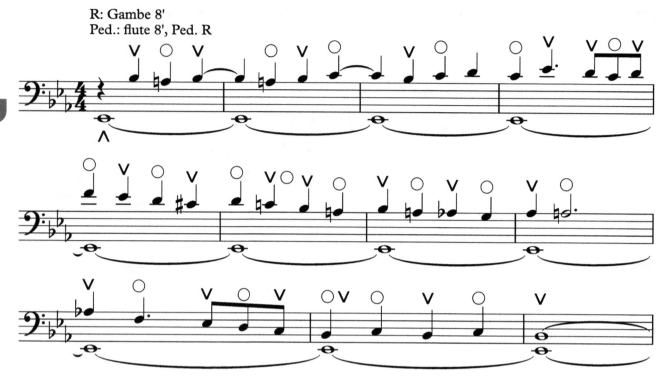

FIGURE 4.34 Charles-Marie Widor, *Organ Symphony No. 9 'Gothique'* op. 70, Andante sostenuto

Multi-pedalling, by contrast, is very rare in the repertoire. It is almost exclusively found in post-Romantic pieces, although one infamous example exists from 1510 by the German organist Arnolt Schlick in his *Ascendo ad Patrem Meum*. A true legato is almost impossible to achieve unless the pedal lines are very carefully planned. Some extended examples of multi-pedalling are the most difficult passages in the entire repertoire (see, e.g., Figure 4.35 as well as Dupré's *Evocation*, Allegro deciso). Once again, the size and shape of the pedalboard can make a large difference as to what is playable and what is not. As such, multi-pedalling should be used with great care and preferably in collaboration with an organist.

Figure 4.35 is the first half of by far the best-known and most-played passage of multi-pedalling. The pedals are registered with the Swell strings alone, forming a lush chordal texture with the right hand whilst the left hand supplies fleeting passagework on the Choir flutes. Note how little each foot moves, often by only a semitone each time. This piece was infamously deemed unplayable in its day by no less an organist than Widor and, whilst it is a recital staple for professional organists in modern times, it still poses an exceptional technical challenge.

FIGURE 4.35 Marcel Dupré, *Trois Préludes and Fugues*, 'Prelude and Fugue in G Minor' op. 7 no. 3 © Alphonse Leduc Editions Musicales. Reprinted by Permission of Hal Leonard Europe Ltd

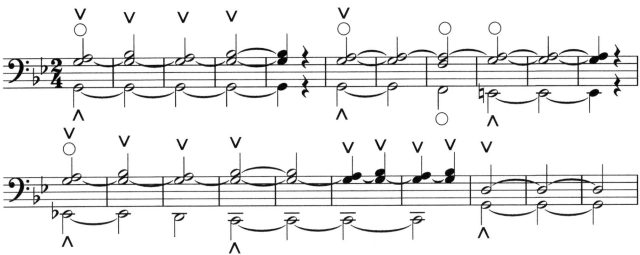

Isolated multi-pedalled chords, by contrast, are more straightforward provided the feet are given time to prepare. In Figure 4.36, there are rests before the pedal chords and the manual passages are relatively simple, giving the organist both physical and mental space to prepare the feet and so making the chords easier to play (see also Litaize *Prélude et danse fuguée* for an excellent example of isolated pedal chords).

FIGURE 4.36 Louis Vierne, *Organ Symphony No. 3* op. 28, Intermezzo

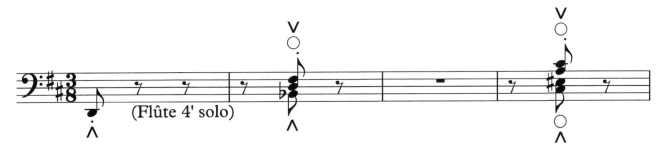

It might be expected that four-note chords are the maximum possible, given that all four parts of the feet are engaged simultaneously. However, it is theoretically possible to go up to five-note chords or even beyond, either using the flat of the foot or with each toe (or heel) taking two notes at the same time. Given the extreme difficulty of execution, such chords should only be used sparingly and ideally in consultation with individual organists. The example in Figure 4.37 is technically playable but requires an uncomfortable twisting of the right ankle for the bottom octave. 'Spreading' the chords as Saariaho does here helps with the execution by allowing the organist to focus on each part of the foot in turn.

FIGURE 4.37 Kaija Saariaho, *Maan varjot* © Chester Music Ltd

The Pedals in Context

The previous examples have isolated the pedal line in order to show what is technically possible. In practice, however, the pedals are rarely used by themselves. The following section therefore looks at typical combinations of pedals both in the context of full pieces, with the manuals, and with other instruments and singers.

Extended pedal solos have occasionally functioned as complete organ pieces or movements in themselves. Notable examples include the 'Épilogue' from Jean Langlais' *Hommage à Frescobaldi* and Wilhelm Middelschulte's 'Intermezzo' (also known as the 'Perpetuum Mobile') from *Konzert über ein Thema von J. S. Bach*. Such movements are often flashy shows of virtuosity; their musical value is sometimes harder to assess. Nevertheless, they do provide a different and still relatively novel option for inventive composers.

In orchestral contexts, it is not uncommon to see the pedals used without the manuals. In these cases, composers almost always specify the rumbling 32′ (remember, however, that this stop is rare outside of concert hall/cathedral instruments). A single judiciously placed pedal note, such as in Figure 4.38, can produce a very striking effect.

FIGURE 4.38 Gustav Holst, *The Planets* op. 32, 'Neptune, the Mystic'

Cluster chords in the pedals alone have long been exploited for their stormy qualities. The Verdi example in Figure 4.39 uses the pedals alone, holding the same cluster for over six minutes; depending on the organist, a part such as this is either very boring or an easy pay check. While this example can theoretically be played by one foot, both feet would normally be used (at least initially) to guarantee a clear articulation.

FIGURE 4.39 Guiseppi Verdi, *Otello*, 1st Act, Allegro agitato

Solo pedal lines can also have a more extended bass part in orchestral music, typically doubling the double basses, bassoons, and/or low brass. This usage is very common in Romantic orchestral scores, Figure 4.40 showing a typical example.

FIGURE 4.40 George Frideric Handel arr. Edward Elgar, *Overture in D minor*

Most of the time, however, the pedals are used simultaneously with the manuals. In their most straightforward usage, the pedals can hold a pedal point while the manuals are busy on top. Such an approach is very easy to play, allowing more concentration space for complex manuals parts. A pedal point can be very effective, especially at loud dynamics, as Figure 4.41 demonstrates (although Bach does not provide registrations, the context and style imply a full plenum).

FIGURE 4.41 Johann Sebastian Bach, *Fantasia super 'Komm, Heiliger Geist'* BWV 651

The Pipe Organ

Unsurprisingly, the most common role of the pedals is to provide the bass line while the manuals provide the melody/accompaniment, Figure 1.7 providing the most basic example. In practical terms, the easiest such pedal parts are slow, conjunct in motion and rhythmically synchronise with the hands. Less experienced organists often struggle with achieving independence between the left hand and pedals, so syncing these two parts will make the music much easier to execute. Figure 4.42 is an excellent example of straightforward yet effective manual/pedal writing, even more so than the previous example:

FIGURE 4.42 Charles Villiers Stanford, *Morning, Evening and Communion Service in C major* op. 115, Magnificat

Note that, even when the pedal is playing the bass line, it does not always need to be the lowest note of the chord. The middle range of the pedals is often underutilised by composers. Just as the basses of the choir regularly sing in the low tenor range and occasionally cross parts with the tenors, so too can the pedals with the lower notes of the left hand. The pedal 16′ can make the bass line clear, even when there is voice crossing. In Figure 4.43, Boulanger adds the low fifth of the chord in the manuals, strengthening the low overtones of the 32′.

FIGURE 4.43 Lili Boulanger, *Psaume CXXX*

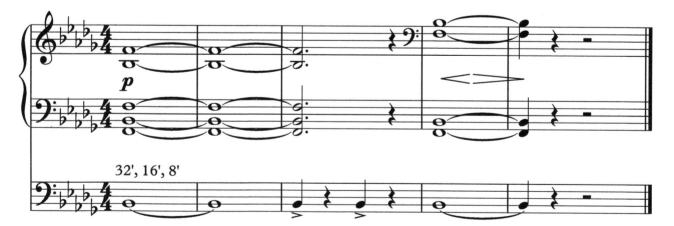

Staccato lines also work very well in conjunction with the manuals. As mentioned in Chapter 1, staccato pedal notes often have a slight percussiveness to them. They can thus lend incision to staccato manual chords, making them appear more marcato than without these pedal notes. Figure 4.44 shows a very effective example; the whole movement should also be studied carefully for how to use staccato pedals.

FIGURE 4.44 Louis Vierne, *Organ Symphony No. 1* op. 14, Allegro vivace

The pedal line can also usefully provide counterpoint to what is occurring in the manuals. The Intermezzo from Vierne's *Organ Symphony No. 3* is an excellent example, with the staccato pedal notes cleverly juxtaposed against more legato manual parts. In Figure 4.45, the pedals and left hand cleverly alternate taking the bass part; the pedals provide a drive and substance to the bass while the left hand offers a rhythmic counterpoint. The whole piece demonstrates an exceptionally complete and sophisticated use of the pedals and should be studied in full.

FIGURE 4.45 Fela Sowande, *Obangiji* © Chappell & Co Ltd

The Pipe Organ

Short pedal flairs are very effective in enlivening textures, especially when the hands are otherwise engaged. The classic work to study in this regard is Karg-Elert's very famous setting of 'Nun danket alle Gott' from his *Choral-Improvisationen für Orgel*. In this work, the pedal line forms a very effective complement to block manual chords, with the writing for both manuals and pedals exemplary. Figure 4.46 shows a twenty-first century example, alternating the pedals and manuals in a call-and-response pattern with very effective results. Note again how alternating toes can be incredibly useful even in a modern idiom.

FIGURE 4.46 Pia Rose Scattergood, *folding, unfolding* © Pia Rose Scattergood

The pedals are also very good for assisting with echo effects. By removing the pedals and taking the bass line in the left hand, a natural echo is created without any need for changes in registration or even changing manuals, as demonstrated in Figure 4.47.

FIGURE 4.47 César Franck, *3 Pièces pour grand orgue*, 'Pièce Héroïque'

Using the pedals in this way works equally well in more complex echo passages. In Figure 4.48, Brahms adds an extra layer to the echo by omitting the pedals for the echoes on Manuals II and III (in this context, the Choir and Swell, respectively). By using the pedals for Manual I (i.e., the Great) alone, Brahms is able to clearly differentiate between the chorale tune on Manual I and the echoes in the other manuals.

FIGURE 4.48 Johannes Brahms, *11 Chorale Preludes* op. 122, 'O Welt, ich muss dich lassen [2nd version]'

When soloistic pedal moments do occur, simplifying the manuals' part is often very helpful both technically and musically, easing the execution and giving more of a spotlight to the pedals. Isolated 'stab' chords in the manuals are very common, especially in Baroque organ music. Figure 4.49 displays all of the typical features of an effective pedal solo in context.

FIGURE 4.49 Johann Sebastian Bach, *Prelude and Fugue in C minor* BWV 549

Giving the pedals the melody is very common at louder dynamics, particularly in French toccatas. With a pedal melody, the hands are free to take more complex toccata figuration (see, e.g., Figure 2.25). It is also possible to couple down solo stops from the manuals to the pedals, most commonly the solo reeds. This is particularly effective when these reeds are wanted in the bass register; the 16′ pedal stops can add extra bass depth to the reed sound. Once again, this approach also frees up both hands, allowing them to supply a more sophisticated accompaniment such as shown in Figure 4.50.

FIGURE 4.50 Louis Vierne, *Pièces de fantaisie*, Suite II op. 53, 'Feux Follets'

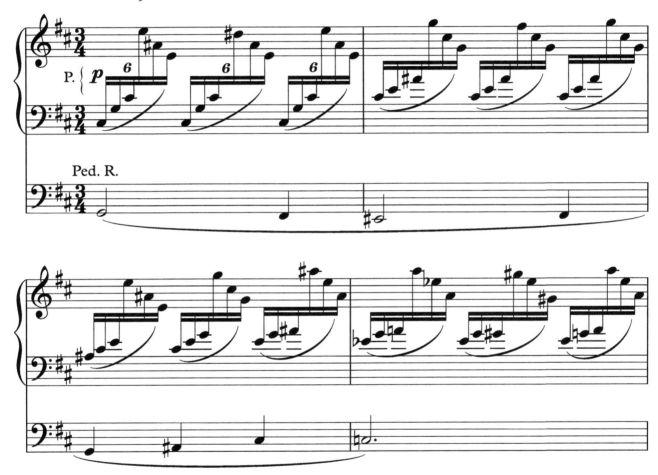

While the 16' pedal stops are normally used by default, there are occasions where the 8' alone for the bass is effective. This pedal registration generally only works in quiet passages, typically with the pedal Flute 8'. Vierne provides an excellent example in Figure 4.51.

FIGURE 4.51 Louis Vierne, *Pièces de fantaisie*, Suite IV op. 55, 'Naïades'

The pedals can also do more than just playing the bass line. In the Baroque period, the pedals were often given the tenor cantus firmus, typically on the Trumpet 8'. This technique is very common in the 'Plein Jeu' of the French Classical school (see Figure 2.26) but German examples also exist as Figure 4.52 demonstrates. Rare examples in Romantic literature are occasionally found (e.g., Howells *Six Pieces*, 'Master Tallis' Testament').

FIGURE 4.52 Johann Sebastian Bach, *Gott, durch deine Güte* BWV 600

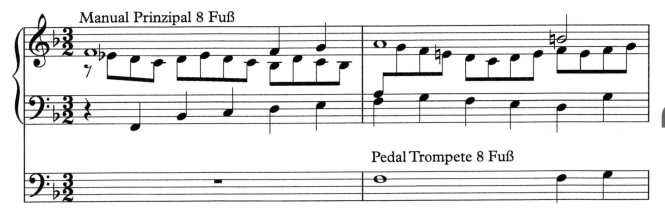

The pedals can even take an alto or soprano melody when a 4′ is used. Some organs have a 4′ flute stop for the pedals (see, e.g., Figure 4.29), but it is most common to couple down 4′ flute or principal from the Great. While only occasionally found in the repertoire (e.g., Messiaen *L'Ascension*, 'Alléluias sereins'), this approach is very common in organ improvisations, typically with the hands accompanying on the Swell; 4′ reeds can also be very effective (see, e.g., Messiaen *Messe de la Pentecôte*, 'Entrée', Demessieux *Te Deum*). There is much unexplored potential here, and composers are strongly recommended to investigate this area further.

An extraordinary example of a pedal melody is Messiaen's 'Les Mages' from *La Nativité du Seigneur*, shown in Figure 4.53. Here, Messiaen couples the Choir 4′ and mutations down to the pedal 4′ (the pedal 4′ can be omitted if unavailable without drastically compromising the desired timbre). The manuals' registration is equally unique: the right hand plays staccato chords with the 16′ and 8′ flutes, while the left hand provides sustained chords with the Gambe 8′ and Flute 4′. This passage is a unique example of the organ's colouristic possibilities and the full piece should be listened to and studied.

The Pipe Organ

FIGURE 4.53 Olivier Messiaen, *La Nativité du Seigneur*, 'Les Mages' © Alphonse Leduc Editions Musicales

The pedals can also function in other roles that are neither the bass nor the melody. In *Rejoice in the Lamb*, Britten uses them with 8′ alone to hold a middle C; the manuals provide chords both above and underneath this pedal point. Such stasis is perfectly suited to the pedals, with Britten's piece showing an innovative way of thinking about the organ.

As is hopefully obvious, the pedals offer a wide and exciting range of compositional possibilities. Just like for the manuals, the pedals are capable of so much more than is often asked of them. With the pedal couplers allowing access to every stop on the manuals, there are almost limitless options for innovation. The full potential for the pedals, and combining them with the manuals, has barely been explored; it is up to composers to discover the true limits of what the pedals can really do.

OTHER TYPES OF ORGAN

Overview

So far, this book has mainly been dealing with regular pipe organs. However, other types of organ do exist. Some, such as the 'regal' and 'positive', are mentioned in historical treatises but have largely fallen into obscurity. These days, there are four main variants which can be reasonably requested: the chamber organ, the harmonium, the theatre organ, and the Hammond organ. Each of these instruments have their own unique idiosyncrasies which separate them from the normal pipe organ and can offer different sonic avenues for modern composers. They can also offer interesting new ways of thinking about the pipe organ itself. It is therefore worth dedicating some space to them to explain these nuances in more detail.

For many of these instruments, notation has not been standardised. The theatre and Hammond organ tradition is largely improvisatory rather than score-based. As such, different textbooks will recommend different approaches to notation, and there are no 'right' answers. In most cases, the principles advocated for pipe organs will work effectively enough for these other instruments. However, there is no substitute for practical collaboration with a player. Many of these instruments are relatively neglected compared to the church organ, so advocates for them are particularly keen to help composers discover them.

Chamber Organ

While the distinction between chamber organs and small regular organs is somewhat blurry, the chamber organ has developed its own identity far enough to warrant further discussion. Chamber organs are normally mechanical-action and have one manual and no pedals, with only a small selection of stops. Unlike regular organs, therefore, they are generally notated without the third pedal stave. They also have a slightly smaller manual compass, often only going from C_2–D_6. As this limited range suggests, chamber organs bear a close affinity to pre-Romantic or even pre-Baroque organ styles, hence making them well-suited to performing early music. The more intimate sound of the chamber organ also gives it a unique character distinct from regular organs, meaning it can offer musical and expressive possibilities its larger relative cannot. Many cathedrals and large institutions these days own a 'box' chamber organ, a small organ with a box-like design (see Figure 5.1) which is generally portable and so can be moved around the building depending on need.

The Pipe Organ. James Mitchell, Oxford University Press. © Oxford University Press 2023. DOI: 10.1093/oso/9780197645284.003.0006

The Pipe Organ

FIGURE 5.1 Chamber ('box') organ

The typical box organ has three stops: a Flute 8′ and Principals 4′ and 2′. Some larger chamber organs have an additional Flute 4′ and very occasionally other stops. Very large chamber organs may have a split keyboard (see 'Historic Instruments' in the Introduction). Rarely, a separate regal add-on may be available, offering a pungent 8′ reed sound. The front panels of the chamber organ can be opened and shut on many instruments, allowing for more subtle control of dynamics. Many box organs can also quickly transpose to A = 415Hz or A = 465Hz, useful for historically informed performances of Baroque music. Given their portability, they can even be hired and transported into a venue if required.

The chamber organ's main usage is usually accompanying Renaissance and Baroque choral and consort music. The chamber organ comes into its own particularly for so-called

Baroque choral 'verse' settings, where a soloist-plus-organ periodically alternates with the main choir. The canticles' settings by William Byrd, Thomas Tomkins, Orlando Gibbons, and Thomas Weelkes all fall into this category and are all staples of cathedral music lists. In this situation, the 8′ alone is used for accompanying the soloist and for quieter full choir passages, while the 4′ is added where the choir is louder. The 2′ is generally too loud for typical choral usage. A brief sample passage is provided in Figure 5.2. The inner voices of the full choir are not present in the original organ part, Gibbons likely relying on players to improvise these inner voices. Modern organists would normally just double the choir parts as indicated by the small notes.

FIGURE 5.2 Orlando Gibbons, *This is the Record of John*

The chamber organ is only very rarely found in modern contexts. Benjamin Britten writes a part for the chamber organ (or harmonium) in his *War Requiem* to accompany the boys' choir. Here, the boys and organ form a 'unit', contrasting with the main choir and orchestra along with the vocal soloists and chamber orchestra. Britten exploits the portable and intimate nature of the instrument; indeed, the main organ is called on as an adjunct only for the final movement. Thomas Adès wrote *Under Hamelin's Hill* for the box organ at Ely Cathedral, with up to three organists playing simultaneously on the small instrument. Jean Guillou wrote *La révolte des orgues* for nine organs (!) and percussion, with eight of the instruments being chamber organs.

One beautiful use of the chamber organ comes from the Japanese composer Satoru Ikeda, whose quasi-minimalist *Water Bubbling* makes clever use of sustained notes to create a shimmering yet melancholic perpetuum mobile. The chamber organ brings an intimacy to this work that strengthens its emotional impact and which is not always possible to replicate on a regular organ. The opening is shown in Figure 5.3.

FIGURE 5.3 Satoru Ikeda, *Water Bubbling* © Satoru Ikeda

The chamber organ still has much untapped potential for modern composers. The instrument can bring the benefits of the organ timbre to smaller chamber setups, with the organist not isolated in the organ loft. There is also much scope for extended techniques such as detailed in Chapter 1. 'Preparing' the instrument is more practical than for the regular organ; not only is it physically easier to access the pipes, but chamber organs are generally used less frequently than the main organ and so can be prepared further in advance and with minimal disruption. Many of the effects listed in Chapter 1 are more audible and reliable on a chamber organ. In addition, many new effects are viable since the player is generally closer to the congregation/audience. Percussive effects (such as tapping the instrument, silently tapping at the keyboard, etc.) and multi-keyboard setups (e.g., playing the organ with one hand and the piano with another) are possible with a box organ while being impractical on regular instruments. Duets between regular and chamber organs are another largely unexplored avenue. The personal nature of the box organ and the more impersonal nature of the main organ contrast neatly with each other, allowing for a varied yet homogenous tonal palette. The chamber organ should therefore be explored not as an inferior type of organ, but as a unique instrument which can offer new and exciting compositional possibilities.

Harmonium

The harmonium used to be a very common instrument in the nineteenth and early twentieth centuries but nowadays is relatively rare. However, its importance in some of the standard orchestral repertoire (e.g., Rossini *Petite messe solennelle*, Mahler *Symphony No. 8*) has prevented the instrument from becoming obsolete. As harmoniums are portable instruments, they can be hired and transported as easily as chamber organs. While not all organists can play the harmonium, many high-level freelance keyboardists have at least a working knowledge of the instrument. The sound of the instrument is normally reedy, like a large harmonica or accordion; however, larger harmoniums are capable of a surprising range of colour. Even though its popularity may have waned since a century ago, it still offers much value and unexplored potential to contemporary composers.

Initially, the harmonium can look like a pipe-less chamber organ, with a single row of stops above the keyboard and two large foot pedals at the bottom of the instrument. Most harmoniums are single-manual with a split keyboard (see 'Building Trends' in Chapter 1); as normal for split keyboards, there is an (almost) duplicate set of stops for each half. Larger instruments with multiple manuals do exist but are very rare. To operate the harmonium, the organist uses the foot pedals to operate a set of bellows, supplying the wind for the instrument. Knee-flaps add an additional level of control for dynamics. A typical harmonium is shown in Figure 5.4.

FIGURE 5.4 Harmonium

There are two main types of harmonium. 'Pressure' instruments such as in Figure 5.4 (also known as 'art harmoniums', famous builders including Debain and Mustel) operate by pushing air onto free reeds, having a range of C_2–C_7 with a split keyboard divided between E_4 and F_4. 'Suction' instruments (such as those built by Mannborg), by contrast, suck the air through the reeds, usually having a range of F_1–F_6 with the split point between B_3 and C_4. Almost all the traditional repertoire is written for pressure instruments, although these days suction instruments are considerably more common than pressure ones. Pressure instruments also have much more expressive potential than suction instruments. By carefully operating the foot bellows and knee-flaps, singing melodies, subtle accents, and even vibrato are possible on pressure harmoniums, effects which are almost impossible on suction instruments. Some harmonium practitioners do not consider the suction instrument a true harmonium, instead calling it just a 'pump organ'.

Indicating registration for the harmonium is more complicated than for the organ. Circled or boxed numbers are used rather than stop names; composers generally indicate registration for each half of the keyboard separately. What these numbers mean depends on whether the instrument is pressure or suction based and, sometimes, which half of the keyboard the stop is located in. The main stops and their effect are summarised in Table 5.1.

Table 5.1 Harmonium Registration

		Pressure Instruments	*Suction Instruments*
Common Stops	①	8'. A warm, round sound. A 'p' after the number indicates a 'percussion' stop on pressure instruments. This stop produces a pitched 'click' in tune with the depressed key, even without any wind in the bellows.	Same as for pressure instruments. A 'p' on suction instruments just indicates a flute-like sound.
	②	16'. A rich, dark sound.	Same as for pressure instruments. While this stop is not universal on suction instruments, particularly in the treble half, there is often a sub-octave "Bass Coupler" in lieu.
	③	4'. A soft and expressive sound.	Same as for pressure instruments although brighter in timbre.
	④	8'. A nasal string sound, akin to the unison doubling on accordion but more subtle. This stop is very useful for filling out the 8' sound.	Same as for pressure instruments.
Less Common Stops	⑤	2' ethereal sound (bass half). 16' solo stop (treble half).	8'. Celeste stop similar to the Voix Céleste on the regular organ.
	⑥	16' celeste stop (treble half only). Commonly labelled as 'C' or 'V. C.', i.e., 'Voix Céléste'.	2' ethereal sound (bass half only). Essentially equivalent to ⑤ on pressure instruments.
	⑦	32' solo stop (treble half only). Karg-Elert describes this stop as essential.	16' 'Sub-bass' (bass half only).
	⑧	8'. Soft 'Violin choir' sound (treble half only).	N/A

There are a few further stops that are commonly indicated, mainly concerning pressure instruments. 'G' indicates the 'Grand-Jeu'; drawing it acts as if ①–④ are drawn (this stop also exists on suction instruments). The 'Forte' stop opens slats on the top of the instrument, therefore boosting the volume, and is indicated by 'F' (Ⓞ indicates the 'Forte expressif', where the foot bellows also control the opening and shutting of the slats). The 'Métaphone', or 'Mét.' for short, acts as a type of mute, pulling an extra wooden panel over to cover the reeds. The 'Prolongement' continuously holds down any depressed note in the lowest octave, freeing up the left hand. Suction instruments also have a tremulant for the treble half; this tremulant is confusingly called a 'Vox Humana'.

Finally, there is 'E', indicating the 'Expression': when drawn, it disconnects the air reservoir and so allows the pedals to directly control the volume, allowing for the subtle accents and vibrato mentioned earlier. The main drawback is, making it hard to produce a sustained tone for loud passages and thick chords. In proper virtuoso harmonium practice, this stop is almost permanently drawn (Karg-Elert requests it in virtually all of his pieces), but some composers leave this stop off for very loud sections.

Not every stop has been detailed here, and not all stops are available on every harmonium. Many composers do not worry about registration, and the music is none the worse for it. However, just as for the organ, detailed registrations can offer new sonic possibilities. Sigfrid Karg-Elert wrote multiple treatises about harmonium registration for both pressure and suction instruments, including *Die Kunst des Registrierens* and the *Elementar-Harmonium-Schule*; composers should investigate these books further if they want to explore registration for the harmonium.

As the harmonium was a popular household instrument in the nineteenth and twentieth centuries, much of its music was written for it in this period. Karg-Elert is one of the most notable names from this period as well as for the harmonium generally. His music includes inventive and detailed registrations for both types of harmonium (he indicates pressure instrument registration with square boxes and suction instrument registration with octagonal boxes). His harmonium sonatas deserve particular mention, virtuosically exploiting the full potential of the instrument; an excerpt from his second sonata is shown in Figure 5.5. The music is visually and contrapuntally dense, and virtually no other composer has pushed the harmonium as far.

FIGURE 5.5 Sigfrid Karg-Elert, *Harmonium Sonata No. 2* op. 46, 'Enharmonische Fantasie und Doppelfuge "B.A.C.H."'

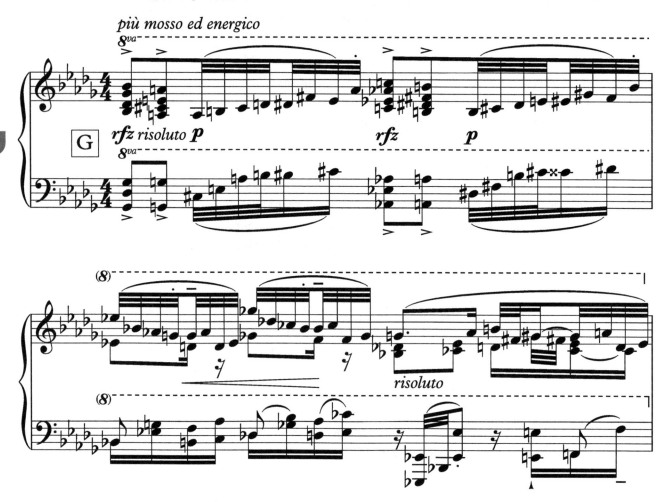

Louis Vierne's *24 Pièces en style libre*, which are popular study pieces for younger organists, are optionally for harmonium and include harmonium registrations. While they are aimed at an amateur audience and so are less technically ambitious than Karg-Elert's music, they are well-written, idiomatic, and a staple of the harmonium repertoire. César Franck also wrote a cycle of harmonium pieces called *L'organiste*. These are also simple but function well for their purpose; Franck's registrations are also quite adventurous, showing the possibilities of the instrument even within a relatively simple context.

The harmonium was the portable organ of choice in the Romantic period, featuring in many situations where regular organs were unavailable. Composers who wrote for the instrument in orchestral contexts include Tchaikovsky (in *Manfred*), Mahler (in his *Symphony No. 8*), Elgar (in his *Sospiri* for string orchestra), and Richard Strauss (in operas such as *Ariadne auf Naxos*). The harmonium also has a very prominent role in Kurt Weill's famous *Die Dreigroschenoper*. The rustic sound of the instrument combines effectively here with a traditional 1920s jazz combo. It is the sole accompanying instrument for 'Mack the Knife' (see Figure 5.6), where Weill exploits its barrel-organlike sound to evoke an urban, working-class atmosphere.

FIGURE 5.6 Kurt Weill, *Die Dreigroschenoper*, 'Moritat vom Mackie Messer'

A remarkable part for the harmonium comes in Franz Schreker's *Kammersymphonie*, where it sustains translucent harmonies under shimmering piano arpeggios and celesta tremolos (see Figure 5.7). The harmonium is uniquely suited to this chordal role: the *ppp* dynamic is not possible on chamber organs and, while potentially doable on regular organs, would lose the intimacy of the sound.

FIGURE 5.7 Franz Schreker, *Kammersymphonie*

The harmonium was particularly beloved by the Second Viennese School. Schoenberg wrote his *Herzgewächse* for the extraordinary ensemble of soprano, celesta, harp, and harmonium. Anton Webern also utilises the harmonium in his *5 Pieces for Orchestra*. The third movement in particular is exceptional (see Figure 5.8), with the harmonium delicately combining with the bell-like sounds of the celesta, harp, mandolin, percussion, and cello harmonics. Virtually no other orchestral instrument would be capable of the softness Webern requires at such a high pitch. The effect is shimmering, delicate, and beautiful.

FIGURE 5.8 Anton Webern, *5 Pieces for Orchestra* op. 10, 'Rückkehr'

In the course of the twentieth century, the harmonium was largely superseded by electrically-powered pipe organs, coinciding with the rise of electricity and mains power in churches. The instrument is still called for in some modern scores, however. Peter Maxwell Davies exploits both the rustic and archaic sound of the instrument in his chamber work *Missa Super l'Homme Armée*. Baroque ornaments and even figured bass appear in the part. Maxwell Davies also cleverly uses some extended techniques, such as weights on the keys and carefully modulating the wind pressure, to push the instrument into new territory. The harmonium has also seen fringe forays into popular music, most notably with the Beatles' tracks 'We Can Work It Out' and 'Being for the Benefit of Mr. Kite!'.

Surprisingly, however, harmoniums found a new country where they have become truly established: India. The portability and heat resistance of the instrument led to its rise under British colonial rule. Indian harmoniums are smaller than European instruments, with the left hand instead of the feet used to pump the organ. The stops are also different from Western instruments. Many Indian harmoniums have 'drone' stops; on some instruments, some stops can add the 22 microtones required by Indian classical music. Naturally, there is very little Western music written for this style of harmonium. However, many characteristics of the Indian instrument are still the same as the Western one. Many modern recordings and video tutorials for the Indian instrument are available online, with contemporary manuals such as Satyaki Brockschmidt's *Harmonium Handbook: Owning Playing and Maintaining the Devotional Instrument of India*, providing a comprehensive survey of the Indian harmonium. Composers looking to add Indian influences to their music are thus recommended to consider what the harmonium can offer.

In summary, the harmonium is nowadays uncommon in European music. However, the instrument has tenaciously kept going despite the rapid technological improvements of the twentieth century. In addition, scholarship on the harmonium has become ever more prominent, with Joris Verdin's recent *A Handbook for the Harmonium* a seminal and comprehensive publication covering every aspect of the instrument. While the harmonium may seem largely obsolete today, it is unlikely it will ever truly die.

Theatre Organ

The theatre organ, also known as the 'cinema' organ or 'unit orchestra', is another remnant of a bygone age. The instrument was invented by UK pipe organ builder Robert Hope-Jones (whose innovations, originally intended for regular pipe organs, helped lead to the theatre organ's distinctive sound) in collaboration with instrument builder Rudolph Wurlitzer. The theatre organ became very popular in the 1910s for accompanying 'silent' movies and for entertaining audiences during film intermissions, with many performers in the 1930s and 1940s becoming household names through records and radio broadcasts. Many theatre organs survive today thanks to preservation by enthusiasts and, for those without easy access to a real instrument, software such as Hauptwerk offers high-quality virtual instruments to a new generation of composers and performers. The theatre organ playing style may also be inspiring to composers for the regular pipe organ wishing to incorporate jazz techniques in an idiomatic way. It is therefore worth discussing the theatre organ, and its unique characteristics and playing style, in more detail.

A typical theatre organ console is shown in Figure 5.9, the horseshoe layout and tongue-shaped stop tabs creating a distinctive organ aesthetic. Like regular pipe organs, theatre organs normally have two or three manuals, with the written range as in Figure 1.2. The bottom manual is called the 'Accompaniment' and, unsurprisingly, is used for left-hand accompaniment patterns. The middle manual is called the 'Great' and typically used for taking the melody or for special percussion effects. The third manual, when available, is usually either a slightly smaller version of the Great called the 'Solo', or a 'coupler' keyboard installed primarily for show. Again, some exceptionally large instruments have four or even more manuals, but given their rarity it is unwise to write for them. The console also has various registration aids such as divisionals to help quick stop changes.

FIGURE 5.9 Console for a Compton theatre organ

Stop-wise, the theatre organ shows distinct similarities but also noticeable differences to church organs. Common stop types include the Flute, Tibia (a type of flute sound which is characteristic of the theatre organ), Diapason (a Principal), String, and Vox Humana. Owing to the compact nature of many instruments, pipes are always shared both across manuals (i.e., the Tibia on the Great and Accompaniment is exactly the same stop) and across octaves (i.e., the 16′, 8′, and 4′ of a stop use the same set of pipes). As such, the different manuals are more unified than on a church organ, allowing for a very blended sound while still offering timbral contrasts. There are also multiple tremulants per manual, used either in isolation or in tandem, which add the characteristic warmth and depth to the theatre organ sound.

It is the percussion section where the theatre organ really defines itself, however, with real percussion instruments are operated through electric relays and pneumatics. There are stops for many keyed percussion instruments including a piano (with 16′, 8′, and 4′), tubular bells, glockenspiels, and tremolo xylophones (all often at 8′ or 4′) on the Great/Solo and various untuned percussion on the Accompaniment and pedals. In addition, many organs have sound effects that can be triggered by foot pistons including bass drums, snare drums, cymbal rolls and crashes, bird calls, and various whistles. The specifics vary from organ to organ, but there is almost always a wide range of effects available.

There are rarely 'scores' of theatre organ music in the traditional sense. The notated sheet music that does exist is normally pedagogical, demonstrating theatre organ style and technique for students and enthusiasts and with different scores using different notational conventions. As advocated earlier in this chapter, traditional pipe organ notation, adapted with the manual and stop names specific to the theatre organ, is perhaps the best option for modern composers. One sheet music example is provided in Figure 5.10, in order to give composers with a starting point when writing for the instrument.

FIGURE 5.10 Tom Horton, *Theatre Organ Originals – Vol. 1*, 'Console Up' © Tom Horton Ltd

Standard theatre organ passagework and figurations are very different from their church organ counterparts and are often influenced by jazz, ragtime, and stride piano. Composers looking to import jazz into regular pipe organ music would be strongly advised to investigate and experiment with these figurations. As ever, there is no substitute for directly engaging with the music, in this case by listening to and transcribing the great theatre organists. Reginald Dixon is probably the most famous name, who in his time was as well-known as Bing Crosby, and many of his recordings are still in circulation and can be found online. Other excellent modern theatre organists include Robert Wolfe, Nigel Ogden, Mark Herman, and Richard Hills. Just listening to these players is an enlightening experience as to what the theatre organ can do.

Further resources are available for those who want more in-depth information. The American Theatre Organ Society (ATOS) produces many excellent online resources, as well as a regular journal with many past editions digitised and available online. The organist Tom Horton, as well as being a fine performer, has produced many resources useful to both composers and performers including *Theatre Organ Originals*, a collection of new compositions for the theatre organ (from which Figure 5.10 is taken) and a highly informative YouTube series that provides video demonstrations of playing techniques, registration, and so forth. The theatre organ is not only an interesting instrument in itself but also offers new ways of thinking about the traditional pipe organ; both composers and performers can learn much by studying this unique instrument.

Hammond Organ

Patented in 1934 by Laurens Hammond, the Hammond organ is the defining organ sound of an entire generation. While occasionally requested by classical composers (e.g., Stravinsky *Circus Polka*), the Hammond is synonymous with black American church music, with the instrument being originally marketed to churches and making its first major appearances in gospel hits of the 1940s. Artists like Jimmy Smith and Booker T. Jones broke the organ into mainstream jazz, rock and soul music in the 1960s, cementing the instrument's place in musical history. The B3, C3, and A100 organ models are particularly famous and are the most valued by players. The Hammond declined in popularity in the 1970s and 1980s, with then-new synthesizers like the Yamaha DX7 appearing to supersede the organ. However, the DX7 has since been relegated to relative obscurity while the Hammond is arguably stronger than ever. Players like Cory Henry have brought the instrument to the cutting edge of modern jazz. Many new 'clonewheels' (i.e., instruments which replicate the B3 and C3 sound) are also being produced, including various sampled keyboards alongside a new instrument line by Hammond themselves, continuing to introduce the organ to a new generation of organists and keyboard players.

The Pipe Organ

FIGURE 5.11 Hammond organ

Hammonds traditionally have two manuals, as shown in Figure 5.11. Unlike regular organs, the top manual (fittingly known as the 'upper manual') is the one typically used for melodies while the 'lower manual' is used for accompaniments and bass lines. While the manuals range is usually C_2–C_7, pedal compasses vary widely. Twenty-five notes (two octaves, from C_2 to C_4) is the standard for 'concert' models. Some Hammonds only have a 13-note C_2 to C_3 pedalboard; other instruments, particularly more modern ones, go up to the top G_4 of the traditional pipe organ. Many clonewheels only have a single manual (usually a split keyboard) and no pedalboard. This single-keyboard setup is by far the cheapest, most portable, and easiest to access; composers should check what is available before writing for larger Hammonds. Not all traditional organists are Hammond players; in fact, jazz pianists are more likely to have experience with the Hammond than church musicians.

The classic tremulant sound of the Hammond was originally obtained with what is known as a 'Leslie speaker'. On modern instruments, there are three speeds of tremolo: stopped (i.e., off), slow, and fast. The speed is adjusted with a toggle usually on the bottom-left of the Hammond's lower manual (in Figure 5.11 this toggle is at the bottom-centre). On many original Leslie speakers, only two speed settings are available, either slow and fast or stopped and fast (this latter setting is achieved by unplugging the slow motors from the speaker). Leslie speakers are completely separate from the organ and are therefore not always available, although the pairing of Hammond and Leslie is relatively standard. Modern digital Hammonds have a digital Leslie in-built.

Registration on the Hammond is done through drawbars. The pedal has two (16′ and 8′) and each manual has nine (16′, 5 1/3′, 8′, 4′, 2 2/3′, 2′, 1 3/5′, 1 1/3′, and 1′). Each drawbar increases in volume the further it is pulled out, going from 0 (off) to 8 (fully drawn). Traditionally, indicating registration is done by specifying how far each drawbar should be drawn in the order presented above; for example, 88 8000 000 means the 16′, 5 1/3′, and 8′ should all be fully drawn and the other drawbars should be fully in. Traditional Hammonds can only have two preset registrations for each manual at a time (using the B_1 and $B\flat_1$ keys on both manuals), although modern digital instruments are less restricted in this regard. Built-in pre-sets can also be available through the bottom octave of the manuals, with said pre-set keys denoted by inverted black and white colouring as in Figure 5.11. Standard combinations for both manuals include:

- 00 8000 000: The 8′ alone, producing a soft yet rich sound. Excellent for quieter moments.
- 88 8000 000: The classic accompaniment sound. This registration is basically the default setting for most styles of music. On the upper manual, adding the percussion creates the classic Jimmy Smith solo sound.
- 00 8400 000: Another mellow accompaniment sound (equivalent to 8′ and 4′ on a regular pipe organ).
- 80 0008 888: The 'Erroll Garner' sound. Combined with a fast Leslie, produces a strongly 'gapped' sound with many overtones.
- 88 8888 888: The full Hammond sound. Combined with a fast Leslie, the effect is overwhelming and is best saved for the climactic moments.

The upper manual also has a 'percussion' stop. When turned on, striking a note produces a tuned 'click', adding an incisive element to solo lines. The percussion tuning can be switched between the second harmonic (sounding an octave above written pitch) and the third harmonic (sounding a perfect twelfth above written pitch). On traditional Hammonds, the percussion only works when using the B_1 preset. Note that none of the drawbars need necessarily be drawn; using the percussion stop alone is fairly common as a special effect.

Just as for the theatre organ, notation is not standardised. While Hammond organ patches are commonly requested in musical theatre keyboard parts, the notation there is often inefficient and rarely takes account of the full intricacies of the Hammond. Notated Hammond music also appears in pedagogical contexts, but again the notation can be unnecessarily confusing (e.g., with varying octave transpositions depending on the piece and registration). Once again, the principles of traditional organ notation are clear and effective and serve well for Hammond writing.

The Hammond has also developed its own array of unique playing techniques, some of which are shown in Figure 5.12. Due to its electric action and tone, the Hammond sounds more percussive than regular organs. As such, rapid repeated notes are very effective and are known as 'sputtering' (a). 'Ghosting' (b) is when the organist does not depress the key fully, creating a type of pitched click like the percussion stop. Effective in jazz solo lines, this technique can also be used for full chords, emulating the sound of funk rhythm guitars. 'Squabbling' (c) is playing a melody in full block chords very staccato and tremoloing on the longer chords, using the 'Erroll Garner' registration mentioned earlier.

FIGURE 5.12 Hammond organ playing techniques

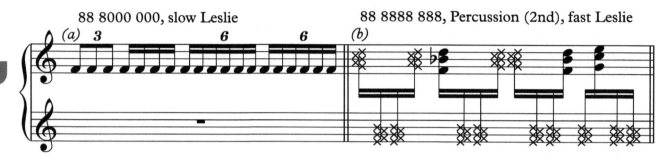

As with the theatre organ, the best way to learn about the Hammond organ is to listen and transcribe the great artists. The best and most innovative players have often been the black jazz and gospel musicians. Particularly recommended are Jimmy Smith, Dr. Lonnie Smith, and Cory Henry, with all three performers turning Hammond playing into a virtuoso art form. Other organists such as Joey DeFrancesco, Barbara Dennerlein, and Keith Emerson have also pioneered Hammond technique in their own unique ways and their recordings are well worth analysing.

Many resources on the Hammond organ exist today. Dave Limina's *Hammond Organ Complete* is a practical guide book and includes CD recordings of each notated example. Free resources are also available online, with video content from The Gospel University and Jazz at Lincoln Center among others. With many new artists, particularly jazz musicians, flocking to the Hammond for its distinct and expressive sound, the popularity of the instrument is only increasing. Composers should therefore explore the full possibilities of this versatile and extraordinary instrument.

THE ORGAN IN ENSEMBLE

Overview

If the organ seems versatile as a solo instrument, then the range of colours and textures possible when combining it with other instruments or voices are practically endless. The organ has much to offer to both larger and smaller ensembles, being able to perform a wide range of roles from delicate colouristic touches to overwhelming masses of sound. It is therefore all the more disappointing that there are so few ensemble works that use organ, and the pieces which do rarely exploit the full capabilities of the instrument. However, such an absence of works provides an exciting space for modern composers: the untrodden ground here allows for innovative new sounds and textures without stretching the budget and resources of performers or venues.

Writing for organ in an ensemble situation requires a subtly different approach compared to solo music, mainly due to the challenge of balancing the organ with other performers. This chapter will therefore focus on these nuances of using the organ in an ensemble, examining in turn choral, orchestral, chamber, and electronic music contexts. For each topic, there will be a short discussion on how organ writing changes depending on the ensemble. Practical experimentation, while again recommended where possible, is probably unfortunately beyond the means of most composers. As such, this chapter turns to analysing various historical examples, giving composers a basis for establishing what works and what does not, as well as providing material for further studying/listening.

Organ and Choir

The pairing of organ and voice has existed virtually since organs were invented. From the time of the earliest notated organ music, the instrument was intended to either double or replace the singers even when not specified, and to this day the organ plays a crucial role in accompanying congregational church singing such as for hymns, chorales, and plainchant. The wind-based sound of the organ complements choral singing very well, and it can offer many unique timbral possibilities for enriching the choir sound. There are also many practical benefits to adding an organ part to choral works outside of just novel sonic possibilities. With organ support, the choir is less likely to go out of tune or struggle with pitching difficult chords; consequently, the vocal parts can also be more ambitious than when the voices are unaccompanied. Excellent modern examples of organ writing in choral music include MacMillan *A New Song*, Escaich *Trois motets*, Martin *Ut Unum Sint*, and Adès *January Writ* (Adès' organ writing is slightly unidiomatic, but the choral/organ combinations are innovative and effective), to provide a varied selection.

It is strongly recommended, if there is an independent organ part, to supply ad lib organ support for extended passages when the choir is unaccompanied. Any slip in tuning from the choir, even if very slight, will be immediately noticeable when the organ re-enters. Good choirs will have no issues with tuning and so will not need the organ's help. However, having the ad lib part available will help less experienced choirs and so make the work more accessible without compromising the composer's intention.

Generally, organ registration should avoid extremes when accompanying the choir more than when the organ is alone. Too quiet, and the choir will not be able to hear it (and so are likely to get slower, slip in tuning, etc.). Too loud, and the organ will drown out the choir. These extremes do have their place in choral music, particularly in solo organ moments, but when doubling the choir in accompanied passages a 'safe' minimum registration would be Swell Founds 8' (or Gambe, Voix Céléste) with a rough maximum as Great Founds 8', 4' with Full Swell coupled (and possibly the pedal 16' or 32' reed). Coupling to the Swell in particular is invaluable for guaranteeing reliable balance in any situation: nuance is key for the choral organist, and the slightest shift of the box can make all the difference in ensuring neither the choir nor organ overwhelm each other.

Note that the organ does not have to play all the time when used in a choral context. Brief organ moments can be as, if not more, effective than extended organ passages. One classic example is Judith Weir's *Illuminare, Jerusalem*: a largely unaccompanied work, the organ's sole appearances on the word 'Illuminare' have a telling and mysterious effect. Figure 6.1 offers a more traditional, yet equally striking, example where the organ punctuates the otherwise unaccompanied choral passage. The spread chords merge with and extend the choral crescendos whilst also supporting the choir's pitch and tuning. This whole work offers much sophisticated interplay between choir and organ and should be studied in full.

FIGURE 6.1 William Walton, *The Twelve* © Oxford University Press

The English choral repertoire in general provides lots of good study material for effective choir and organ writing. Charles Villiers Stanford is one of the most-performed composers from this tradition, with both his canticle settings and anthems well worth study for their often straightforward yet very effective organ and choral writing. Herbert Howells's compositions are a paragon of organ music without specific registration indications: while they can be played as written very effectively on small organs, creative performers with large instruments can bring out the various contrapuntal lines with the full timbral resources of the instrument (see the Online Resources for one demonstration of this with *Like as the Hart*). His canticle settings have become standard repertoire even for amateur choirs; particularly famous are the services for King's College Cambridge (*Collegium Regale*) as well as for Gloucester and St. Paul's cathedrals. Both William Walton (*The Twelve*) and Benjamin Britten (*Rejoice in the Lamb*, *Missa Brevis*, *A Hymn of St Columba*, etc.) combine the choir with organ very effectively in a twentieth-century context. Edgar Bainton's *And I Saw a New Heaven*, Edward Bairstow's *Blessed City, Heavenly Salem*, Kenneth Leighton's *Second Service*, and Gerald Finzi's *Lo, the Full Final Sacrifice* and *God is Gone Up* are all also cathedral choir staples and well worth studying.

In more modern times, John Rutter's organ accompaniments (see, e.g., *The Lord Bless You and Keep You*) are generally accessible and extremely effective, while Matthew Martin offers an innovative and idiomatic take on the tradition as shown in Figure 6.2. Notice how, because of the more involved organ part, even simple choral writing can sound fresh and new by being recontextualised against the organ. The simplicity of choral writing also saves valuable choir rehearsal time and so makes the work more likely to be performed, with the organist able to practice their part independently beforehand (see also MacMillan's *A New Song* for a similar and very frequently performed example).

FIGURE 6.2 Matthew Martin, *Ut Unum Sint* © Faber Music

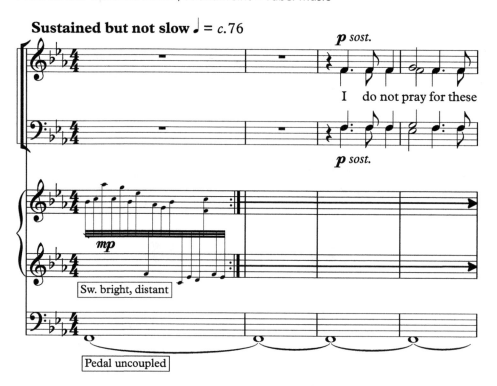

Interestingly, substantial choral organ parts are surprisingly rare outside of English-speaking countries. There is only one German choral work with organ that has really entered the standard canon, Brahms's *Geistliches Lied* (shown in Figure 6.3). The organ writing is spare but very effective, with a well-judged combination of linear counterpoint and more homophonic writing. The final section is particularly well-written, the organ naturally getting louder with the choir by gradually rising up through the compass. The phrase breaks provide a convenient place to add stops in a quasi-symphonic fashion.

FIGURE 6.3 Johannes Brahms, *Geistliches Lied* op. 30

In France, large churches have a separate organ solely for accompanying singers. Duets between this choir organ ('orgue de chœur') and the main organ ('grand orgue'), often in alternation with each other, are common in French choral works. Many of the mass settings have the choral passages accompanied by the choir organ, with the main organ offering cataclysmic interjections; see, for example, the *Messe solennelle* settings by both Vierne and Langlais. Much of this music has a monumental, epic quality unmatched by anything else in the repertoire (although organists outside of France usually have to play both organ parts on one instrument). One particularly remarkable work is Yves Castagnet's *Messe "Salve Regina"* where extraordinary virtuosity is required to produce a truly titanic sound as shown in Figure 6.4. In terms of single-organ choral music, Duruflé's *Requiem* achieves a variety of textures and sound rarely matched in any other choral literature, pushing the organ (and organist) close to the limits of technical virtuosity.

FIGURE 6.4 Yves Castagnet, *Messe "Salve Regina"*, Sanctus © Symétrie

The discussion so far has been concerned with the full SATB choir. Much of the same advice applies to male-voice (TTBB) or female-voice (SSA) choirs, perhaps to an even greater extent than normal choirs. Reduced groups such as these are common even in cathedral settings: UK cathedral choirs frequently dedicate one service a week to choristers alone (S) with occasional but not infrequent services for the lower voices or 'lay clerks' alone (ATB). In all these cases, organ accompaniment can be even more valuable for filling out the textures. The existing repertoire with organ for these formats is very limited; for trebles alone there are Britten's *Missa Brevis* and Poulenc's *Litanies à la Vierge noire*, while for lay clerks there are only occasional anthems like Ernest Walker's *I Will Lift Up Mine Eyes*. The reduced choral forces make it easier for the organ to overwhelm the singers, so organ dynamics should perhaps be slightly scaled back when compared to writing with a full choir. The smaller number of singers allows a greater intimacy than with the full choir, so exploiting this intimacy in the organ writing (or even using the chamber organ rather than the main instrument) can be very effective. The limited repertoire for these groups means there are excellent opportunities here for modern composers to innovate and establish themselves.

Organ and Orchestra

Virtually every major composer, outside of the impressionists and a few others such as Tchaikovsky, has attempted to integrate the organ into the orchestra at some point. Even Stravinsky, who famously said of the organ that "the monster never breathes," gave the instrument a prominent role in his *Canticum Sacrum*. The expansive sound of the instrument is frequently requested for the most grandiose works or for pieces of a religious or quasi-religious nature. Unfortunately however, even composers famous for their orchestration ability such as Wagner, Strauss, Mahler, Stravinsky, and Bernstein struggle with the basic fundamentals of organ notation by, for example, going beyond the organ's written range (see Figure 1.3 for a typical problematic example). Satisfying and innovative organ parts, such as those written by Boulanger and Duruflé, are very rare in the traditional orchestral canon.

However, this situation is gradually improving. The rise in digital instruments means that organs are appearing in more concert halls than ever before; it is now possible even to hire organs to bring in for concerts, as mentioned in Chapter 1. Excellent modern organ parts like in Judith Weir's *Stars, Night, Music and Light* bring the instrument back to the contemporary classical mainstream. The organ is therefore a very useful orchestral instrument for modern composers, offering much room for orchestrational experimentation and innovation while still being within the confines of the standard symphony orchestra line-up.

Player availability is almost never an issue in practice if an instrument is available. Orchestral pianists can (and do) play simple organ parts when called to, with many freelancers having at least a basic competence in the organ. For more complex organ parts, it is necessary to hire in a specialist organist. There are enough orchestral organ parts in the standard repertoire, however, that many orchestras have established relationships with freelance organists who they can call in if needed. As such, it is not unreasonable to request an organist as part of a typical orchestral line-up. However, pianists should not be expected to play complex organ parts and vice versa.

Surprisingly, the organ is often easily overpowered by the orchestra, even when all the stops are drawn. The Swell and Choir reeds in particular do not project nearly as well as their real orchestral counterparts. As such, delicate orchestration arguably suits the organ better than the traditional bombastic fare of many orchestral organ parts, although this loud writing can still serve a useful orchestrational role. The softer colours of the organ also offer much potential, being particularly useful as digital organs (which are particularly common in non-religious venues) can often render quieter sounds more convincingly than the full tutti. The opposite problem, where organs are too loud for the orchestra, is much rarer and easier to fix; removing a couple of stops or moving onto a 'quieter' manual can often solve the problem while keeping the same timbre. Composers should therefore worry more about overscoring rather than underscoring orchestration when including the organ.

The earliest examples of the orchestral organ are as a basso continuo instrument, mainly in religious music. Modern organists tend to use a chamber organ (see Chapter 5), although there is historical evidence the large church organs would have been used. In this continuo context, the organ was often given solo opportunities, particularly in the Benedictus of the mass. Notable examples include Bach in his cantata *Wir müssen durch viel Trübsal* BWV 146, Haydn in the *Missa brevis Sancti Joannis de Deo* (also known as the 'Little Organ Mass' and shown in Figure 6.5) and Mozart in his *Missa Brevis No. 12 in C major* (the 'Organ Solo' mass). While relatively simple and often without an independent pedal part as in Figure 6.5, these solos are very effective and in modern times are typically given a soft, sparkling neo-Baroque registration such as 8′, 4′, and 1 1/3′ (with the accompaniment registered with 8′ and possibly 4′).

FIGURE 6.5 Joseph Hadyn, Missa brevis Sancti Joannis de Deo Hob.XXII:7, Benedictus

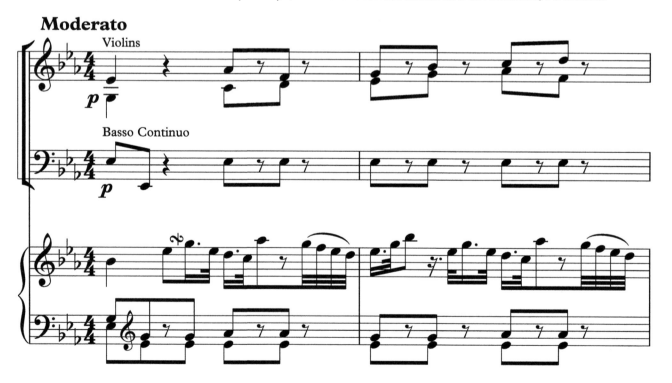

Into the Romantic period, composers were enamoured with the sheer power the organ could provide. In many of these works, the organ part is ad lib. Unfortunately, much unidiomatic writing abounds in the standard orchestral canon and numerous Romantic organ parts require substantial adaption to make them work (see, e.g., Figures 1.3 and 1.4). Traditional Romantic orchestral organ writing can broadly be grouped into three categories:

1. The organ plays sustained chords which blend with the full orchestral tutti, generally at louder dynamics (e.g., Elgar *Pomp and Circumstance March No. 1*, Respighi *Fontane di Roma*, Strauss *An Alpine Symphony*).
2. The organ is given an *ff* solo, generally sustaining a single chord (e.g., Mahler *Symphony No. 8*, Strauss *Also sprach Zarathustra*) although sometimes it is given more extended passages (e.g., Vaughan Williams *Sinfonia Antartica*).
3. The pedals are used alone as a bass part, almost always with the 32′ (see, e.g., Figures 2.8, 4.20, 4.38, 4.39, and 4.40).

The first usage is by far the most common; just like the harps, the organ offers a certain undefinable quality despite often being inaudible in the thick orchestral textures. Given the issues of the orchestra overpowering the organ mentioned earlier, many Romantic orchestral organ parts are remarkably unsatisfying to play on anything except the largest and loudest instruments. Rare exceptions do occur: Koechlin's *La course de printemps* features some astonishing orchestral organ writing, particularly in the movement 'Flûte de Krishna'. Strauss writes an interesting part in *Also sprach Zarathustra* as shown in Figure 6.6, a rare example of the organ's soft side being used soloistically in an orchestral context (the word 'Magnificat' is in the original organ part):

FIGURE 6.6 Richard Strauss, *Also sprach Zarathustra* op. 30, 'Von der grossen Sehnsucht'

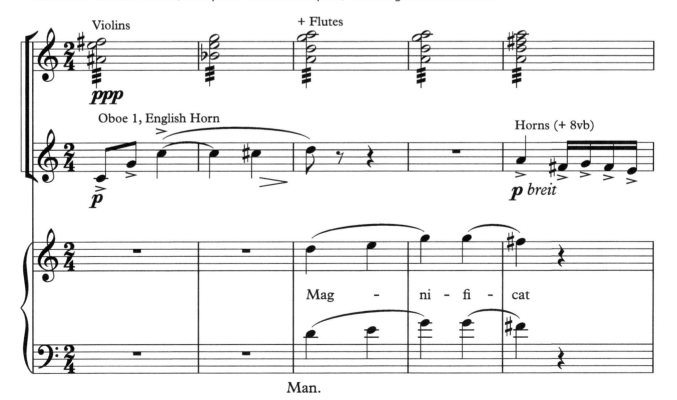

The English Romantics, including Elgar, Holst, and Vaughan Williams, all write better organ parts in this regard than their German counterparts. The finale of Elgar's *Enigma Variations*, quoted in Figure 3.24, presents a typical idiomatic example. The English Romantic oratorios also present much good organ writing; in these works, the organ is frequently more important than in the purely orchestral works. Recommended scores for study are Walton's *Belshazzar's Feast*, Elgar's *The Dream of Gerontius*, and Howell's *Hymnus Paradisi*. All three have interesting and prominent organ parts, and each combines the organ with the orchestra in fascinating ways.

Remarkable examples do also occur outside of western Europe. Bartók wrote a small but interesting part in his ballet *The Miraculous Mandarin* and Scriabin composed an effective Romantic organ part in his *Symphony No. 5* ('*Prometheus: A Poem of Fire*'). Arguably the most notable parts in this regard however are by Czech composer Leoš Janáček. While some of the notation leaves something to be desired, the actual uses of the organ are very effective. Janáček dedicates a whole movement to a solo organ toccata in his *Glagolithic Mass*, but just as interesting is the organ solo in the orchestral rhapsody *Taras Bulba*, shown in Figure 6.7.

FIGURE 6.7 Leoš Janáček, *Taras Bulba*, 'The Death of Andrei'

For standard orchestral repertoire, the consistently best composer for organ writing is Ottorino Respighi. The three parts of his Roman Trilogy feature the organ in progressively more ambitious roles. *Fontane di Roma* has an ad lib organ part for the third movement. The writing is idiomatic, avoiding many of the pitfalls other composers have fallen into. *Pini di Roma* only improves on this basis, the organ featuring prominently in the second and fourth movements. The organ is no longer ad lib but a necessary part of the whole piece; the fourth movement is particularly clever in its use of the instrument. *Feste Romane* pushes the boundaries of the organ even further, with important parts in the first and fourth movements. The latter features one of the most extraordinary orchestral organ passages in standard orchestral repertoire. The pipe organ is used to imitate the barrel organ in conjunction with the piano, winds, and trumpets as seen in Figure 6.8. *Vetrate di Chiesa* is also exceptional and is quoted in Figure 3.16.

FIGURE 6.8 Ottorino Respighi, *Feste Romane*, 'La Befana' © Ricordi

Some of the most interesting and idiomatic orchestral organ writing is found in the *Psaume CXXX* of Lili Boulanger. This is her only choral-orchestral work to feature the organ, but the extraordinary usage of the instrument is virtually unmatched by any other composer. Boulanger was a gifted organist herself, and so the organ writing is natural, technically assured and expertly uses a wide range of registrations. It is in her orchestration, however, where her organ writing truly stands out. The delicate colours of the organ, so rarely used by other orchestral composers, are masterfully combined with other instruments and the choir. Each registration is treated as a separate orchestral colour; sometimes the pedals are used alone, sometimes the organ sustains chords while other instruments are more animated, and sometimes the organ either doubles the harp or provides harp-like accompaniment. Too many passages stand out to all be quoted here, but the passage shown in Figure 6.9 is truly exceptional. The left hand provides the only sustained chords in the texture while also doubling the harp part. The right-hand arpeggio pattern doubles the flutes in inversion. The pedals alone provide the bass. All of this is a backing for two solo singers, providing a gently pulsing and shimmering accompaniment.

FIGURE 6.9 Lili Boulanger, *Psaume CXXX*

A few other examples of modern orchestral organ music will suffice for this section.

George Crumb wrote an important organ part in his large-scale work *Star-Child*. The main organ part is standard Romantic fare, doubling the loudest moments of the piece. In 'Musica Mundana 2', however, the solo organ is creatively used for one of the many background ostinatos that dominate the later part of the work. While Crumb requires the full organ earlier in *Star-Child*, the 'Musica Mundana' ostinato is on Flute 8′ alone. As such, a separate chamber organ would potentially be very effective here where available.

Steve Reich wrote many parts for electric organs, including in his choral-orchestral work *Tehillim*. Here, Reich requests '2 Electric Organs (or Synthesizers)'; he provides more detail in the performance notes, specifying "either four synthesisers or two double manual electric organs [...] A mild double reed timbre (stop/preset) should be used for all." The writing is not very well suited to the organ as it does not taking the subtle differences between different manuals into account. Reich desires the double-manual quality of the organ above anything else, with the parts always doubling the singers. There is also no pedal line. This part is therefore not a true organ part and is better suited to synthesizers. Similar instances occur in other minimalist works, for example, Glass *Einstein on a Beach*. For more successful minimalist organ writing (albeit in a non-orchestral context), see, for example, Glass *Dance No. 4*, McDowall *Church Bells Beyond the Stars*, Wammes *Miroir*, and Dove *Seek him that Maketh the Seven Stars*.

Kaija Saariaho offers many interesting and innovative takes on the orchestral organ. As well as her notable concerto *Maan varjot* (see Figure 4.37), there is also the organ part for her orchestral work *Orion*. In *Orion*, Saariaho exploits the instrument's indefinite sustain, particularly at the more extreme ends of the register. The organ is integrated into the orchestra extremely effectively, using the full range of dynamics and colours and innovatively complementing the other instruments. Occasionally the ambition of the organ writing strays close to being unidiomatic (the pedal clusters in the second movement are extremely difficult to play) but overall Saariaho provides a unique and effective organ part.

The organ has seen a prominent role in many film scores, mainly being used for its religious associations. Perhaps the most famous recent example is by Hans Zimmer in *Interstellar*, but other notable examples include *Ben-Hur*, with a score by Miklós Rózsa, *The Grand Budapest Hotel*, with music by Alexandre Desplat, and Wendy Carlos's score to the original 1982 version of *Tron* (the organ having a major solo in the end credits music). The organ has even made forays into musical theatre, with a major solo role in Stephen Sondheim's *Sweeney Todd*. The same principles for these kinds of music apply as for orchestral music; specific issues relating to recording the organ are covered in 'Organ and Chamber Ensembles'.

The orchestral Hammond organ is potentially also of much interest to modern composers, more so than for other variants of organ in Chapter 5. The instrument has also seen occasional usage in the orchestra, particularly as a keyboard patch in musical theatre ensembles or jazz bands, but the keyboard parts rarely exploit the full capabilities of the instrument even without the pedalboard. The versatility of the Hammond sound can offer many options to orchestral composers of all genres, and there are many exciting possibilities for it still waiting to be discovered.

Concertos

Concertos for the organ are relatively rare, with Poulenc's *Organ Concerto* being the only one to really enter standard repertoire. The organ concertos of Handel and Rheinberger are charming but are given only very occasional outings. Other more modern concertos do exist, such as by Hindemith, Leighton, Rouse, and Escaich among others, but they have not yet established a real footing in the repertoire. There are currently no major concertos for the theatre or Hammond organs. Given the unique aspects of the instrument, the organ concerto therefore offers much potential for the modern composer looking to break away from traditional concerto conventions.

Many of the most popular organ concertos feature a reduced orchestra, often just strings with or without percussion such as Poulenc's concerto. Such an arrangement has undisputable economic and practical advantages, allowing these concertos to be performed in smaller venues with more limited budgets (particularly as the best organs are often found outside of concert halls). Nevertheless, concertos such as Escaich's show just how much potential there is in organ concerti with full orchestra; the second movement of his concerto is particularly inspiring in this regard.

Orchestral works with an organ obbligato part are considerably more common, although again many have struggled to enter the standard repertoire. Strauss's *Festliches Präludium*, quoted in Figure 1.3, was written to inaugurate the new organ of the Vienna Philharmonic. By far the most famous example, however, is Saint-Saëns's *Symphony No. 3* (the so-called 'Organ' Symphony). This piece dominates concert programmes over the other organ-orchestra repertoire, even the Poulenc concerto. The organist is often given a separate billing in programmes alongside the conductor, despite the relative simplicity of the part. Nevertheless, Saint-Saëns's writing is highly effective and justly famous. Figure 6.10 shows a particularly noteworthy extract (see also Figure 4.3).

FIGURE 6.10 Camille Saint-Saëns, *Symphony No. 3 'Organ'* op. 78, Poco adagio

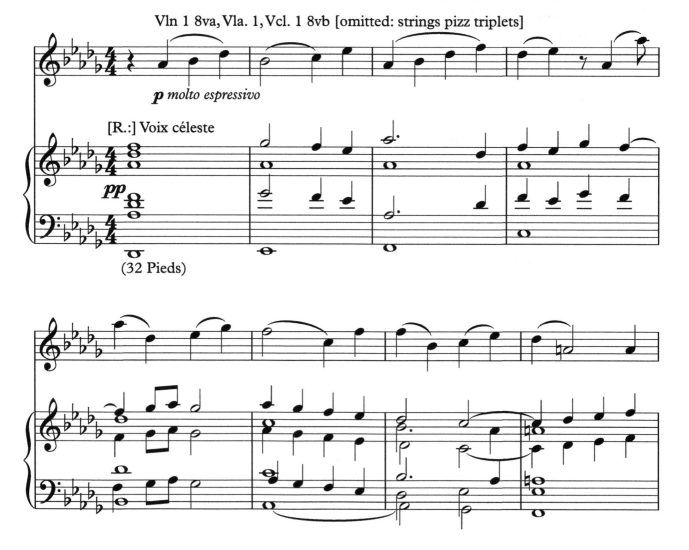

The repertoire for solo organ and orchestra has also expanded slowly from the twentieth century onwards. Samuel Barber's incredibly virtuosic *Toccata Festiva*, like much of his other music, is moderately well-known in America but is not as mainstream in other countries. Aaron Copland's *Symphony for Organ and Orchestra* similarly is popular in America but less well-known abroad. Striking modern examples include James MacMillan's *A Scotch Bestiary*, a quasi-concerto where an astonishing range of timbres and textures are drawn out of the organ. Kaija Saariaho's sensitive ear for orchestral colour is applied to the organ obbligato in *Maan varjot* (quoted in Figure 4.40). Sofia Gubaidulina's *The Rider on the White Horse* is similarly inventive, with both the softest and loudest sounds of the organ used incredibly effectively (see, e.g., Figure 2.4) The virtuosity of many modern organists makes the lack of organ-orchestral works all the more disappointing. Even Poulenc's concerto rarely reaches the technical ambition of the solo works of, for example, Duruflé and Messiaen. It is hoped that through this book, by helping to show the full versatility of the organ, composers are encouraged to explore the full potential of this exciting genre.

Organ and Chamber Ensembles

Perhaps unsurprisingly, the organ has been rarely used as a chamber instrument. Its large size, traditional lack of availability outside of churches and its impersonal nature (the player often a long distance away from the other musicians) have deterred composers from attempting to include it in traditional chamber groups. Organ chamber ensembles with more than two players are particularly rare, although some striking modern examples do exist, for example, Hindemith *Kammermusik VII*, Weir *In the Land of Uz* and Schnittke *Requiem*. However, the organ has potential to be an incredibly useful modern chamber instrument, where its versatile range of colours can augment and fill out both larger and smaller chamber setups. In an era when new music commissions are more common for chamber groups or chamber orchestras than a full symphony orchestra, the possible value of the organ in these ensembles cannot be overlooked.

There is perhaps the misconception that the organ is too loud to balance with solo instruments. The diversity of quieter registrations available on the organ have only rarely been exploited outside of the solo repertoire. Additionally, it is often easy to reduce the volume with only minimal, if any, changes in registration needed. Just like with choral accompaniment, the maximum recommended registration for accompanied passages is approximately Great Founds 8′ and 4′ with the Full Swell coupled; when accompanying instruments such as the cello, this maximum may have to be slightly quieter (e.g., without the Great 4′). Even with this limit, the organ can produce a wide range of textures and tonal colours, and so has definite potential within smaller ensembles.

Chamber organs, in contrast to the regular pipe organ, have seen much modern success in Renaissance and Baroque chamber setups. In this context, the organ has become as standard as the harpsichord, with many music institutions owning a chamber organ specifically for these types of music. Competent continuo players are expected to be able to perform on both instruments, often switching between the two depending on the piece. The chamber organ's small size makes balance issues less problematic than for larger organs, their portability means they can be hired in if unavailable, and the organist is usually very close to and can interact with the other musicians. The chamber organ, as its name suggests, is therefore perfectly designed for chamber music and has much to offer the modern composer in this regard.

Hammond organs have also established themselves firmly as part of traditional jazz combos. The organ trio, comprising Hammond, guitar, and drums, was popularised by Jimmy Smith and has since become a standard ensemble on the jazz circuit. In traditional gospel music, pairing the Hammond with the drums alone is common, this ensemble also being augmented with piano and bass. Many classic tracks from the 1960s feature a Hammond as part of the ensemble, including the famous organ part for Bob Dylan's 'Like a Rolling Stone'. As the primary focus of this book is the pipe organ, and Hammond music is often improvised rather than notated, examining all of the Hammond ensemble examples is beyond the scope of this book. Composers should instead investigate the many resources and playlists dedicated to the instrument, many of which are available for free online.

Four-handed organ music (two players at one console) is considerably rarer than four-handed piano music. Nevertheless, examples do exist and can even receive regular performances, such as Tomkins's *A Fancy for Two to Play*. There is also surprising amount of potential for the genre, even on small organs: not only is finding a second organist to duet with often surprisingly easy, an extra player can help add in additional contrapuntal lines, useful on an instrument that often favours static hand positions over more complex pianistic textures (see Leighton *Martyrs* and Laurin *Fantasy and Fugue on the Genevan Psalm 47* for how useful this contrapuntal freedom can be). Registration can also be controlled at every moment with much more precision than a single player is able to. The same ergonomic issues arise as for piano four-hand repertoire, although the organ's multiple manuals can also help mitigate these difficulties such as in Rutter's *Variations on an Easter Theme*. Normally there is only one pedal part between both players.

An analysis of Liszt's rarely performed *Ossa Arida*, for unison men's choir and organ four-hands, illustrates both good and bad writing for the genre. The opening is very effective, with the stacked thirds suiting the organ well; while technically playable by one person (involving some complex pedalling), Liszt's presented execution is technically easier and less contrived. Afterwards, however, the second player mostly just doubles the first player an octave or two lower (see Figure 6.11). Such writing is largely redundant: with the addition of pedals and 16′ in the manuals, having one player alone would work just as well as what Liszt wrote.

Four-handed music is most effective when each hand (or player) has an independent textural or contrapuntal role from the others.

FIGURE 6.11 Franz Liszt, *Ossa Arida*

Organ and instrument duets are undeservedly rare. It is relatively easy to engage an additional solo performer for the occasional church service, which can provide nice musical variety for regular congregation. Organ plus brass is common for arrangements (there are numerous modern organ/trumpet arrangements, particularly of English Baroque trumpet tunes, while Liszt arranged his own *Hosannah* for bass trombone and organ). However, the general lack of original music for any pairing offers composers much room for experimentation in this area.

The Pipe Organ

The pairing of organ with string instruments has produced pieces like Sofia Gubaidulina's landmark composition *In Croce* for cello and organ, as well as smaller yet charming works such as Saint-Saëns's *Prière* (cello and organ) and Gounod's *Vision de Jeanne d'Arc* (violin and organ). Saint-Saëns's piece provides an excellent example of duet writing and is shown in Figure 6.12. The organ part can be played on a chamber organ or harmonium (although there is a pedal line ad lib). Saint-Saëns balances the two instruments very effectively, the thematic material being shared between them while Saint-Saëns carefully makes sure the organ does not overwhelm the cello. For a more symphonic treatment of the organ in a similar duet context, see Hugo Riemann's arrangement of Max Bruch's *Kol Nidrei* for cello and organ.

FIGURE 6.12 Camille Saint-Saëns, *Prière* op. 158

Duets between organ and piano are also unjustly rare. Many churches own a piano alongside an organ and the two instruments complement each other very well. Joel Raney's piano and organ arrangements of various hymns use both instruments to the full, the two keyboards combining together very effectively. More common in the repertoire are duets between piano and harmonium, often accompanying a choir, such as for Rossini's *Petite messe solennelle*. Vincent d'Indy exploits this combination fully in his *Sainte Maria Magdalene* op. 23. In the extract shown in Figure 6.13, the piano is treated like a harp, with arpeggio figuration to contrast with the sustained harmonium chords. In this example, the harmonium is the top part while the piano is underneath (harmonium registration is explained in Chapter 5).

FIGURE 6.13 Vincent D'Indy, *Sainte Marie Magdaleine* op. 23

Larger chamber ensembles with organ are even rarer than duets in the traditional repertoire. One extraordinary example is Lili Boulanger's *Pie Jesu* for soprano solo, organ, string quartet and harp. Boulanger's organ writing is excellent as ever and, just like in her other music, it is in combining the organ with other instruments where she truly excels. The organ plays throughout, providing a woodwind-like sound; the strings form a small group, often playing unison lines in octaves; and the harp adds a gentle percussiveness to the ensemble. The organ part is always quiet and delicate, with the strings and harp never having to compete in terms of volume. Even at the loudest moments, the organ never goes beyond Founds 8′, 4′ on any manual. Many passages stand out, as is common in Boulanger's work; however, the following passage quoted in Figure 6.14 shows best how the ensemble is more than the sum of its parts.

FIGURE 6.14 Lili Boulanger, *Pie Jesu*

The organ has a special affinity with brass instruments and, by extension, the brass quintet and brass band. Brass groups are frequently employed for ceremonial religious or civic occasions and so numerous pieces have been written combining the choir, organ, and brass. Notable examples include Vaughan Williams's arrangement of *The Old Hundredth Psalm Tune* (written for the 1953 coronation of Queen Elizabeth II), Lili Boulanger's *Psaume XXIV* (which also includes a harp part), and James MacMillan's epic *Tu es Petrus*. The organ and brass can both match each other at loud dynamics while delicately complementing each other at quieter dynamics. Brass mutes offer a wide range of colours with again no issue of projection. Spatial elements can also be explored: the brass players can be positioned in various locations around the venue (e.g., the nave/concert platform, organ loft, side galleries, etc.) and so offer new antiphonal and spatial options.

An excellent example of organ and brass together is Sigfrid Karg-Elert's final chorale from his *Choral-Improvisationen für Orgel*, 'Wunderbarer König', featuring the small ensemble of organ, two trumpets and two trombones with an ad lib timpani part. Karg-Elert exploits the full range of textural possibilities and combinations of organ and brass: the unison brass and organ are in dialogue in a quiet opening; the organ accompanies the trumpets and then trombones at a louder dynamic; and the full ensemble comes together for the final fanfare, shown in Figure 6.15.

The Pipe Organ

FIGURE 6.15 Sigfrid Karg-Elert, *Choral-Improvisationen für Orgel* op. 65, 'Wunderbarer König'

There are of course a theoretically infinite number of ensembles involving the organ, with only the most common ones covered here. Nevertheless, there is much unexplored ground for using the organ in ensembles not discussed earlier. Woodwinds can work very effectively as organ duet partners, despite how it may first seem: these instruments can both blend yet also contrast with the organ when needed, and the reed stops sound sufficiently different to their woodwind counterparts to still be useful timbral resources. Percussion instruments also work very well in duet, the rhythmic incision of the percussion complementing the smoother tone of the organ. Nico Muhly's *Beaming Music* for marimba and organ, for example, shows how effective the combination can be.

Organ and Electronics

Combining organ and electronics largely relies on the same principles as for using the organ in orchestras or chamber ensembles, albeit with a few specific nuances. Digital or sampled organs (see 'Software Instruments' in the Introduction) tend to merge better live with electronics than real pipe organs do. For recorded media, it is also very easy to adjust the level of the organ in the mix, allowing an even greater control of dynamics than is possible live (in *Interstellar*, Zimmer often 'cheats' crescendos by adjusting the organ mix instead of using stop changes, in spite of recording with a real organ). As has hopefully been demonstrated throughout this book, the organ is capable of more than just the stereotypical full organ sound, particularly when these sounds can be electronically modified and manipulated such as by using reversed organ samples (see, e.g., 'Inuart Battle' from the video game *Drakengard*, an extraordinary track more innovative than much music in more conventional genres). Inspiring examples of organ combined with electronica include Vangelis 'Nucleogenesis, Pt. 1', von Hauswolff 'Theatre of Nature', and Baptiste Lagrave's astonishing 2019 duo performance with French organist Thomas Ospital. Composers looking for novel sounds in electronic music should therefore consider exploring the organ; it may have exactly the sound needed.

As can be seen, there is an extraordinary amount of uncovered ground relating to the organ in ensemble, as well as the organ more generally. The instrument has been long misunderstood by non-specialists, a situation which this book hopes to help change. The organ has so much potential both as an ensemble and a solo instrument, with numerous unexplored textures and timbres easily accessible once the capabilities of the instrument are known. This book has therefore had one major aim: to show not just what the organ was, or what the organ is, but what the organ can be. If composers are inspired to go out and write for the instrument, then this book has succeeded in its goal.

Appendix
NATIONAL ORGAN STYLES

Understanding the main national and historic organ design styles can be very useful for a composer. It allows for a better engagement with the standard repertoire and the sound worlds they inhabit. It also can be valuable knowledge for modern organ compositions when writing for specific organs in these styles. Software such as Hauptwerk allows any composer (including non-classical musicians) to access and play around with instruments in any style from the comfort of your own home. Furthermore, eclectic organs are essentially amalgams of these various styles, usually borrowing the most features from the 'home' national style (e.g., a UK cathedral eclectic organ will normally have predominantly English Romantic features, a US one will have the American Classic style strongly represented and so on). Taking account of these styles can therefore help make the organ, and therefore the composition, sound at its best.

This appendix therefore presents a chronological list of the main styles, complete with representative organ builders, composers, and a brief summary of organ design and performance practice. Sample organ specifications with commentaries for each of these building styles are available in the Online Resources, including an example specification of a real modern eclectic organ. Composers wishing to study national styles in more detail should also consult the relevant chapters in *The Cambridge Companion to the Organ* and Jon Laukvik's seminal *Historical Performance Practice in Organ Playing*.

Italian Renaissance (c. 1550–1650)

Notable organ builders: Costanzo Antegnati
Representative Composers: Giovanni Gabrieli, Claudio Merulo, Girolamo Frescobaldi

Sample Organ—Basilica di Santa Barbara, Mantua, Italy

The Italian Renaissance organ style is one of the earliest major organ styles in the West. The organs, despite their typically small stop-list (mostly comprising principals and a couple of flutes) are often capable of more substance, clarity, and richness than many instruments several times their size. Most organs in the Italian Renaissance style have many of the typical features of historic organs such as pedal pull-downs, divided sharp keys, and a short octave. What sets the Italian style apart from any organ style before or since is the absence of mixtures. Instead, each mixture is broken down into individual mutations, providing an extremely fine control of the principal chorus. Many Italian organs also have a principal celeste, an extremely beautiful stop that is incredibly rare outside of Italy.

Sadly, the Italian Renaissance is surprisingly poorly represented in the modern organ world. The broken mixtures and principal celestes are found in almost no other style of organ, be it Baroque, Romantic, or even eclectic. Nevertheless, new 'historic' instruments in this style are slowly becoming more prevalent, and so composers now do not have to go to Italy to get to write for these beautiful, and unique, instruments.

Spanish Renaissance/Baroque (c. 1500–1700)

Notable organ builders: Echevarría (shared surname)
Representative Composers: Correa de Arauxo, Antonio de Cabezón, Juan Cabanilles

Sample Organ—Capilla de San Enrique, Burgos Cathedral, Spain
While the Spanish organ tradition spans from the 1500s to the present day, the most notable period for Spanish organs and organ composition is during the Spanish Golden Age. Spanish organs generally had a split keyboard at $C_4/C^\sharp_4$ rather than multiple manuals. Consequently, Spanish organ composers explored the possibilities of the split keyboard more than virtually all other organ traditions, save perhaps the English Tudor composers. Spanish composers such as de Arauxo produced sophisticated and unique textures with this split, often with one hand playing a virtuosic solo line accompanied by the other hand (see, e.g., de Arauxo's 'Siguese otro tiento de medio registro de dos tiples de séptimo tono', no. 54 from his *Facultad organica*). The other major unique feature of Spanish organs are the trumpets. The Spanish were the first to have en chamade reeds, and Spanish organ cases are instantly recognisable by the protruding horizontal reed pipes. The reeds themselves have a distinct sound, similar to those of other Baroque traditions but with a unique character of their own.

Unfortunately, like the Italian Renaissance tradition, the Spanish organ style is generally relegated to historic instruments alone rather than being reflected in later organ design. The music is perhaps the least performed of the major organ styles, with reliable editions of the music not always easy to find. Nevertheless, the Spanish organ has again seen a slight resurgence through modern interest and new 'historic' instruments, so the vibrancy and brilliance of these instruments is slowly being brought to the next generation.

German Baroque (c. 1600–1750)

Notable organ builders: Arp Schnitger (north Germany), Gottfried Silbermann (central Germany), Johann Holzhey (south Germany)
Representative Composers: J. S. Bach, Dieterich Buxtehude (north Germany), Samuel Scheidt (north Germany), Johann Froberger (south Germany)

Sample Organ—Freiburg Cathedral, Germany
There is a distinct regional split in organ design and composition between north, central, and south Germany in the seventeenth century. South German organs are stylistically similar

to Italian instruments, with the music favouring one-manual textures without pedals. These features made this music very transmittable and popular in its day in contrast to, for example, the north German and French Classical styles.

Lean choruses define the north German sound: both flutes and principals produce a very 'pronounced' sound, flutes are not added to the principal chorus, and each manual is designed to work largely as independent uncoupled sections (known in modern terminology as 'Werkprinzip' design, although this term was only coined in the twentieth century). As in other Baroque styles, a low wind pressure gives the pipes a breathy and incisive quality. The north German style is perhaps most known for the brilliant yet lean tutti sounds which for many listeners define the traditional full organ sound.

The central German style is the main tradition in which Bach grew up and worked. In contrast to the Werkprinzip sectionalisation of the organ, central German organs had all the pipes in one section. These organs less brilliance and fewer reeds compared to their north German counterparts but more diversity in softer sounds, particularly strings. Bach merged both north and central German styles in his music, with the north German influence most prominent in his grander pieces and the central German predilection for colour in his softer works.

Unsurprisingly, the north and central German styles in particular are arguably the most important organ schools in the instrument's history. Counterpoint features very prominently, unsurprising given that all German organ traditions came out of vocal polyphony, and the writing suits the organ so perfectly that it has essentially become the gold standard. This music rarely contains any registrations or dynamics, with the organist left to intuit them based on the musical style of the piece, thereby making the music suitable for practically every organ no matter its size or style. With the prominence of Bach, as well as other composers such as Buxtehude and Froberger, these styles of organ are an essential component of many modern eclectic organs.

French Classical (c. 1650–1770)

Notable organ builders: Clicquot (shared surname), Dom Bédos
Representative Composers: François Couperin, Nicolas de Grigny, Louis-Nicolas Clérambault, Louis-Claude Daquin

Sample Organ—Chapelle royale, Versailles, France

The French Classical style is all about the French courtly values of grace and elegance. Much of the music is for manuals alone, although the pedals do sometimes have a significant part. The music can be very hard to adapt to eclectic instruments since French Classical organs have an abundance of mutations (and a pedal Trumpet 8′) that many non-French organs simply do not have. Registration of this music is typically indicated in piece titles and more rarely in the score itself. The specifics of registration vary between different historical sources and are a popular topic for debate among organists. To give a rough outline a few of the most common terms found in scores:

- *Plein Jeux*: Flutes and Principals 16′, 8′, 4′, 2′, Mixtures, Pedal Trumpet 8′
- *Grand Jeux*: Reeds, Cornets (the 'Grand Jeu' is on the Grand-Orgue while the 'Petit Jeu' is on the Positif)

- *Jeu Doux*: Bourdon [Flute] 8′, Montre [Principal] 8′ (sometimes with the Prestant [Principal] 4′), Pedal Flute 8′ where specified
- *Tierce*: Bourdon 8′, Prestant 4′, Nazard 2 2/3′, Doublette [Principal] 2′, Tierce 1 3/5′, Larigot 1 1/3′

Other registrations either clearly specify a solo stop (e.g., Cromorne, Voix Humaine) or can have a range of performance options (e.g., Duo, Trio). Performance practice is similarly complex, with a wide range of notated ornaments as well as the concept of 'inégalité' (lit. 'unequalness') where groups of quavers are not always performed with equal note lengths. The French Classical school notoriously requires a lot of prior specialist knowledge to perform, more so than most other organ styles, and giving a full breakdown is beyond the scope of this book. However, the information given should be enough give a solid introduction to this tradition; the style's influence on later French organ music and its modern popular resurgence give it continuing relevance to this day.

German Romantic (c. 1830–1930)

Notable organ builders: Friedrich Ladegast, Wilhelm Sauer
Representative Composers: Johannes Brahms, Franz Liszt, Max Reger, Sigfrid Karg-Elert

▶ Sample Organ—Thomaskirche, Leipzig, Germany

In stark contrast to the Werkprinzip Baroque style of organ design, the Romantic styles, and German Romanticism in particular, were about blending many different types of stops to create a rich symphonic sound. While Baroque organs use a low wind pressure to get a more 'breathy' sound, the high wind pressure of German Romantic instruments enabled stops to better mix together. The reeds are less prominent than on any other style of organ, instead blending into the general tutti. The crescendo pedal (or 'Rollschweller') was beloved by the German Romantics and, while rarely specified in the scores, is crucial to the classic sound of Reger and Liszt among others.

While German Romantic music is a fundamental part of the modern organists' repertoire, it is often less idiomatic than that from other organ schools. Many of the German Romantic composers are self-described 'awkward organists', with awkward manual and pedal writing that does not lie easily under the hands and feet. Additionally, the need for a crescendo pedal makes much of this music difficult to adapt to the many organs which do not have one. Nevertheless, the rich expressivity and intense emotionality of German Romanticism has continued to prove popular with organists and audiences alike, and therefore the style enjoys a key role in the modern organ world.

French Romantic (c. 1830–1940)

Notable organ builders: Aristide Cavaillé-Coll
Representative Composers: César Franck, Charles-Marie Widor, Louis Vierne, Marcel Dupré, Maurice Duruflé, Jeanne Demessieux

▶ Sample Organ (a) — Église Saint-Sulpice, Paris, France
Sample Organ (b) — Église de la Sainte-Trinité, Paris, France

The reputation of the French Romantic organ is down to virtually one builder, Aristide Cavaillé-Coll, and his instruments are some of the most important and prestigious in the world. Like for Romantic organs of other countries, the French instrument aimed to emulate the sound of the orchestra. However, there are a few notable features that set French organs apart. The reeds are markedly more fiery and pungent than in either Germany or England, lending a raw and exciting edge to the tutti organ sound. These reeds could be added or removed by foot levers known as 'ventils', one of the only registration aids traditionally available on these organs aside from foot pedals for every coupler. As such, registration changes in French Romanticism are generally limited to adding or removing reeds which, in retrospect, has actually made the music more 'transferable' to non-French organs than its German or English counterparts.

This transferability is partly why, in the present day, French Romantic composers are arguably the most popular of the Romantic schools. The ease of registration means that the music is quick and easy to set up and prepare, an element invaluable to many concert organists in particular. French Romantic organ writing is also arguably one of the most idiomatic organ styles in general, with both the manuals' and pedals' writing lying excellently under the hands and feet. The French also have a unique affinity with organ improvisation, with French-style improvising being an obsession for many high-level organists more than any other type. More modern French organ music, such as by Olivier Messiaen and Thierry Escaich, is also fundamentally based on the Romantic and Classical styles, so understanding these antecedents will elucidate the current French organ scene.

English Romantic (c. 1850–1960)

Notable organ builders: Henry 'Father' Willis, William Hill & Son, Harrison & Harrison Ltd
Representative Composers: Edward Elgar, Charles Villiers Stanford, Charles Hubert Hastings Parry, Herbert Howells, Judith Bingham

▶ Sample Organ—King's College chapel, Cambridge, UK

While some early Tudor composers such as Henry Purcell and William Byrd both played the organ and wrote important works for the instrument, the UK's main global organ contribution was in the Victorian period. The English Romantic organ was inspired by the French and German Romantic styles but, under the pioneering work of Henry Willis, developed its own unique character. Defining features include electro-pneumatic or tubular-pneumatic key action (allowing for lightness of touch even with all stops drawn), divisional pistons, the Tuba stop, and an enclosed Choir (or Solo on four-manual instruments) with many warm, expressive solo reeds as well as extra strings and flutes. These developments make the English Romantic organ style arguably the best suited to orchestral transcriptions and accompaniments.

While much English Romantic organ music is arguably more idiomatic than its German counterpart, the style has struggled to have the centrality of the French and German Romantic styles, certainly in terms of solo organ pieces. However, the importance of Anglican choral repertoire, particularly in the UK and US, has ensured the continued relevance of English Romanticism to the organ world. In addition, the English Romantic sound has had some major representations in film, most notably in the soundtracks to *Tron* and *Interstellar* (recorded with the organs of the Royal Albert Hall and the Temple Church, London respectively). As such, English Romanticism has a very important role in public perception of the organ sound; given the beauty and richness of the best English instruments, this is no bad thing.

North American Modern (1930–present)

Notable organ builders: Ernest Skinner, Æolian-Skinner Organ Company, Holtkamp Organ Company, Austin Organs

Representative Composers: Leo Sowerby, Calvin Hampton, William Albright, William Bolcom, Vincent Persichetti, Thomas Kerr, Rachel Laurin

Sample Organ—Grace Cathedral, San Francisco, USA

A general 'North American' organ style is surprisingly hard to pin down. Perhaps the most definitive, distinctly American type of organ is the so-called 'American Classic' championed by G. Donald Harrison at the Æolian-Skinner Organ Company in the 1940s and 50s. Harrison sought to update earlier American symphonic-style instruments, such as built by E. M. Skinner, by making them more versatile (e.g., including clean principal choruses suitable for Baroque and Renaissance music) and hence developing the first types of truly 'eclectic' instruments. Characteristic features of these organs include flute celestes, percussion stops, and a balanced crescendo pedal. North America was also a leading developer in neoclassical historically oriented instruments, with organ builders such as Fritts, Taylor and Boody, and Brombaugh all helping repopularise older design principles such as mechanical action, Baroque pipe voicing, and unequal temperaments.

Sadly, most North American organ composers have not been able to enter the mainstream canon outside their home continent, just like the situation for North American classical music more generally. The eclecticism and diversity of North American organs makes the American style less clearly definable than for other countries. Even in the USA itself, the most distinctive features of the North American style, such as the crescendo pedal, are by no means universally available on the organs themselves. This stylistic void, however, leaves space for a new wave of composers to define themselves. It is very possible that the next major revolutions in organ music will come from America in the current, and upcoming, generations.

Glossary

Action The system used to connect the keys and manuals to the pipes and wind system. See 'Mechanical Action' and 'Electric Action' below for more specifics.

Anches The French term for the Reeds. On older French Romantic organs, reed stops can be pre-drawn and added/disengaged by using a foot lever, hence 'anches préparées' as seen in the music of, for example, César Franck (this foot lever usually also adds/removes upperwork such as the 2′ and Mixtures).

Antiphonal A division normally found only on large American organs. This division is typically separated from the main organ case to produce an antiphonal effect, hence the name.

Bombarde A common division for the fourth manual. Typically houses the en chamade solo reeds alone.

Bourdon See 'Flute'.

Box See 'Swell Box'.

Brustwerk A division common on German Baroque organs. It is usually positioned below the Hauptwerk and essentially functions as an unenclosed Swell.

Case The façade and wooden housing which covers the pipes, action, and wind system of the organ. Many organ cases are elaborate artistic feats designed by leading architects of the day. Most pipes are contained inside the case, but some of the loudest reeds such as the Tuba are placed outside (see 'En Chamade').

Chamber Organ A small organ, usually with only one manual and no pedals, that is designed to fill a small room rather than a large church (hence why they are different from one-manual historic organs). Such organs are typically found on the floor of the building rather than in an organ loft and are often portable. The sound is much more intimate than a regular organ.

Channel An abbreviation of 'memory channel' and part of combination action. Individual sets of generals and divisionals (normally between six to ten of each) can be stored on each channel, with generals and divisionals usually having independent sets of channels. Many modern organs will have upwards of 100 channels, allowing hundreds of different registrations to be electronically pre-set.

Chorus Stops, usually of one family, which are designed to work and blend together as one unit. Common examples include the principal chorus and reed chorus.

Choir One of the main divisions/manuals on the organ. It has varying functions depending on the organ, normally either providing solo colours or acting as a step between the Great and the Swell. The term 'choir' can also be an alternative spelling for 'quire', the part of a cathedral behind the nave and where choral evensong is commonly held.

Chorale The German Lutheran equivalent of a hymn.

Cipher A common organ fault where drawing a stop causes a note to sound even when no keys are pressed.

Combination Action The (normally electronic) system where organ registrations can be pre-programmed, stored, and then recalled. Combination action is therefore a crucial part of modern registration aids. Generals and divisionals are a part of the combination action. Combination actions usually have multiple channels, allowing multiple sets of generals and divisionals to be stored simultaneously.

Compass The written range of the organ. The organ compass for both the manuals and pedals is shown in Figure 1.2.

Glossary

Console The area where the organ is played from (see Figure 1.1). Organ consoles normally contain a number of manuals, a pedalboard, a range of stops and various registration aids. Some large organs have more than one console, allowing them to be played from multiple locations.

Cornet A mutation mixture made of 8′, 4′, 2 2/3′, 2′ and 1 3/5′ flutes. The Cornet was popular in French Classical organ music and retains its prominence thanks to its use by many of the great twentieth-century French organ composers.

Coupler A stop that allows different manuals to be connected together. Couplers generally only work one way; for example, the 'Swell to Great' coupler allows Swell stops to be played on the Great manual but not vice versa.

Crescendo Pedal A expression pedal which adds or removes stops the more the pedal is open or shut respectively. Some crescendo pedals are 'Rollschweller', where the foot pushes a treadmill-like track rather than a pedal per se. Whilst crescendo pedals are moderately common on large American and German Romantic organs, they are very rare otherwise.

Diapason Generally another name for the Principal. However, the Stopped Diapason 8′ is a Flute stop and string varieties of diapason can sometimes be found on English organs (where they are normally called 'Violin Diapason' or similar).

Division The section of pipes (and consequently stops) each manual controls, for example, the Choir manual controls the Choir division. On large organs, some manuals may control more than one division (e.g., some large organs have both a Choir and Positive division on the same manual). 'Floating' divisions are those which are not attached to any specific manual; however, they can typically be coupled to any of the manuals.

Divisional Pistons A registration aid allowing the organist to quickly change stops on each independent manual. On older instruments divisionals may be unalterable, but on electric instruments they can usually be changed and pre-programmed. Specific divisionals settings are normally based on the instrument, venue and personal taste and so composers should not expect them to be modified for individual pieces except in special circumstances. Most large organs have between six to eight divisional pistons per manual, as well as a separate set for the pedals. On UK organs, the Great and pedal divisionals can often be linked together, that is, pressing one simultaneously operates the other.

Echo A division most commonly found on French Classical and US instruments. On French organs, this division is unenclosed and is used for straightforward echo effects (see 'French Classical—Chapelle royale, Versailles' in the Online Resources for one example). On American organs, however, its normal function is to provide very soft flutes and strings, acting like an enclosed version of the Antiphonal. Echo divisions are very rare.

Eclectic An organ design style where the organ is created to be as versatile as possible, playing music from any period or country equally well. In practice, true eclecticism is impossible and compromises often need to be made, for example, whether the organ has tracker or mechanical action.

Electric Action On organs with electric action, pressing a key connects a circuit which then opens the valve to let wind through the pipes. Electric-action organs typically have a lighter touch than mechanical-action instruments, allowing faster and ergonomically awkward passages to be executed more easily. The sacrifice, however, is the subtle expressivity and note-shaping that defines mechanical-action organs.

En Chamade A term typically referring to when a solo reed stop is placed outside the main case and points horizontally into the building. The sound of en chamade reeds is therefore direct and penetrating and they are normally the loudest stops on the organ.

Enclosed See 'Swell Box'.

Expression Pedal A foot pedal that usually opens and shuts a set of shutters, allowing for gradated crescendos and diminuendos. Virtually all modern Swell divisions have an expression pedal, commonly known as the 'Swell pedal'. More rarely, other divisions may also have dedicated expression pedals. Crescendo pedals in North America usually also take the form of expression pedals. See also 'Swell Box'.

Floating See 'Division'.

Flue A flute, principal or string pipe. The flues are commonly combined together to form the 'Foundation' stops of the organ.

Flute A type of organ stop which, as the name suggests, produces a flute-like sound. The flutes are the second-most common type of stop found on an organ after the principals.

Foundation A group of stops typically comprising the flues, occasionally with the Swell Oboe. The foundation stops are the bedrock of the Romantic sound and will typically be used in Romantic music when no other registration is specified.

General Pistons A registration aid allowing the organist to instantly change every stop on the organ. Generals can be pre-programmed with any stop combination imaginable. Most large organs have six to ten generals available at one time, with multiple memory channels allowing multiple sets of generals to be stored ready for usage. Large organs can cycle through generals by using a 'Stepper' or 'Sequencer'.

Grand Jeu One of the typical registrations for French Classical organ music, referring to the reed choruses of the organ backed up by Cornets and often some principal stops.

Grand-Orgue The French term for the Great.

Great The main division/manual of the organ. Every manual can be coupled to the Great, and the Great typically contains the loudest stops on the organ (except for the Tuba).

Hauptwerk See 'Great'. Also the name for the main virtual organ software currently in use.

Larigot The French name for the 1 1/3' mutation stop.

Leslie Speaker An amplifier/loudspeaker unit named after its inventor, Donald Leslie. The rotating drum in the speaker creates the characteristic tremolo sound, with both slow and fast speeds possible. The Leslie/Hammond organ pairing is standard and many of the most famous Hammond tracks involve this speaker.

Loft An abbreviation of 'organ loft', a common name for the gallery area containing the organ console. Many consoles are found high up in the building in specially built enclaves or galleries, often situated next to the main organ case. Large organ lofts typically also contain furniture such as shelves (for music), chairs or even sofas.

Manual An individual keyboard on the organ. Most organs have two or three manuals, but larger ones can have four or rarely even more.

Mechanical Action Also known as 'tracker action'. When an organ has mechanical action, depressing a key directly controls the valve that lets wind flow into the pipes. This allows for more expressive playing, as the organist can subtly vary how fast this valve opens and closes. However, mechanical-action organs can feel very heavy to play, and so are less suited to loud fast figuration or passages requiring awkward hand positions.

Mixture An organ stop connected to more than one rank of pipes. The number of ranks is indicated by the Roman numeral on the stop. Said ranks usually also change across the compass, with lower-pitched ranks substituting for higher ones as the organ ascends in range.

Mutation An organ stop that does not sound in unison or octaves with the written pitch. Mutations are typically based on the harmonic series and are used to 'mutate' the sound of 8' and 4' stops, hence the name. Common lengths and sounding pitches are given in Figure 2.28.

Nazard The French name for the 2 2/3' mutation stop. Some French Classical composers request a Jeux de Nazard, that is, Flutes 8', 4', 2 2/3'.

Glossary

Oberwerk A division usually found on German Baroque organs (although more common in countries like the Netherlands than Germany itself). It is usually placed above the Hauptwerk. On small organs, it may also replace the Hauptwerk.

Pistons The buttons on the console which operate registration aids. Some pistons (typically those linking to couplers) are 'reversible', meaning they can both add and remove the coupler when pressed. See also 'General Pistons' and 'Divisional Pistons'.

Plein Jeu One of the typical registrations of French Classical organ music, referring to the full principal chorus from 16′ up to the mixtures. The pedal is usually registered with a Trumpet 8′.

Plenum Another name for the full organ, often referring to a full Baroque principal chorus.

Positive See 'Choir'. The Positive division typically sits away from the main case and behind the player. A 'Positive Organ' is another name for a chamber organ.

Principal The main type of stop on the organ. Principals typically produce a strident, bright sound.

Rank A single group of pipes of similar construction sounding the full chromatic range of the organ. Each stop typically controls only one rank; mixtures, however, control as many as their Roman numeral indicates.

Récit The French term for the Swell.

Reed A group of stops on the organ, typically named after and intended to emulate orchestral woodwind and brass instruments. The specifics of reed stops are discussed in Chapter 2.

Registration The art of choosing, adding and removing stops.

Registrant A console assistant who specifically helps with changing stops.

Registration Aid A device which helps with either pre-setting or changing registration without needing to physically draw or remove stops. Most of these devices are electronic and so can be pre-programmed as necessary. Large organs have a wide range of registration aids for both the hands and feet. The use of registration aids should not usually be specified in the score.

Reversible Pistons See 'Pistons'.

Rollschweller See 'Crescendo Pedal'.

Rückpositiv The German term for a Choir division that sits away from the main case behind the player (lit. 'back-Positive').

Sequencer See 'Stepper'. Unlike steppers, sequencers work independently of the generals.

Specification The stop-list for an organ. Specifications often contain other technical details of the organ in question, as well as occasional photographs and recordings.

Solo The most common division for the fourth manual in the UK/USA. The Solo division is typically enclosed, therefore often being used to replace the Choir (which is often not enclosed on four-manual organs). This division normally contains additional sets of flutes and strings, as well as a wide range of solo clarinets and oboes. The Tuba/solo reed is also usually relocated to this manual from the Choir.

Stepper A registration aid, normally indicated with a plus symbol, that allows the organist to cycle through generals. Although these are not uncommon on large organs, particularly in Europe, they are often considered unidiomatic and composers should normally write as if for normal generals rather than the stepper specifically.

Stop The draw-knobs or switches on the organ console that control the sound and timbre of the organ.

String A type of stop that emulates the character of string instruments. They are normally only found on the Swell.

Swell One of the main divisions/manuals on the organ. Typically, the Swell is voiced to be quieter than the other manuals. It also is the only manual to reliably be enclosed.

Swell Box A box-like structure with shutters that surrounds the Swell pipework. These shutters are controlled by an expression pedal called the 'Swell pedal', allowing for a fine control of Swell dynamics. Similar boxes are also occasionally found for other divisions; any division with a box is described as 'enclosed'.

Swell Pedal See 'Expression Pedal' and 'Swell Box'.

Tibia A type of flute rank that is characteristic of the theatre organ, to the point where 'Tibia' is a name for a stop category on these instruments.

Tierce The French name for the 1 3/5′ mutation stop. In French Classical organ music, the Jeux de Tierce is similar to the Cornet but with Principal stops from 4′ upwards.

Tirasse The French term for the pedal couplers.

Touch The technique of playing a keyboard with either the hands or feet, including factors like how the key is pressed and how it is released. Occasionally, the term is used to refer to key action, for example, an organ can have a 'light' or 'heavy' touch.

Tracker Action See 'Mechanical Action'.

Tremulant A stop which, when drawn, causes the wind supply to fluctuate in much the same way as a vibraphone motor. The Swell almost always has a tremulant, but the stop is rarer for the Choir and Great manuals.

Unification An innovation by Robert Hope-Jones, which has become a fundamental part of theatre organ design, where individual ranks could be used on different manuals and at different octaves simultaneously. This design choice allows for wide range of stops and colours in a very compact design.

Unit Orchestra Another name for the theatre organ.

Voicing In organ terminology, how a pipe is physically modified to achieve a desired tonal quality. Features altered through voicing include the initial sound onset ('speech'), the timbre of sound produced and general loudness of the pipe.

Voluntary A piece of organ music used in a church service. Typically, the term 'voluntary' itself refers to the piece at the end of the service, but it can also be used for the piece(s) beforehand as well.

Werkprinzip A modern term indicating a neo-Baroque approach to organ design, typically where each division is based on a separate principal chorus. This style of organ design was very popular in the mid-twentieth century, the reaction against the excesses of Romantic organ building leading to the rise of the neoclassical organ. This term has also been retrospectively applied to the equivalent sixteenth and seventeenth-century design principles.

Zungen See 'Reeds'.

Index

For the benefit of digital users, indexed terms that span two pages (e.g., 52–53) may, on occasion, appear on only one of those pages.

Tables and figures are indicated by *t* and *f* following the page number

1', 30–31*f*, 108*f*, 137
1 1/7', 107*f*, *See also* Septième
1 1/3' 32*t*, 52*f*, 137, 146, 166. *See also* Larigot
1 3/5', 32*f*, 52*f*, 53*f*, 85*f*, 90*f*, 111–12, 166. *See also* Tierce
2', 30*f*, 30–32, 32*t*, 35*f*, 36, 37, 38*f*, 50*f*, 51, 53–54, 62, 85*f*, 89*f*, 108*f*, 124–25, 128*t*, 137, 165, 166
2 2/3', 32*t*, 36, 52–53*f*, 53*f*–54, 62, 80*f*, 85*f*, 88*f*, 89*f*, 106*f*, 119*f*, 120*f*, 122*f*, 137, 166. *See also* Nazard
4', 22, 29–32*f*, 32*t*, 34, 35*f*, 36, 37, 38–39*f*, 40–41, 42, 43*f*, 44, 45, 48*f*, 48–49*f*, 50*f*, 50–51, 52–54, 55, 57*f*, 62, 68*f*, 69*f*, 73*f*, 74*f*, 79*f*, 80*f*, 83*f*, 84*f*, 85*f*, 87*f*, 88*f*, 89*f*, 90*f*, 103*f*, 107*f*, 107, 108, 111*f*, 112, 115*f*, 119*f*, 120*f*, 121–22, 124–25*f*, 128*t*, 133–34, 134*f*, 137, 140, 146, 149*f*, 150*f*, 153, 157, 165, 166
5 1/3', 52, 137
8', 21–22, 28, 29*f*, 29–30*f*, 31–32, 32*t*, 34–35*f*, 36, 37–41*f*, 41*f*, 42*f*, 42, 43*f*, 44*f*, 45, 46*f*, 48*f*, 48–51*f*, 52–54, 55, 57*f*, 60*f*, 62, 68*f*, 69*f*, 74*f*, 79*f*, 80*f*–81, 83*f*, 84*f*, 85*f*, 86*f*, 87*f*, 88*f*, 89*f*, 90*f*, 102*f*, 103*f*, 104*f*, 107*f*, 107–8, 108*f*, 110*f*, 111*f*, 114*f*, 115*f*, 117*f*, 119*f*–21*f*, 121–22, 124–25*f*, 128*t*, 133–34, 134*f*, 137, 140, 146, 149*f*, 150*f*, 150, 153, 157, 165, 166
10 2/3', 107*f*
16', 30*f*, 30, 31*f*, 32*t*, 32, 34, 36, 37*f*, 37, 38*f*, 40–41, 41*f*, 42*f*, 42–43, 44, 44*f*, 45, 48*f*, 48–50, 50*f*, 57*f*, 60*f*, 62, 67–68*f*, 69*f*, 73*f*, 74*f*, 79*f*, 83*f*, 84*f*, 85*f*–86*f*, 87*f*, 88*f*, 89*f*, 90*f*, 92, 93, 102*f*, 103*f*, 104*f*, 105*f*, 107*f*, 107–8, 108*f*, 109, 111*f*, 112*f*, 114*f*, 115*f*, 117*f*, 119–20, 121–22*f*, 128*t*, 133–34, 134*f*, 137, 140, 148*f*, 149*f*, 150*f*, 154–55, 165
32', 30*f*, 30, 32*t*, 36, 37*f*, 40–41, 48–49, 49*f*, 50, 57*f*, 60*f*, 69*f*, 79*f*, 83*f*, 84*f*, 85*f*–86*f*, 103*f*, 107*f*, 112*f*, 112*f*, 114*f*, 128*t*, 140, 147, 152*f*

ABRSM, 101
acoustic, 5, 21, 67, 75, 81, 82–83
action
   electricaction, 16, 25, 57, 75, 80–81, 86, 137–38, 167
   mechanical/tracker action, 15–16, 24, 25, 57, 75, 80–81, 104, 123, 168
   stop action, 24, 25
Adler, Samuel, 1–2
   The Study of Orchestration, 30
Æolian-Skinner Organ Company, 168

America/American, US, 7–8, 37, 42, 55, 61, 64, 135, 153, 163, 168. *See also* North America
American Classic, 42, 163, 168
American Guild of Organists (AGO), 7–8
American Theatre Organ Society (ATOS), 7–8, 135
Anches. *See* reed
Anglican, 6, 19, 167–68. *See also* Christianity
Antegnati, Constanzo, 163
Antiphonal, 15
articulation, 15–16, 21, 23, 28, 66, 68, 69, 80, 81, 94–95, 97, 99, 100–1, 103, 112
   legato, 23, 66–67*f*, 68–69, 71–72, 73–74, 77, 78–79, 80, 89, 94, 95, 96, 97, 99–100, 101, 103, 106, 107–8, 110, 115
   non legato, 68, 95, 99
   staccato, 23, 68, 71–72, 74, 79–81, 82, 90, 103, 115, 121, 137–38
Austin Organs, 168
Ave Maris Stella, 23

balance, 3, 15, 22, 30, 31–32, 36, 50, 51, 56, 57–58, 87, 89, 140, 153–54
Baroque, 7, 13–14, 16–17, 18, 36, 44–45, 47, 49, 56, 66, 70–71, 75, 94, 100, 104, 118, 120, 123–25, 132, 146, 153–54, 155, 164–65, 166, 168. *See also* English; German
Basilica di Santa Barbara, 17–18, 39, 163
Basilica of Valère, 1
basso continuo, 146*f*, 153–54
Bassoon, 32*t*, 40, 42, 90*f*, *See also* reed
Blatter, Alfred, 1–2
Bombarde, 15, 48–49
Bourdon, 31*f*–32, 36, 37–38*f*, 38*f*, 60*f*, 79*f*, 85*f*, 89*f*, 90*f*, 108*f*, 115*f*, 119*f*, 120*f*, 122*f*, 150*f*, 166. *See also* flute
box
   Choir box, 46, 63*f*, 89, 93
   Swell box, 13, 15, 21–22, 27, 30, 34, 37, 38, 39, 42, 56, 61–63, 89, 96–97, 106, 140
box organ. *See* chamber organ
British Institute of Organ Studies (BIOS), 7–8
Brockschmidt, Satyaki
   Harmonium Handbook: Owning Playing and Maintaining the Devotional Instrument of India, 132
Brombaugh, John, 168
Burgos Cathedral. *See* Capilla de San Enrique

Index

The Cambridge Companion to the Organ, 163
Capilla de San Enrique, 18, 164
case, 13–14*f*, 47, 55
cathedral, 1, 2, 4, 6, 13, 18, 112, 124–25, 141–42, 145, 163. *See also* church
Catholic, 19. *See also* Anglican; Christianity
Cavaillé-Coll, Aristide, 166, 167
Celesta (stop), 55
celesta (instrument), 131
celeste, 32*t*, 32–33, 37, 39–40*f*, 42, 128*t*, 163–64, 168. *See also* Voix Céleste
'cello, 103, 131, 153, 156
chamber organ, 2–3, 17, 18, 22–23, 24, 94, 123–27, 131, 145, 146, 150, 153–54, 156
Chapelle royale, Versailles, 17, 165
Chimes, 55
choir, 13–14, 50, 114, 124–25, 139–45, 149, 154–55, 156, 159, 167. *See also* choral
Choir (manual), 29, 30, 31–33, 32*t*, 36, 37, 38, 39, 40–41, 43, 45, 46–47, 51, 52, 53–54, 55–56, 57–58, 60, 61*f*, 62, 73–74, 87, 88–89, 108, 110, 117, 121, 146
choral, 8, 44, 50, 77, 80–81, 94, 124–25, 139–45, 149, 150–51, 153, 167–68. *See also* choir
chorale. *See* hymn
chords, 16, 17–18, 19–21, 25, 28, 38, 50, 57, 66, 67, 68–70, 76–86, 90, 92, 105–6, 107, 110–12*f*, 114, 115, 116, 118, 121, 122, 129, 131, 137–38, 139–40, 147, 149, 156. *See also* voicing
   broken/cascading chords, 21, 24, 82–83, 85
   cluster chords, 23, 112
chorister, 145
Christianity, 5–6. *See also* Anglican; Catholic; religion
church, 1, 2, 4, 5, 6, 8, 15, 36, 55, 75, 123, 132, 133–34, 135, 136, 139–40, 143–44, 146, 153, 155, 156, 167–68. *See also* cathedral
Clarinet, 32*t*, 33, 40–41, 46–47, 60, 62. *See also* reed
Clarion, 32*t*, 40, 42, 45. *See also* reed
Clicquot, 165
Common Praise. *See* hymn
compass, 10*f*, 17, 18, 19, 41, 44, 51–52, 62, 94, 95*f*, 98, 99, 106, 123, 136, 142
console, 9–10*f*, 14*f*, 15, 25–26, 29, 133*f*, 154
continuo. *See* basso continuo
Contra Fagotto. *See* Bassoon
contrapuntal, 67, 68–69, 76–77, 82–83, 129, 141–42, 154–55. *See also* counterpoint
Cor de Nuit, 89*f*, 119*f*, *See also* flute
Cornet, 32*t*, 38*f*, 45, 51, 53–54*f*, 62
counterpoint, 20, 66, 76, 78, 91, 115, 142, 165. *See also* contrapuntal
coupler, 13, 16, 17, 21, 22, 32–33, 34–36, 40, 45, 48, 50–51, 55–58, 59, 61, 80–81, 87, 88, 93, 97, 107, 108, 119, 121, 122, 128*t*, 133, 140, 153, 167
   Sub/Super Octave coupler, 40, 48, 58, 84*f*, 134*f*
crescendo pedal, 15, 63–64, 93, 166, 168
Cromorne, 32*t*, 40, 46–47*f*, 166. *See also* Clarinet; reed

Crosby, Bing, 135
Ctesibius, 1
Cymbale, 51, 89*f*, *See also* mixture

DAW, 2, 7, 25–26
DeFrancesco, Joey, 138
Dennerlein, Barbara, 138
Diapason, 36, 133–34
   Open Diapason, 36 (*see also* principal)
   Stopped Diapason, 37 (*see also* flute)
divisionals, 34, 59, 60–62, 64, 93, 133, 167
Dixon, Reginald, 135
Dom Bédos, 165
double bass, 21, 103, 113
Doublette, 31*f*, 36, 166. *See also* principal
Dulciana, 90*f*, *See also* principal
DX7. *See* Yamaha DX7
dynamic range, 5, 21–22, 25, 34, 36, 43. *See also* dynamics
dynamics, 13, 16–17, 21–22, 27, 28, 30, 34, 36, 37, 40–41, 43, 47, 48, 56, 57–58, 59, 67, 72, 79, 80–81, 87, 89, 106, 113, 119, 124, 127, 131, 145, 147, 151, 159, 161, 165
   crescendo, 13, 15, 21–22, 27, 34, 37, 56, 61–62, 63, 64, 87, 97, 140, 161
   diminuendo, 13, 15, 21, 34, 63, 87
   forte, 27
   fortissimo, 13, 16–17, 21–22, 34, 36, 47, 57, 61–62, 79, 147
   mezzo-forte, 56, 89
   mezzo-piano, 37, 39
   piano, 21–22, 27
   pianissimo, 13, 16–17, 27, 34, 36, 43, 61–62, 85
   pianississimo, 131

Echevarría, 164
echo, 87, 116, 117
Echo (manual), 15
eclectic, 9, 13–14, 16–17, 28–29, 32–33, 42, 52, 92, 163, 164, 165, 168
Église de la Sainte-Trinité, 52, 167
Église Saint-Sulpice, 94, 167
Emerson, Keith, 138
en chamade, 47, 164
enclosed. *See* box
England/English, 6, 38, 47, 60–62, 87, 141–42, 164, 167. *See also* UK; US
   English Baroque, 155
   English Romantic, 20, 28, 36, 37, 41, 42, 47, 52, 68–69, 70, 99, 148, 163, 167–68
'Erroll Garner' (registration), 137–38
Evangelishes Gesangbuch, 6
extended techniques, 2, 15–16, 22–26, 126, 132

Fifteenth, 36, 106*f*, *See also* principal
fingering, 71, 77, 89, 94–95

Flageolet, 36. *See also* flute
Flageolet-nasard. *See* Nazard
flute, 22, 29, 30, 31–33, 32*t*, 34, 36, 37–40, 42*f*, 42, 43*f*, 44*f*, 50*f*, 50–51, 52–53, 53*f*–54, 55, 62, 73*f*, 80*f*–81, 85*f*, 85, 87, 89*f*, 90*f*, 110*f*, 110, 111*f*, 115*f*, 119*f*, 120*f*, 121–22*f*, 124, 128*t*, 133–34, 147, 149, 150, 163–64, 165, 166, 167, 168
Flute Celeste, 32*t*, 32–33, 37, 168. *See also* celeste; flute
Flute Harmonique, 37, 61*f*, 90*f*, *See also* flute
Forte (harmonium stop), 129
foundations, 28, 31–32, 34, 37, 38, 41, 43*f*, 46*f*, 49*f*, 50–51, 57*f*, 62, 68*f*, 69*f*, 74*f*, 79*f*, 83*f*, 84*f*, 87*f*, 103*f*, 107*f*, 117*f*, 140, 153
four-hands, 154–55*f*
Fourniture, 51. *See also* mixture
France/French, 27, 38, 41, 42, 43, 51, 52–54, 55, 74, 78–79, 90, 106, 107, 119, 143–44, 161
    French Classical, 17, 44, 45, 46–47, 49, 52, 54, 70, 99, 120, 164–66
    French Romantic, 7, 20, 28–29, 39, 40, 41, 42, 44, 45, 52, 57, 77, 78–79, 87, 94, 166–68
Freiburg Cathedral, 164
Fritts, Paul, 168
Full Organ. *See* Tutti
Full Swell, 31–32, 42, 80*f*, 85*f*, 87*f*, 117*f*, 140, 153

Gamba, 32*t*, 37, 39, 40, 62, 79*f*, 110*f*, 122*f*, 150*f*, 158*f*, *See also* string
Garner, Erroll. *See* 'Erroll Garner' (registration)
Geigen, 36. *See also* principal
generals, 17, 34, 56, 58–62
Germany/German, 6, 63, 64, 110, 121, 142, 148
    German Baroque, 7, 16, 44, 70, 164–65
    German Romantic, 15, 19, 28–29, 41, 52, 57, 68–69, 83, 87, 104, 148, 166
ghosting, 137–38
glissando, 75, 86*f*, 104
gospel, 135, 138, 154
Gospel University, 138
Graduale Romanum/Graduale Triplex, 6
Grand Jeux, 45*f*, 54, 165
Grand-Orgue (manual). *See* Great
GrandOrgue (software), 7, 33
grand orgue, 143–44*f*
Gran Pieno. *See* Tutti
Great, 13–15, 30, 32*t*, 32, 36, 37–38, 40–41, 42, 43, 45–46*f*, 47, 48–49, 50–51, 52, 53–58, 60, 61*f*, 62, 80–81, 87, 88–89, 93, 117, 121, 133–34, 140, 153
Grosse Quinte, 107*f*, *See also* 10 2/3'; mutation; Nazard

Hammond organ, 2–3, 54–55, 75, 86, 97, 123, 135–38, 151, 154
Harp (stop), 55
harp (instrument), 85, 131, 151–50*f*, 156–59
Harrison, G. Donald, 168
Harrison & Harrison Ltd, 167

Hauptwerk. *See* Great
Hauptwerk (software), 2, 7, 15, 17, 33, 64, 132–33, 163
Hautbois. *See* Oboe
Henry, Cory, 135, 138
Herman, Mark, 135
Hill, William, 167
Hills, Richard, 135
historic organs, 15, 16, 17–18, 22, 94, 124, 163–64
Hohl Flute, 37. *See also* flute
Holtkamp Organ Company, 168
hydraulis, 1
hymn, 4, 6, 19*f*, 139–40, 156
Hymns Ancient and Modern, 6

IMSLP, 8
inégalité, 166
Italy/Italian, 17–18
    Italian Renaissance, 17–18, 39, 163–65

jazz, 130, 132–33, 135, 136, 137–38, 151, 154
Jazz at Lincoln Centre, 138
Jeu Doux, 46–47*f*, 54*f*, 166
Jones, Booker T., 135

keyboard, 1–2, 6, 9, 10–12, 13, 14–15, 18, 19, 20, 36, 65, 66, 67, 68, 75, 91, 126, 127, 128, 133, 135, 136, 137, 151, 156
    split keyboard, 18, 124, 127–28, 136, 164
King's College, Cambridge, 141–42, 167

Ladegast, Friedrich, 166
Larigot, 32*t*, 52, 90*f*, 166. *See also* 1 1/3'; mutation
Laukvik, Jon
    Historical Performance Practice in Organ Playing, 163
lay clerk, 145
Liber Usualis, 6
Limina, Dave
    Hammond Organ Complete, 138

manual, 2, 10, 13–15, 17, 19, 21, 22, 23, 24, 27, 28, 30, 34–36, 37, 39, 40–41, 45, 46, 47, 48–49, 51, 52, 54–56, 57–58, 59–60, 61, 62, 63, 65, 66, 67, 68, 75, 76, 77, 78–79, 85, 86–91, 94, 97, 104, 106–7, 109, 111, 112, 113–19, 121–22, 123, 127, 133–34, 136–37, 146, 150–51, 154–55, 157, 164, 165, 166, 167
    four-manual, 13, 15, 16, 28, 39, 42, 47, 62, 133, 167
    one-manual, 16, 17, 18, 123, 164–65
    two-manual, 13–15, 16, 18, 28, 32–33, 47, 133, 136, 150–51
    three-manual, 13–15, 47, 55, 57, 133
Marsden Thomas, Anne
    The New Oxford Organ Method, 6
    Pedalling for Organists, 98
Microtones, 24, 132
MIDI, 6, 15, 25–26
Missa de Angelis, 73–74

Index

mixture, 30, 32t, 36, 50–52, 53–54, 73f, 74f, 79f, 88f, 89, 105f, 107f, 163–64, 165
Montre, 36, 166. *See also* principal
mutation, 30, 32–33, 38, 45, 50–51, 52–54, 121, 163–64

National Pipe Organ Register (NPOR), 8
Nazard, 32t, 52–53, 80f, 85f, 89f, 119f, 120f, 122f, 166. *See also* 2 2/3'; mutation
New English Hymnal, 6. *See also* hymn
Nkoda, 8
North America. *See* America/American; US
notation, 4, 11, 13, 22–23, 27, 86, 123, 134, 137, 145, 148
  notation software, 1–2, 4, 7
notes en commun, 78–79

Oboe, 32t, 33, 35f, 40–42, 43, 50–51, 57–58, 62, 89f, 90f, *See also* reed
Octave (stop), 36. *See also* principal
Octavin, 31f, 37, 38f, 108f, *See also* flute
Ogden, Nigel, 135
Online Resources, 8, 9, 17–18, 19, 22–23, 28–30, 32–33, 39, 52, 59, 61–62, 92, 94, 141–42, 163
orchestra, 1–2, 8, 11–12, 30, 37, 40–41, 56, 70, 73, 80–81, 94, 103, 112, 113, 125, 126–27, 130, 131, 132–33, 139, 145–53, 167
Orchestral (manual), 15
Organ Historical Trust of Australia (OHTA), 8
Organo Pleno. *See* Tutti
orgue de choeur, 143–44f
Ospital, Thomas, 161

Paris. *See* Église Saint-Sulpice, Église de la Sainte-Trinité
pedal
  expression pedal, 13–14, 63, 96–97 (*see also* box)
  sustain pedal, 6, 21, 65, 66, 68–69, 71–72, 78–79, 85, 91
pedalboard, 10, 21, 55, 79, 92–93, 95–96, 98, 100, 104, 106, 110, 151
  split pedalboard, 98
pedalling, 94–95, 95f, 96f, 97, 98, 99, 101, 103, 104, 107–8, 154–55
  heel, 94–95, 96, 98, 99, 101, 103, 104, 105–6, 111–12
  double pedalling, 21, 92, 100, 105–10f
  multi-pedalling, 92, 100, 105–6, 110–12f
  toe, 94–95, 96, 98–99, 103, 104, 105–6, 111–12, 116
pedals (keyboard), 2, 10, 11–12, 13, 17, 19–20, 21, 30, 32t, 32, 34–37, 45, 48–50, 52–53, 54, 55, 56, 61, 62, 67, 74, 76, 77, 79, 82, 83–84, 85, 88, 89, 92–122, 123, 134, 136, 137, 140, 146, 147, 149, 150–51, 154–55, 156, 163–65, 166, 167
percussion (stops), 55, 128t, 133, 134, 137–38, 168
percussion (instrument), 98, 125, 131, 152, 161
pianist. *See* piano (instrument)
piano (instrument), 6, 10–12, 15–16, 19, 20, 21, 23, 65, 66, 67, 68–69, 70, 71–72, 73–74, 81, 86, 91,

98, 126, 131, 134, 135, 148, 154, 156. *See also* dynamics; keyboard
Piccolo, 36, 108f, *See also* flute
Pipe Organ Database, 8
piston, 17, 55, 56, 58–62, 93, 96–97, 106, 134, 167. *See also* divisionals; generals
Piston, Walter, 1–2
plenum, 36, 113
Posaune *See* Trombone (stop)
Positive, 13–14f, 123. *See also* Choir (manual)
Prestant, 36, 122f, 166. *See also* principal
principal, 29, 31–33, 32t, 34, 35f, 36–37, 38, 39, 40, 45, 50–51, 52, 87, 88f, 121f, 124, 133–34, 163–64, 165, 166, 168
pull-downs, 17, 163–64. *See also* pedals (keyboard)

Quarte de nasard, 85f, *See also* flute
Quintatön, 73f, *See also* flute
Quint, 52. *See also* mutation; Nazard

rank, 51
Récit. *See* Swell
reed, 13, 22, 29, 31–33, 32t, 34, 35f, 36, 40–51, 52, 54–55, 57f, 57–58, 62, 68f, 69f, 73–74, 74f, 79f, 83f, 84f, 87, 103f, 107f, 117f, 119, 121, 124, 126–28, 129, 134f, 140, 146, 150–51, 161, 164, 165, 166, 167
regal, 123, 124
register, 20, 21, 43, 53, 69, 119, 151
registrant, 25, 29, 34, 58, 61–62. *See also* registration; registration aid
registration, 2, 4–5, 7, 13, 14–15, 18, 19, 20, 21–22, 23, 24, 25, 26, 27–64, 67, 70, 75, 87–89, 97, 106, 107–8, 109, 110, 113, 116, 120, 121, 128–30, 135, 137–38, 140, 141–42, 146, 149, 153, 154, 156, 165–66, 167
  hand registration, 58, 61–62, 64
registration aid, 5, 17, 25, 34, 56, 58–64, 93, 96–97, 133, 167. *See also* crescendo pedal; divisionals; generalsl; piston
Renaissance, 17–18, 39, 77, 124–25, 153–54, 163–64, 168
reservoir, 9, 23, 129
Rollschweller. *See* crescendo pedal
Romantic, 7, 9, 13–14, 16–17, 19, 20, 28, 36, 37, 38, 39, 41, 42, 44, 45, 46, 50–51, 52, 55–57, 58, 61–62, 66, 68–69, 73–74, 78–79, 87, 94, 100, 103, 109, 110, 113, 120, 123, 130, 147–48, 150, 163, 164, 166–68. *See also* English; French; German
Royal Albert Hall, 167–68
Royal College of Canadian Organists (RCCO), 7–8
Royal College of Organists (RCO), 7–8

Salicional, 29f, 29, 39, 60f, 115f, 120f, *See also* string
SATB. *See* choir; choral
Sauer, Wilhelm, 166
Septième, 52, 107f, *See also* 1 1/7'; mutation

Index

Sesquialtera, 51. *See also* mixture
side-chaining, 64
Skinner, Ernest, 168
Smith, Jimmy, 138
Smith, Dr. Lonnie, 138
software. *See* GrandOrgue; Hauptwerk (software); notation
Solo (manual), 15, 42, 167
Soubasse. *See* Subbass
Spain/Spanish
    Spanish Renaissance/Baroque, 18, 164
specification/stop-list, 3, 8, 13–14, 16, 29–33t, 40–41, 51, 163–64
Spitfire Audio, 7
Spotify, 8
sputtering, 137–38
squabbling, 137–38
Stocken, Frederick
    The New Oxford Organ Method (*see* Marsden Thomas, Anne)
stop, 1–2, 3, 5, 7, 13, 15–17, 18, 21–22, 24, 25–26, 27, 28–29, 30–33, 34, 36–51, 52, 53–55, 55, 58, 59, 61–62, 63, 65, 67, 85, 87, 93, 98, 107, 108, 112, 119–20, 121, 122, 123, 124, 127, 128–29, 132, 133–34, 137–38, 142, 146, 150–51, 161, 163–64, 166, 167, 168
    stop change, 13, 15, 16–17, 21–22, 24, 27, 34, 58–59, 62, 133, 161
    stop name, 29–32t, 34, 36, 37, 39, 40–41, 48–49, 51, 52, 55, 128, 134
strings (stop), 29, 32–33, 36, 37, 39–40, 44, 44f, 51, 90f, 108, 110, 128t, 133–34, 165, 167
strings (instrument), 66, 80, 94–95, 130, 152, 157. *See also* cello; violin
Subbass, 31f, 108f, 148f, *See also* flute
substitution
    finger substitution, 66, 68–69, 77, 78–79, 95
    foot substitution, 95f
Swell, 13–15, 21–22, 27, 30, 31–33, 32t, 34, 36, 37, 38, 39, 40–45, 46, 47, 48–49, 50–51, 52, 53–55, 56, 57–58, 60, 61f–62, 63, 64, 87, 88–89, 93, 96–97f, 106, 110, 117, 121, 140, 146, 153. *See also* Full Swell
    Swell pedal, 56, 64, 93, 96–97f (*see also* box; pedal)
symphonic, 7, 16–17, 19, 56, 73, 74, 86, 87, 91, 142, 156, 166, 168

Taylor and Boody, 168
temperament, 17–18, 168
Temple Church, 167–68
texture, 19–21, 24, 28, 30, 44, 51–52, 65, 66, 67, 68, 69, 74, 75–79, 80–81, 82–83, 84, 88, 89, 91, 106, 109, 110, 116, 139, 143–44, 145, 147, 149, 153, 154–55, 159, 161, 164–65

theatre organ, 2–3, 7, 44–45, 54–55, 97, 123, 132–35, 137, 138, 151
thumb legato, 66–67f, 77
Tibia, 133–34. *See also* flute
Tierce, 32t, 52, 53, 70, 85f, 122f, 166. *See also* 1 3/5'; mutation
toccata, 42, 45, 48–49, 51, 72, 80–81, 82, 84, 119, 148
touch, 15–16, 66, 68, 78–79
Tremulant, 37, 44f, 54–55, 119f, 129, 136–37
Trombone (stop), 40–41, 48–49
trombone (instrument), 155, 159
trumpet (instrument), 148, 155, 159
Trumpet (stop), 32t, 40–41, 42–43f, 45–46f, 47, 49–50f, 120–21f, 164, 165
Tuba, 13, 32t, 36, 40–41, 45, 47, 48, 57–58, 62, 167. *See also* reed
tuning, 17–18, 137, 140. *See also* microtones
Tutti, 11f, 12f, 23f, 60f, 70f, 71f, 74f, 75f, 105f, 106f, 116f
Twelfth, 52. *See also* mutation; principal

UK, 5, 7–8, 13–14f, 15, 32–33, 37, 44, 52, 61, 92, 132–33, 145, 163, 167–68. *See also* England/English
Unda Maris, 60f, *See also* string; Voix Céléste
US, 7–8, 13–14, 32–33, 37, 44, 52, 92, 163, 167–68

Verdin, Joris
    A Handbook for the Harmonium, 132
Versailles. *See* Chapelle royale
Viole de Gambe, 150f, 158f, *See also* Gamba; string
Violin (stop), 39
violin (instrument), 128t, 146f, 147f, 156
voice leading, 66, 77, 82
voicing (chord), 21, 40, 77
voicing (pipe), 13, 168
Voix Céléste, 32t, 39, 50–51, 60f, 62, 79f, 111f, 128t, 140, 150f, 152f, 158f, *See also* celeste; string
Volles Werk. *See* Tutti
Vox Angelica, 39. *See also* celeste; string
Vox Humana, 32t, 40, 42, 44–45, 54–55, 119f, 129, 133–34, 166

Werkprinzip, 165, 166
Willis, Henry 'Father', 167
Wolfe, Robert, 135
Wurlitzer, Rudolph, 132–33

Yamaha DX7, 78–79
YouTube, 8, 135

Zimbelstern, 55
Zungen. *See* reed

Index of Composers

For the benefit of digital users, indexed terms that span two pages (e.g., 52–53) may, on occasion, appear on only one of those pages.

This index refers to composers only; performers/scholars and works without a specific composer (e.g. hymnbooks) are listed in the general index. Page numbers next to composers' names indicate where the composer is mentioned without referencing a specific work. **Bold numbers** indicate musical examples.

Adès, Thomas
  Fool's Rhymes op. 5, 32
  January Writ, 139–40
  Under Hamelin's Hill op. 6, 125
Alain, Jehan
  Litanies, 82
  Variations sur un thème de Clément Jannequin, 47
Albright, William, 168
Ammerbach, Elias Nikolaus
  Orgel oder Instrument Tabulatur, 77
de Arauxo, Correa, 164
  Facultad organica, 164

Bach, Johann Sebastian, 76–77, 83, 98, 164, 165
  Fantasia and Fugue in G minor BWV 542, **36f**
  Fantasia super 'Komm, Heiliger Geist' BWV 651, **113f**
  Gott, durch deine Güte BWV 600, **121f**
  Nun komm, der Heiden Heiland BWV 599, **66f**
  Nun komm, der Heiden Heiland BWV 658, **99f**
  O Mensch, bewein' dein' Sünde groß BWV 622, **75f**
  Prelude and Fugue in D major BWV 532, 71, **100f**
  Prelude and Fugue in G minor BWV 535, **76f**
  Prelude and Fugue in A minor BWV 543, **98f**
  Prelude and Fugue in C minor BWV 549, **118f**
  Toccata and Fugue in D minor BWV 565, **68f**
  Trio Sonata No. 1 BWV 525, **88f**
  Wir müssen durch viel Trübsal BWV 146, 146
Bainton, Edgar
  And I Saw a New Heaven, 141–42
Bairstow, Edward
  Blessed City, Heavenly Salem, 70, **85f**, 141–42
Barber, Samuel
  Toccata Festiva op. 36, 153
Bartók, Béla
  The Miraculous Mandarin, 148
Bauckholt, Carola
  Gegenwind, 24
Beatles, The
  Sgt. Pepper's Lonely Hearts Club Band
    'Being for the Benefit of Mr. Kite!', 132
  'We Can Work It Out' (single), 132
Bernstein, Leonard, 145
Bingham, Judith, 167

Boëllman, Léon
  Suite Gothique op. 25,
    'Toccata', **83f**
Bolcom, William, 168
  Gospel Preludes
    'What a Friend We Have in Jesus!', 86
Boulanger, Lili, 145
  Pie Jesu, 157, **158f**
  Psaume XXIV, **79f**, 97, **108f**, 159
  Psaume CXXX, **86f**, **109f**, **114f**, 149, **150f**
Brahms, Johannes, 87, 166
  11 Chorale Preludes for organ op. 122
    'Es ist ein Ros', **77f**
    'O Welt, ich muss dich lassen [2nd version]', **117f**
  Geistliches Lied op. 30, **143f**
Briggs, Kerensa
  Light in Darkness, **44f**
Britten, Benjamin
  A Hymn of St Columba, 141–42
  Missa Brevis op. 63, 141–42, 145
  Rejoice in the Lamb op. 30, 122, 141–42
  War Requiem op. 66, 125
Bruch, Max
  Kol Nidrei op. 47 (arr. Riemann), 156
Bruhns, Nicolaus
  Praeludium in G major, **109f**
Buxtehude, Dieterich, 98, 164, 165
  Prelude, Fugue and Chaconne in C major BuxWV 137, 30
  Toccata in F major BuxWV 157, 71
Byrd, William, 124–25, 167

Cabanilles, Juan, 164
de Cabezón, Antonio, 164
Carlos, Wendy
  Tron, 151, 167–68
Castagnet, Yves
  Messe "Salve Regina"
    'Sanctus', **144f**
Chang, Vicky
  Suite for Organ
    'Cloudy Sky', **88f**
Charpentier, Jacques
  Messe pour tous les temps
    'Sortie', 70

Index of Composers

Chen, Chelsea
   Taiwanese Suite
      'Mountain of Youth', **46f**
Clérambault, Louis-Nicholas, 165
   Suite du deuxième ton
      'Basse de Cromorne', **47f**
      'Flûtes', 39
Copland, Aaron
   Symphony for Organ and Orchestra, 153
Couperin, François, 165
   Messe pour les couvents
      'Récit de Cornet', **54f**
Crumb, George
   Star-Child, 150

Davies, Peter Maxwell
   Missa Super l'Homme Armée, 132
Dearden, Nathan James
   storms don't last forever, **53f**
Demessieux, Jeanne, 166
   6 Études op. 5
      'Tierces', 107–8
      'Sixtes', 107–8
   7 Meditations sur le Saint-Esprit op. 6
      'Lumière', **73f**
   Te Deum op. 11, 121
Desplat, Alexander
   The Grand Budapest Hotel, 151
Dove, Jonathan
   Missa Brevis
      'Gloria', **82f**
   Seek him that Maketh the Seven Stars, 150–51
Downes, Kit
   WEDDING MUSIC
      'Rat Catcher', 24
      'Optics', 53
Dubois, Théodore
   12 Pièces pour orgue
      'Marche des Rois Mages', 24
Dupré, Marcel, 54, 77, 91, 166
   Evocation op. 37
      'Allegro deciso', **75f**, 110
   Trois Préludes et Fugues op. 7, 4–5, 97
      'Prelude and Fugue in B Major', 83–84
      'Prelude and Fugue in G Minor', 38, 70, **111f**
Duruflé, Maurice, 27, 39, 54, 74, 77, 86, 91, 145, 153, 166
   Prélude, Adagio et Choral varié sur le thème du 'Veni Creator' op. 4, 94
   Prélude et Fugue sur le nom d'Alain op. 7, **38f**, 47
   Requiem op. 9, 143–44
      'Kyrie', 73–74
   Scherzo op. 2, 37, 74, 90, 100
   Suite op. 5, 74
      'Sicilienne', 40, 90, 94, **108f**
      'Toccata', 82–83
Dylan, Bob
   Highway 61 Revisited
      'Like a Rolling Stone', 154

Elgar, Edward, 148, 167
   The Dream of Gerontius op. 38, 148
   Imperial March op. 32 (arr. Martin), **41f**
   Pomp and Circumstance Marches op. 39
      'March No. 1', 147
      'March No. 4' (arr. Sinclair), 30
   Sospiri op. 70, 130
   Variations on an Original Theme 'Enigma' op. 36, 148
      'Variation XIV', **78f**
Escaich, Thierry, 3, 52, 151–52, 167
   Cinq Versets sur le Victimae Paschali, **31f**
   Evocation IV, 30, 80–81
   Poèmes pour orgue
      'Eaux natales', 80–81, 90, **108f**
   Récit, **23f**
   Trois motets, 139–40

Finzi, Gerald
   God is Gone Up op. 27 no. 2, 71–72, 141–42
   Lo, the Full Final Sacrifice op. 26, **46f**, 83–84, 141–42
Fletcher, Percy
   Festival Toccata, **56f**
Frances-Hoad, Cheryl
   Psalm 1, 25
Franck, César, 166
   L'Organiste, 130
   Trois chorals pour orgue, 44
   Trois pièces pour grand orgue
      'Pièce héroïque', 81, 95, **117f**
Frescobaldi, Girolamo, 163
Froberger, Johann, 164

Gabrieli, Giovanni, 163
Gibbons, Orlando, 124–25
   This is the Record of John, **125f**
Gigout, Eugène
   10 Pièces pour orgue
      'Toccata', **68f**
Ginastera, Alberto
   Turbae ad Passionem Gregorianum op. 43, 23
Glass, Philip
   Dance No. 4, 150–51
Gounod, Charles
   Vision de Jeanne d'Arc, 156
Grainger, Percy
   Marching Song of Democracy, 48
   The Immovable Do, 24
de Grigny, Nicolas, 165
   Veni Creator Spiritus
      'Plein Jeu', **50f**
Gubaidulina, Sofia
   In Croce, 23, 156
   The Rider on the White Horse, **31f**, 153
Guillou, Jean
   Jeux d'orgue
      'Au miroir des flûtes', 85
   La révolte des orgues, 125

Index of Composers

Guilmant, Alexandre
  Organ Sonata No. 1 op. 42
    'Allegro', **101*f***

Hailstork, Adolphus
  Toccata on 'Veni Emmanuel', **72*f***
Hakim, Naji
  Toccata, 44–45
Hampton, Calvin, 168
Handel, Georg Frideric, 151
  Overture in D minor (arr. Elgar), **113*f***
von Hauswolff, Anna
  All Thoughts Fly, 17
    'Theatre of Nature', 161
Haydn, Josef
  Missa brevis Sancti Joannis de Deo
    Hob.XXII:7, **146*f***
Henze, Hans Werner
  Toccata senza fuga, 83
Hindemith, Paul, 28, 76–77, 151
  Kammermusik VII, 153
Holst, Gustav, 148
  The Planets op. 32
    'Saturn, the Bringer of Old Age', **37*f***
    'Uranus, the Magician', 75
    'Neptune, the Mystic', **112*f***
Horton, Tom, 135
  Theatre organ Originals – Vol. 1
    'Console Up', **134*f***
Howells, Herbert, 34, 141–42, 167
  Hymnus Paradisi, 148
  Like as the Hart, 19, 28, 141–42
  Six Pieces
    'Master Tallis' Testament', 120

Ikeda, Satoru
  Water Bubbling, **126*f***
d'Indy, Vincent
  Sainte Maria Magdalene op. 23, **157*f***
Irrepressibles, The
  Mirror Mirror
    'In This Shirt', 36

Jackson, Francis
  Evening Service in G, 87
Janáček, Leoš
  Glagolithic Mass, 148
  Taras Bulba
    'The Death of Andrei', **148*f***
Jenkins, Karl
  6000 Pipes
    'Secret Orchids', 70
Johnson, Mikhail
  Si Di Staar Deh, **53*f***

Karg-Elert, Sigfrid, 129–30, 166
  Choral-Improvisationen für Orgel op. 65
    'Ein Feste Burg', **71*f***, 83, 94
    'Nun danket alle Gott', 116
    'Wunderbarer König', **160*f***
  Die Kunst des Regestrierens op. 91
  Elementar-Harmonium-Schule op. 99,
  Harmonium Sonata No. 2 op. 46,
    'Enharmonische Fantasie und Doppelfuge
      "B.A.C.H," **130*f***
Kerr, Thomas, 168
  Anguished American Easter, 1968, **39*f***
  Suite Sebastienne
    'Reverie (for Celestes)', **40*f***
Koechlin, Charles
  La course de printemps
    'Flûte de Krishna', 73, 147

Lagrave, Baptiste, 161
Langlais, Jean, 107
  7 Études de Concert
    'Alleluia', **105*f***
    'Trilles', 96
  Hommage à Frescobaldi
    'Épilogue', 112
  Messe solennelle, 143–44
  Suite médiévale
    'Tiento', 44–45
  Trois paraphrases grégoriennes op. 5
    'Hymne d'actions des grâces
      'Te Deum'', 70, **74*f***
Laurin, Rachel, 168
  Fantasy and Fugue on the Genevan
    Psalm 47, 154
Leighton, Kenneth, 28, 34, 37, 151
  Martyrs, 154
  Missa di Gloria
    'Gloria', 87
  Paean, **83*f***
  Second Service, 141–42
Lemare, Edwin
  2 Pieces for Organ op. 83
    'Moonlight and Roses', **90*f***
Levin, Ben
  Small Animal PNG Attachment Open Wide From My
    Star's New Hand, **20*f***
Ligeti, György
  Two Etudes for Organ, 25
    'Harmonies', **78*f***
  Volumina, 23
Liszt, Franz, 166
  Deux légendes (arr. Saint-Saëns)
    'St. François d'Assise: La predication aux
      oiseaux', 30
  Fantasia and Fugue on 'Ad nos ad salutarem undam',
    104
  Hosannah, 155
  Ossa Arida, 154–55
Litaize, Gaston
  Prélude et danse fuguée, 31, 111
  Reges Tharsis, 47

Index of Composers

MacMillan, James
- *A New Song*, 40, 139–40, 142
- *A Scotch Bestiary*, 153
  - '2. Reptiles and Big Fish (in a small pond)', 49
- *Tu Es Petrus*, 159

du Mage, Pierre
- *Suite du premier ton*
  - 'Tierce en taille', 70
  - 'Grand Jeu', **45f**

Mahler, Gustav, 145
- *Symphony No. 8* ('Symphony of a Thousand'), 126–27, 130, 147

Martin, Matthew
- *Ut Unum Sint*, 71, 139–40, **142f**

Martlew, Zoë
- *Starlude*, **90f**

Mathias, William, 34

McDowall, Cecilia
- *A Prayer of St Columba*, 31
- *Church Bells Beyond the Stars*, 150–51
- *O Antiphon Sequence*
  - 'O Sapientia', **43f**
- *Sacred and Hallowed Fire*, **105f**

Mendelssohn, Felix, 37, 87
- *Organ Sonatas* op. 65
  - Sonata No. 3 ('Con moto maestoso'), **102f**
  - Sonata No. 5 ('Andante'), **103f**

Merulo, Claudio, 163

Messiaen, Olivier, 3, 15, 16, 27, 37, 52, 54, 77, 78, 107, 153, 167
- *L'Ascension*
  - 'Alléluias sereins d'une âme qui désire le ciel', 121
  - 'Transports de joie d'une âme devant la gloire du Christ qui est la sienne', **75f**
- *La Nativité du Seigneur*
  - 'Les bergers', **80f**
  - 'Jésus accepte la souffrance', 49
  - 'Les mages', **122f**
  - 'Dieu parmi nous', 20, 82
- *Les Corps Glorieux*
  - 'Combat de Mort et de la Vie', **60f**
  - 'Joie et clarté des Corps Glorieux', 28–29, 44, 46–47, 60
- *Livre d'orgue*
  - 'Pièce en Trio', 88
- *Livre du Saint Sacrement*, 77
  - 'Adoro te', 67
  - 'Le Dieu caché', 31, 60
  - 'La manne et le Pain de Vie', 51–52
  - 'La Transsubstantiation', **89f**
  - 'Les deux murailles d'eaux', 84
  - 'Offrandre et Alleluia final', 84
- *Meditations sur le mystère de la Sainte Trinité*, 63
- *Messe de la Pentecôte*
  - 'Entrée', 121
- *Verset pour la fête de la Dedicace*, 40, 46–47

Middelschulte, Wilhelm
- *Konzert über ein Thema von J. S. Bach*
  - 'Intermezzo'/'Perpetuum Mobile', 112

Mitchell, James
- *Festival Toccata*, **48f**

Moore, Undine Smith
- *Variations on "There is a Fountain,"* **104f**

Moussa, Samy
- *A Globe Itself Infolding*, 32

Mozart, Wolfgang Amadeus
- *Missa Brevis No. 12 in C major K. 259*, 146

Muhly, Nico
- *Beaming Music*, 161

Mulet, Henri
- *Carillon-Sortie*, 83–84

Muse
- *Origin of Symmetry*
  - 'Megalomania', 36

Nishimura, Akira
- *Vision in Flames*, 27

Parry, Charles Hubert Hastings, 50–51, 167
- *Elegy*, **28f**
- *Fantasia and Fugue* op. 168, **99f**

Pärt, Arvo
- *Annum per Annum*, 25

Persechetti, Vincent, 168

Poulenc, Francis
- *Litanies à la Vierge noire*, 145
- *Organ Concerto*, **79f**, 151–53

Price, Florence
- *Adoration*, 81

Purcell, Henry, 167

Rachmaninoff, Sergei, 72, 91
- *The Bells*, 106

Raney, Joel, 156

Reger, Max, 166
- *Choralfantasie über 'Freu dich sehr, o meine Seele'* op. 30, **104f**
- *2 Choralfantasien* op. 40
  - 'Wie schön leucht't uns der Morgenstern', **70f**
- *12 Stücke* op. 59
  - 'Fugue', **102f**
- *12 Stücke* op. 65
  - 'Consolation', **107f**
  - 'Te Deum', **39f**
- *7 Stücke* op. 145
  - 'Siegesfeier', **69f**

Reich, Steve
- *Tehillim*, 150–51

Renaud, Albert
- *Deux Toccatas* op. 108 no. 1, **73f**

Respighi, Ottorino
- *Feste Romane*, 148
  - 'La Befana', **149f**

Fontane di Roma, 147, 148
Metamorphosen
    'Modus XII', 103
Pini di Roma, 148
    'I pini presso una catacomba, lento', **103*f***
Vetrate di Chiesa, 103
    'S. Gregorio Magno', **74*f***
Rheinberger, Josef, 151
Rossini, Giacomo
    Petite messe solennelle, 126–27, 156
Rouse, Christopher, 151
Rózsa, Miklós
    Ben-Hur, 151
Rutter, John
    The Lord Bless You and Keep You, 142
    Variations on an Easter Theme, 154

Saariaho, Kaija
    Maan varjot, **112*f***, 151, 153
    Orion, 151
Saint-Saëns, Camille
    Prière op. 158, 156
    Symphony No. 3 'Organ' op. 78, 152
        'Maestoso', **94*f***
        'Poco adagio', **152*f***
Sano, Nobuyoshi (with Takayuhi Aihara)
    Drakengard
        'Inuart Battle', 161
Scattergood, Pia Rose
    folding, unfolding, **116*f***
Scheidt, Samuel, 164
Schittke, Alfred
    Requiem, 153
        'Tuba Mirum', 81
Schlick, Arnolt
    Ascendo ad Patrem Meum, 110
Schoenberg, Arnold
    Herzgewächse op. 20, 131
Schreker, Franz
    Kammersymphonie, **131*f***
Scriabin, Alexander
    Symphony No. 5 ('Promtheus, Le Poème du Feu'), 148
Simpson, Ralph (arr.)
    King of Kings, **82*f***
Sondheim, Stephen
    Sweeney Todd, 1, 151
Sowande, Fela
    Obangiji, **115*f***
Sowerby, Leo, 168
    Carillon, 55
Stanford, Charles Villiers, 141–42, 167
    Morning, Evening and Communion Service in A major op. 12
        'Magnificat', 71–72
    Morning, Evening and Communion Service in C major op. 115
        'Magnificat', **114*f***

Strauss, Richard, 145
    Also sprach Zarathustra op. 30, 147
        'Von der grossen Sehnsucht', **147*f***
    An Alpine Symphony op. 64, 147
    Ariadne auf Naxos op. 60, 130
    Festliches Präludium op. 61, **11*f*, 12*f***, 152
Stravinsky, Igor, 145
    Canticum Sacrum, 145
    Circus Polka, 135

Tchaikovksy, Pyotr Ilyich, 145
    Manfred, 130
Tomkins, Thomas, 124–25
    A Fancy for Two to Play, 154
Tournemire, Charles
    L'Orgue mystique, Cycle de Noël op. 55
        'Office No. 7 Epiphania Domini', **107*f***

Vangelis
    Albedo 0.39
        'Nucleogenesis, Pt. 1', 161
Vaughan Williams, Ralph, 148
    The Old Hundredth Psalm Tune, 159
    Symphony No. 7 ('Sinfonia Antarctica'), 1, 147
Verdi, Guiseppi
    Otello
        '1st Act, Allegro agitato', **113*f***
Vierne, Louis, 44–45, 77, 166
    Messe solennelle op. 16, 143–44
    Organ Symphony No. 1 op. 14
        'Allegro vivace', **115*f***
        'Finale', **49*f***, 83–84
    Organ Symphony No. 3 op. 28
        'Finale', **57*f***, 82–83, **103*f***
        'Intermezzo', **111*f***, 115
    Organ Symphony No. 6 op. 59
        'Scherzo', **85*f***
    Pièces de fantaisie, Suite II op. 53
        'Feux follets', 52–53, **110*f***
        'Toccata', **84*f***
    Pièces de fantaisie, Suite III op. 54
        'Carillon de Westminster', **43**
        'Sur le Rhin', 42, **107*f***
    Pièces de fantaisie, Suite IV op. 55
        'Cathédrales', 42
        'Les cloches de Hinckley', 58
        'Naïades', 70, **110*f***
    24 Pièces en style libre op. 31, 130

Wagner, Richard, 145
Walker, Ernest
    I Will Lift Up Mine Eyes, 145
Wallen, Errollyn
    Tiger, **42*f***
Walmisley, Thomas
    Evening Service in D minor
        'Magnificat', **106*f***

Index of Composers

Walton, William
   Belshazzar's Feast, 148
   The Twelve, 48, **141***f*
Wammes, Ad
   Miroir, 150–51
Webern, Anton
   5 Pieces for Orchestra op. 10
      'Rückkehr', **131***f*
Weelkes, Thomas, 124–25
Weill, Kurt
   Die Dreigroschenoper
      'Moritat vom Mackie Messer', **131***f*
Weir, Judith
   Ettrick Banks, **38***f*, 44, 80–81
   Illuminare, Jerusalem, 140
   In the Land of Uz, 153
   Stars, Night, Music and Light, 80–81, 145

Whitlock, Percy
   Five Short Pieces
      'Folk Tune', 41
      'Paean', **48***f*
Widor, Charles-Marie, 110, 166
   Organ Symphony No. 5 op. 42 no. 1
      'Toccata', **72***f*
   Organ Symphony No. 6 op. 42 no. 2
      'Cantabile', **42***f*
      'Finale', **69***f*
   Organ Symphony No. 9 'Gothique' op. 70
      'Andante', **110***f*

Xenakis, Iannis
   Gmeeorh, 23

Zimmer, Hans
   Interstellar, 1, 151, 161, 167–68
      'S.T.A.Y.', 39

Printed in the USA/Agawam, MA
September 18, 2023

851697.068